THE GREEN GROCER

THE GREEN GROCER

ONE MAN'S MANIFESTO FOR CORPORATE ACTIVISM

RICHARD WALKER

MANAGING DIRECTOR OF ICELAND FOODS

DK LONDON
Senior Acquisitions Editor Stephanie Milner
Managing Art Editor Bess Daly
Editor Fiona Holman
Jacket Co-ordinator Lucy Philpott
Jacket Designer Nicola Powling
Pre-production Manager Sunil Sharma
DTP Designers Manish Chandra Uperti, Umesh Rawat
Production Editor David Almond
Senior Production Controller Stephanie McConnell
Publishing Director Katie Cowan
Art Director Maxine Pedliham

First published in Great Britain in 2021 by
Dorling Kindersley Limited
DK, One Embassy Gardens, 8 Viaduct Gardens,
London, SW11 7BW

Copyright © 2021 Dorling Kindersley Limited
A Penguin Random House Company
10 9 8 7 6 5 4 3 2 1
001–323339–Apr/2021

Text copyright © 2021 Richard Walker

A CIP catalogue record for this book
is available from the British Library.
ISBN: 978-0-2414-9223-9

Printed and bound in the United Kingdom

For the curious
www.dk.com

MIX
Paper from
responsible sources
FSC™ C018179

Dear Reader,

Thank you for buying this book, all the proceeds from which will go to the Iceland Foods Charitable Foundation. You are clearly interested in making the world a better place, and every one of us can make a difference. To echo the words recently sent to my wife and me by Sir David Attenborough:

'Congratulations on all you have done to save the planet and wishing you future success.'

Richard Walker

Iceland has made ethics affordable and shown that responsible shopping isn't just for the middle classes. Richard's passion for the environment has seen the grocer's campaigns on palm oil and plastic bags often upstage its upmarket rivals.

Ashley Armstrong, Retail Editor, *The Times*

Richard Walker has long stood out from the crowd of mainstream business leaders as someone who completely 'gets' the scale and urgency of the climate and ecological emergencies, and how we need something different from business as usual if we're going to overcome them. From banning GM foods, to phasing out palm oil and plastics, and making the case for nature's recovery, Richard has consistently demonstrated real leadership and activism on corporate environmental and ethical issues in his own business, but also been a lead advocate for action from government and elsewhere.

Craig Bennett, CEO of The Wildlife Trusts, and former CEO of Friends of the Earth

Richard is a rare species – an MD of a successful retail chain, that genuinely cares, not just for his customers (although he certainly does), but for the greater good. In this book he outlines how businesses can and must play a pioneering role in how we treat the planet and each other. Decisions that don't cost the earth.

Julia Bradbury, broadcaster

Right up there with Chouinard's seminal work *Let My People Go Surfing* as a sustainable business insight. A leader of modern sustainable business, Walker inspires through his own actions. His environmental vision and consciousness shows that it's no longer all about the profit and that purpose and sustainability is core to success.

Kenton Cool, world-leading mountaineer and 14-time Everest summiteer

With honesty, clarity and insight, Richard Walker shares the inspiring story of Iceland's corporate transformation from quarterly profits to quarter-century impact. A must read for all business leaders.

Christiana Figueres, Former Executive Secretary of the United Nations Framework Convention on Climate Change (UNFCCC) 2010–16, architect of the 2015 Paris Climate Agreement and co-founder of Global Optimism

Richard Walker is one of a new generation of business leaders, who is not only focused on quality and delivery, but actively looks to disrupt, drive positive change and enhance the planet along the way. Iceland's success as a brand activist and community champion is a lesson for businesses big and small. Richard's personal thought leadership on the environment is already shaping the future of retail.

Liv Garfield, CEO of Severn Trent

The actions Richard has taken at Iceland show how corporations can lead and thrive in a world beset by natural decline and climate shocks. We're in the early years of what must be a decade of climate action – Richard's refreshingly honest and highly topical book is essential reading for business leaders, investors, policy

makers and environmentalists who want to get stuff done.
Emma Howard Boyd, Chair of the Environment Agency

Not so long ago most company chief executives believed that the business of business was business. But in a world facing climate and Nature emergencies exacerbated by crippling social inequalities, this is not credible or viable. Solving these challenges must now be a core business purpose. Richard Walker has made it his, and this is his story. I hope many follow his lead.
Tony Juniper, environmentalist

Richard Walker has shown true leadership within his own company and of the industry in his willingness to pursue an environmental agenda, even at the expense of profit.
Adam Leyland, Editor, *The Grocer*

Richard has been at the vanguard of tackling environmental and social issues for many years, enabling him to write from first hand and with practical knowledge of what can be achieved through a clear vision and commitment to driving solutions to some of the world's biggest problems.
Deborah Meaden, businesswoman and star of *Dragons' Den*

Richard Walker is one of the most impressive business leaders in the UK, combining strong leadership skills and common sense with a real desire to effect change. He's always prepared to face tough questioning about his decisions, and as a result of his firm bold direction, Iceland has become known as a company that genuinely cares about the welfare of its customers and the environment.

Piers Morgan, broadcaster, journalist and writer

Please buy this book [...] it is a brilliant appraisal of humanities' predicament. A remarkable insight: honest, pragmatic, hopeful and realistic – this is the challenge that capitalism needs to make sure we survive. It isn't about business, it's about the business of survival on planet Earth. If you read one book in 2021 and want a better 2022 then this should be it.

Chris Packham, broadcaster and environmental campaigner

The reason *The Green Grocer* is such an important book in the campaign for a more sustainable world is that the writer Richard Walker and his business, Iceland, put what they say into practice. Leading the charge on reducing plastics, food waste and deforestation are all tangible examples of a passion to do the right thing. Often more is said than done but not in this case.

Lord Price, former cabinet minister, former MD of Waitrose and Chairman of Fair Trade UK

Richard is one of the UK's most progressive business leaders. It takes real courage to put corporate activism above corporate reputation, but that's exactly what he's done at Iceland. Unafraid to tackle the social and environmental issues that matter, or engage with critics and competitors to accelerate progress, his commitment to a cause bigger than his own company is truly inspirational.

Paul Polman, former CEO of Unilever and founder of IMAGINE

A book full of passion and pragmatism. A vital illustration of how you can make a difference.
Mark Rose, CEO of Fauna & Flora International

It's easy to be green if you can afford to shop at Waitrose. Richard Walker sells to those that can't. But as a passionate environmentalist he doesn't want them left behind. Should be read by all those living in their green bubble.
John Sauven, Executive Director, Greenpeace UK

I loved reading this book. In *The Green Grocer*, Richard Walker has achieved that rare thing – a totally accessible response to the nature and climate crisis that is unfussy, and yet filled with passion and respect for the natural world. You won't find convoluted theory and bloviated descriptions written in shepherds' huts (thankfully). But you will find lively insight from the shop floor, the nation's chiller cabinet and very windy beaches. The effect is a bright green manifesto for change that makes you turn 'why?' into 'why not?'
Lucy Siegle, journalist and writer

We live in a world of commitments, pacts and promises but rarely do we see examples of real action and impact from industry. This straight-talking, optimistic book proves the power of business to lead the world into a more responsible, kinder, fairer, greener 21st-century future. We need more leaders like Richard Walker to challenge the status quo, to redefine the corporate role as an environmental protagonist, a protector versus a plunderer, whilst delivering on the new metrics of

bottom line success. It's possible. This book proves it.
Sian Sutherland, co-founder of A Plastic Planet

This is a rare treat – a business book with true purpose. Filled with openness and optimism, Richard throws down the gauntlet to society's need to radically reinvent our approach to business for the good of people and planet; equality and fairness; and for a future filled with hope rather than fear. At this pivotal point in society, with multiple crises accelerating at alarming pace, from Covid-19 to climate change, biodiversity loss to the plastic pollution crisis, the manifesto sets out a powerful case of how to do business better and speak truth to the powers destroying the planet. It also shows that better stewardship of the planet will ultimately mean a better life for us all.
Hugo Tagholm, CEO of Surfers Against Sewage

The Green Grocer is a remarkable book; if you care about the future of our planet and society, this is essential reading. From running one of the biggest businesses in the UK, to being a leading activist for climate change, Richard shows how these can, and should, be the dual role of our future leaders.
James Timpson, CEO of Timpsons

Richard made Iceland cool. This transparent account of his successes and failures on his journey to a sustainable business is a fascinating one.
Kate Wylie, Chief Sustainability Officer at Chanel

PROLOGUE

'TIME DOESN'T DO REFUNDS.'

DAVID HIEATT[1]

I'd spent so long avoiding working for the family firm that when my first day came in winter 2012, I was surprisingly nervous. Unusually for me, I was early reporting for duty as a trainee shelf-stacker at Iceland Greenford in west London – store number 1217. I sat waiting in my parked car to avoid the grey cold morning, staring at the ubiquitous red and orange fascia, wondering why I'd decided to give up my perfectly successful (and anonymous) property career.

. . . .

Twelve months of store training later, I was based in Iceland's hulking, brown-brick head office on Deeside Industrial Estate in North Wales. Despite now being in my 30s, I still spent too much time being almost apologetic for my presence among the senior leadership team. Confidence was a recurring issue – I hadn't earned the right to be there, unlike everyone else around me. I'd joined the business because I was the boss's son.

The root cause of this crisis of confidence was that as 'Walker Junior', I had some pretty large shoes to fill. Trying to emulate my Dad was sure to end in disaster. So how on earth was I going to make my own mark?

. . . .

Twenty years earlier when I was a kid, I remember talking to my English teacher at school. At one point we were having some sort of career discussion on what I should do with my life. He told me a quote from a famous writer – the exact words and author I can't even remember, but the sentiment has stayed with me vividly: 'given my privilege, ensure I make use of it'.

....

Fast forward to January 2020 and I'm ridiculously nervous once again, this time because I'm about to meet my all-time favourite hero, Sir David Attenborough. Like an eager schoolboy, I was overflowing with questions and desperate to garner as much wisdom from the 93-year-old as I possibly could during what was scheduled to be a brief 15-minute encounter at the Wounded Buffalo Sound Studios in Bristol.

'Was he still optimistic that humanity could save itself? Did he have any regrets? What should I be focusing on in my life? Is running a supermarket trivial when compared to the big issues facing our planet?'

Attenborough himself had declined the top job at the BBC so that he could focus on what he knew was his life's mission of bringing the wonders of the natural world to as many people as possible. Instead of seeking the status of Director-General – and being instantly forgotten – he helped change how we see the world.

We stood in the small but significant sound recording room, dominated by a giant blank screen: this was where Sir David had watched and narrated *Blue Planet II*. Of course, I never did ask the legendary broadcaster and environmentalist those questions. Not only wasn't there the time to do so, but I realised how ridiculous it was to ask anyone else what path I should take.

However, the following week when listening to an interview he was giving to launch the BBC's Our Planet Matters platform, his half-whispered words jumped out of the radio and hit me straight between the eyes: 'The moment of crisis has come.'

As if he was reading my mind, Sir David had shown me the way.

CONTENTS

INTRODUCTION
LIGHTBULB MOMENTS
Why I care

'I BELIEVE THAT WHEN YOU FIND PROBLEMS, YOU SHOULD ALSO FIND SOLUTIONS.'

NGOZI OKONJO-IWEALA[1]

As we stood in the crackling rain, surveying the charred remains of a recently incinerated ancient rainforest, I wiped a tear from my eye. The air smelled leaden.

'I promise you I'll do something.'

But it was a daft thing to say to the Dayak tribesman, really. First, he couldn't speak any English. Second, I had no firm idea what that 'something' was. But as I left that fragile world of West Kalimantan, on the Indonesian island of Borneo, where humans and nature were increasingly bumping up against each other, I was determined to work that out during my long four-day journey home.

. . . .

Our world is changing, and businesses must change if they are to survive. As I write, grandmothers are taking to the streets; children are striking from school; evidence is piling up on the scale and speed at which we are damaging our planet. All of this is being shared and amplified, as social media rewrite the rules on how we trade information. Meanwhile, politicians try to keep up with their own rapid, sometimes knee-jerk, policy decisions.

I am perhaps best known as a business leader. I am Managing Director of Iceland Foods, a budget food retailer that is one of the UK's best-known brands. I'm privileged to have 30,000 colleagues standing alongside me, and together we serve over 5 million customers every week, in one thousand stores across the United Kingdom.

I don't use the word 'privileged' lightly. Through lucky circumstance, I find myself in a unique position: appreciating and representing the needs of countless people. I learn about our customers' levels of confidence via our daily sales figures or from listening to staff feedback. On weekly store visits I get to know the communities that we serve and what is important to them. We might have conversations about their hopes or concerns, or simply share a joke and a smile. In many ways, our business ecosystem is a barometer of modern Britain.

But I am also a climber and a surfer. I have travelled the globe and met extraordinary people, in my search for discovery and meaning; to feel 20 seconds of pure euphoria and oneness with the ocean when riding a perfect wave. I've gone to inordinate efforts to seek out untouched mountain ranges;. feeling the unique sense of triumph that comes from being the first person to set foot on an unclimbed Kyrgyzstani summit.[2] Or the wonderous adventure of joining an expedition to climb the Tibetan side of Everest[3], where I looked out towards the endless Himalayan peaks and saw the curvature of the Earth.

Such travels have given me a deep love of the natural world. But so have my experiences closer to home. The community projects I am involved in – such as helping inner city kids engage more with the nature on their doorstep, or mobilising passionate activists around the UK to help improve their local beach, river or street quality – prove to me that the environment has the power to both heal and inspire anyone.

This affinity to nature has become more profound since my wife Rebecca and I became parents to two beautiful children. My daughters have an innate fascination with butterflies and birds, bugs and spiders, worms and bees. They are at their happiest discovering the unique beauty around them – watching peregrine falcons nesting on the sandstone cliffs near our home in Cheshire, or rock pooling for hermit crabs along north Cornish beaches. I have developed a strong sense of purpose to try and protect these things they love.

Yet our planet's problems should not be viewed through the narrow lens of privilege. Real change will only come from the beliefs and actions of the millions of families doing their best to get by, rather than the evangelical stance of middle-class environmentalists with time and money to spare.

Younger people are now making value judgements about where they work, and how they spend. More than that – research has shown that people of all generations are looking to business leaders, and those leaders are realising their success is predicated on society giving them a licence to operate.[4]

With faith in politicians at an all-time low, I know all too well that people now want – indeed *expect* – corporations to take action and solve the most troublesome problems facing us all.[5] Not just existential threats like climate change or nature's destruction, but everything from plastic pollution and deforestation to pressing social issues like isolation and poverty. At times, some of these problems seem unsolvable, which is all the more reason for people like me, in a unique position to use the weight of our own £4 billion business, to help try to change things for the better.

My experiences have shown me that we can only truly meet the challenges we're facing societally and globally by working together. The idea that businesses only exist to make shareholder profit should be killed off for good. Shareholders now expect their businesses to inspire and encourage change.

In Iceland's case this means empowering 'ordinary' people by offering them ethical choices that were traditionally only available to better-off consumers. It means collaborating with unexpected and sometimes unnatural partners. Most importantly, it means capturing the passion of a workforce that lives, works and is embedded within their communities.

At Iceland, our sustainability strategy is simply called 'Doing it Right'.[6] But this really isn't a book about Iceland Foods. It is about a business and leadership philosophy I'm developing. One that is based on looking far beyond short-term profit: setting seemingly impossible goals and single-mindedly pursuing them; coping with the many internal and external challenges that will inevitably be encountered along the way; and focusing on the long-term benefits for business, community and the planet.

It also means taking risks, through what I call 'corporate activism'. In the last few years I have been privileged to lead campaigns on plastics and palm oil that have achieved global significance: bringing about massive increases in public awareness of the issues of plastic pollution and deforestation, nudging other businesses to change their operating models and even helping to drive government policy changes. I discuss these in detail in Chapters 3 and 4.

My approach isn't entirely new. As I discuss in Chapter 1, Iceland has a long, proud track record as the plucky, northern-based, straight-talking discounter: achieving real change on important environmental issues by disrupting markets and shaking up the status quo. And in Chapter 2, I look at the many other businesses and industries that are driving positive shifts for people and the planet ... as well as their profits.

....

I joined the company in 2012 at the age of 32 and then took on my current job six years later. When I took board responsibility for sustainability in 2017, I was clear that I needed to set out an agenda that was not just about planetary, but business and individual sustainability as well.

That doesn't just mean delivering long-term environmental progress for the benefit of all. We also have to maintain prices at levels that hard-pressed customers can afford, to enable them to feed their families. And overriding this balancing act, we have to ensure that the business can continue to generate a profit. Profits that enable us to keep doing good. Profits that 30,000 people depend on for a pay cheque each week.

Every decision we make faces three ways: balancing not just environmental responsibility (by trying to have as low an impact as possible), but also our social responsibility to our customers (by offering the best quality food at the lowest possible price and supporting the communities we serve) alongside sustained business performance (to provide for our staff and shareholders). That's my definition of 'true sustainability'.

Too often, people get caught up with just one element of those three key responsibilities without taking a broader view. If customers can't buy caged hens' eggs any more because they are deemed lower welfare than free-range eggs – then they might not be able to afford to provide high quality protein for their families. If we fail to sell more environmentally friendly paper bags because customers prefer the robustness of plastic bags – then they aren't properly sustainable because the customer doesn't want them. And if our sales drop by 20 per cent following the installation of doors on our fridges in an attempt to lower energy usage – then that isn't sustainable either because the business would go bust. These are just three examples of the many hard choices and trade-offs we face every single day – which demand innovative, rather than superficial, responses.

Unlike most in my sector, I have been fortunate in joining a privately-owned and family-controlled company. It gives us much greater freedom than many businesses to take a genuinely long-term view. Yet regardless of my personal enthusiasms, like any organisation our people still have to be persuaded to get behind a cause from within, rather than have it imposed upon them from above. I hope that means the experiences I have to share are relatable, even to businesses not as large as my own.

I also want to stress that as a (relatively) young leader, I realised early on that seeking out and listening to the experts is invaluable – whether that's one of our amazing 'Talking Shop' representatives, who are the voice of store colleagues; our customers; community activists as far apart as Birkenhead and Borneo; inner city kids campaigning for green spaces; or the leading environmental experts I work with on charity boards.

So, it is with their help that I am respectfully sharing the lessons I have learned on my journey – and that of our business – thus far. Lessons that have become all the more focused and urgent since the global outbreak of Covid-19. In Chapter 5, I consider what opportunities might emerge from the terrible pandemic for both society and the natural world. Finally, in Chapter 6, I look at how the multiple crises we face require us to rethink old assumptions, what radical policies the government should now consider in order to catapult a green recovery, and how they can utilise the private sector to do this.

I am fuelled by hope.

My hope in writing this book is that it might provide practical help, guidance or inspiration to any business, large or small, or any citizen, powerful or idealistic, who believe that our best days are ahead.

. . . .

But what, specifically, has made me such an advocate for the environment? Quite simply, seeing at first hand the degradation of the natural world I had grown up loving.

In 2006 I went on a surf mission to Taghazout in Morocco. I'd been excited about the trip for months, and when I got there, I wasn't disappointed – world-famous waves like Killer Point and Boilers were in peak condition, firing towards the barren coastline with ferocious precision. Among the assembled band of ragtag surfers from all around the world, there was a palpable sense of nervousness and excitement as we gathered on the beach.

But despite such a long-anticipated trip, despite the primo conditions – I cut it short. Because it wasn't just the firing waves that greeted me as I stood on the white sandy beaches and paddled in the water. I also looked in sheer horror at the amount of plastic detritus strewn *everywhere* – which extended to hypodermic needles as well as the usual haul of plastic bottles, trays and bags. It was overwhelming. Nauseating.

That trip was over ten years ago. Since then there has been more new plastic produced than there was over the previous century.[7] Talk about paradise lost. Every time I have surfed since then, I've witnessed at first hand the growing sewage of plastic in our seas and on our beaches. After I came to work for Iceland, it rapidly dawned on me that *we* were actually a significant contributor to the problem because pretty much every product we sold was packaged in plastic.

In addition to the scourge of plastic pollution I had witnessed so personally, through time spent within the business I realised there were many other environmental problems – from deforestation to carbon emissions – to which Iceland was not only a contributor ... but also a potential changemaker. Moreover, it occurred to me that as a business serving the most deprived communities around the UK, we have an authority – an obligation, even – to advocate for environmental solutions that are both applicable and just, for everybody.

I became determined to make it my mission to try and do something about it – indeed, it was the knowledge that I *could* do something about it that kept me working in the family business in the first place.

. . . .

I spent the first three decades of my life desperately trying not to follow in my Dad's footsteps. I knew that everyone would say that I could never match up to his track record as the legendary Founder and Chairman of Iceland, so I carefully ploughed my own furrow: graduating in Geography from Durham University, travelling around the world, qualifying as a chartered surveyor at a London firm before setting up my own property companies, first in Poland and later in the UK.

Having traded through many trials and tribulations – not least the 2008 financial crisis – these companies eventually amalgamated into Bywater Properties: a commercial property developer focused on building the most sustainable workspaces possible, which today has a portfolio valued at over £250 million. I remain its Chairman and, above all, immensely proud of what we have achieved.

I suppose these journeys were part of a necessary process: to grow up and become my own person, taking some hard knocks and developing a thick skin along the way, as well as gaining a little bit more maturity and confidence. And I think I proved, to my personal satisfaction at any rate, that I could succeed in business on my own account.

But then two things happened.

In 2010, after months of knowing that something wasn't quite right, we received the devastating news that my Mum, Rhianydd, had developed early-onset Alzheimer's disease. She was then only 64. Creeping uncertainty was pushed aside by a blunt diagnosis – and no cure.

And then in 2012, my Dad led a £1.55 billion management buyout of the company, effectively putting it back under family control. This was a long-term investment with no exit plan, not a quick 'turnaround and sell' opportunity. Therefore, sooner or later I stood to inherit a major shareholding in a business of which I had only the second-hand knowledge that can be derived from years of family conversations around the kitchen table.

These two events gave me a powerful motive – and an opportunity. I wanted to protect the legacy of the business my dear Mum had named and jointly founded; and her illness also made me acutely aware that life is short. Since early-onset dementia is often a hereditary condition, I also realised that I might only have 20 years left to get things done.

So, after giving it a lot of thought, I arranged to meet Dad and tell him that I wanted to give Iceland a try.

'Don't bother,' he said. 'Collect rents – it's a much easier life.'

Not very encouraging. Was this reverse psychology? Or proof of the fact that my joining Iceland had never really been on the cards. Growing up, we never even discussed it.

I was living in London at the time, and for some reason we'd met in the august marble lobby of the Corinthia hotel. It felt significant yet transitory. But I was undeterred: 'I'll do it properly – start at the bottom and work my way up.'

'OK,' he said, looking at me sceptically. 'Just one bit of advice – don't fuck it up.'

Determined not to, I threw myself into a three-year secondment stacking shelves and manning the tills full-time in some of our London stores, starting in the western suburb of Greenford, a vibrant melting pot of Irish, Indian and Polish communities. I didn't hide the fact from colleagues of who I was – that wouldn't have been right. It was awkward for perhaps one hour, but after rolling up my sleeves and getting stuck in I quickly became one of the team.

Under the wing of Simon Felstead, undoubtedly one of our best and most committed store managers, I embraced every single second. The early morning bread deliveries, the banter throughout the day, the post-work nights out ... they were all an opportunity to immerse myself in Iceland's irreverent culture, and perhaps an opening to learn more about myself too. Within a year I had scraped through being signed off as Store Manager at the Iceland branch in Swiss Cottage.

That first year in stores taught me so much. First and foremost, how to lead. Despite the fact that almost all prices, product selections and even layouts are centrally controlled, a good manager can put 20 per cent on the sales, no question. He or she can do that through the power of leadership: galvanising a team together to create a tangible sense of purpose, a sense of camaraderie; belonging, even.

It was also a way to learn about the nuts and bolts of Iceland from the sharp end. The real insights come from the stores, not from head office. I found so many unnecessary processes or procedures that had been handed down from upon high, but which were unnecessary or counterproductive.

But most of all I was humbled. I learned a great deal from our colleagues and customers – not only about retail, and how hard the work can be, but also about life: resilience, how to be smart on limited budgets and, above all, being kind to each other. The respect I have for our store colleagues is limitless.

I then moved to our head office near Chester and started running our International business, which exports Iceland food to almost 30 countries around the world, as well as serving chains of franchised stores in several more countries – mainly in areas popular with British expats such as Spain, but also including, oddly enough, Iceland the country.

I'd resolved to give working at Iceland three years and see how it went. And during any time off, every holiday away or weekend at home I observed the natural world groaning under the strains imposed upon it by the human race.

It was about this time I started actively listening to some of the experts. I had been a long-term donor to environmental charities, some of them leading campaign groups. However, like many people, I simply completed a direct debit or wrote a cheque every once in a while and thought I had done my bit.

It occurred to me that these people really understood the scale of what we were facing, the causes and, most importantly, potential solutions. So, I started to ask questions – about our oceans and rainforests, about the loss of habitats and the damage being done to the planet. I was used to dynamism and bold action in business, but I found real inspiration in some of the people I talked to in the third sector – people who were not just committed, but more pragmatic than I expected – and, above all, brave and hopeful.

This helped me to realise that what I wanted from life was to help make a difference to causes that I think really matter. I wouldn't be satisfied if I ended up on my deathbed reflecting that I'd 'only' added another 1,000 Iceland stores, or even if I'd created another 30,000 jobs. But I might feel that I'd used my time wisely if I could say that alongside doing all of that I'd also made a useful contribution to fighting for nature's recovery, for a stable climate and for better social equality.

This was what made me resolve to stay with the business and to make the fullest possible use of its power to do good, and as a platform to drive positive change for all of our stakeholders – not just to mine ever-more profit for our shareholders.

I knew this was going to be easier for me than for most business leaders, because we have had the powerful advantage of being privately owned since 2005. As mentioned earlier, in 2020, 50 years after the company was founded we managed to buy out our only outside shareholder (a South African private equity firm), returning the business to full family ownership.[8] This gives us much more bandwidth than most businesses, allowing us to do pretty much what we like.

Companies quoted on the stock market – or those controlled by money managers – are fixated on short term results. Fund managers want to see their portfolio valuations increasing quarter by quarter, in order to attain their resulting bonuses. So, the companies they own are under constant pressure to deliver consistent sales growth, often with scant regard for the social and environmental consequences.[9]

Our ownership structure has kept Iceland off this

crazy treadmill and allowed us to take a much more extended view – we phrase this as being 'long-term greedy'. Make the right long-term decisions for our staff and customers, and the profits will follow. The underlying health of the business is paramount, and we try to avoid short-termism at all costs. We can make investments and bear short-term costs in the interests of long-term growth, which a quoted company would never be able to bear without the CEO being voted out of their job.

In this context, it is interesting to note that the average tenure of a FTSE 100 CEO in the UK is just five and a half years.[10] By contrast, my Dad has been Chairman of Iceland Foods – with one break – since 1970.

....

Today's urgent environmental crisis can only be addressed by engaging the population as a whole – not just the rich and vocal middle class who can afford to shop at Marks & Spencer or Waitrose. The sort of people who can easily pay more for premium food that is organic, or grown locally, low-input, low-impact and high-satisfaction.

Businesses that cater for the better-off, and charge more for environmentally friendly products, are not offering real sustainability in my eyes – such choices must be affordable to everyone, otherwise environmentalism isn't scalable.

It's time to 'democratise environmentalism'.

We also need to engage people of all ages, and to recognise the huge gulf that exists between generational experiences. Many of those baby boomers now approaching retirement have enjoyed free university education, a high level of job security, steadily increasing prosperity, opportunity and affordable homes. In many cases they will also have accumulated a comfortable pension pot to boot.

Compare and contrast this with your average 25-year-old in the UK today: still living at home with their parents, weighed down with student debt and no realistic prospect of ever setting foot on the housing ladder. And now, they must try to build a career facing a grim jobs market in a shell-shocked, post-Covid economy.

Maintaining the balance between 'Doing It Right' and running a healthy and sustainable business is a permanent high-wire act – without a safety net. And staying on course is made harder by the fact that, if you go out with a clipboard and ask the question, most people of any stripe will say that they are willing to pay a bit more for something that is kinder to the environment or socially beneficial.

However, long experience has shown us that in practice, this just isn't true. If we raise the price of something in our stores, the majority of the public will vote with their feet for a cheaper alternative in a competitor's store down the road.

No one should blame them for this. More than ever, people need affordable food and it is our responsibility to get it to them and to ensure that it is also of good quality. In the wealthy, highly developed UK today – a G7 country – I've become outraged at the seemingly Dickensian levels of hardship that some of our society are trapped in.

At the start of the 2020s we have 4.2 million kids living in poverty[11] and last year The Trussell Trust, a charity working to end the need for foodbanks in the

UK, gave out 700,000 emergency food packs to children.[12] Malnutrition is on the rise[13], and there are now more food banks in this country than branches of McDonald's.[14]

Inequality, in all its forms, is growing for more than 70 per cent of the global population.[15] The old assumptions that underpin our capitalist system are under attack as never before. This is little wonder when you pause to consider that, according to Oxfam, the 26 richest people in the world now have the same combined wealth as the poorest 3.8 billion people.[16]

Simultaneously, we are waking up to the fact that we have been sleepwalking into environmental disaster.

Domestically, Britain is one of the most nature-depleted countries in the world. We have lost half of all our wildlife over the last 50 years, including 90 million wild birds.[17] This silent, creeping tragedy has seen unique ecosystems such as wildflower meadows disappear by 97 per cent since 1930[18], and only 20 per cent of UK peatlands survive in a near-natural state.[19] Iconic species such as tortoiseshell butterflies, hedgehogs and nightingales might soon become assigned to the natural history books.

Globally, scientists have issued chilling warnings of an impending man-made apocalypse. Approximately 2.5 per cent of the world's insect population is being wiped out every year, which is sure to cause catastrophic consequences for mankind.[20] Humans are now driving species to extinction at around 1,000 times the natural rate.[21]

All this matters, not just because of the intrinsic value of nature, but because by diminishing nature and her 'ecosystem services' we are weakening the very web of life upon which we all depend – with Covid-19 showing exactly what the direct consequences for humanity can be.

The emergency of the natural world is twinned with the unfolding climate crisis – and again, it will ultimately be us humans who pay the price. The planet is getting hotter: the 2010s were the hottest decade ever recorded[22], and the same goes for the last five years[23], culminating in July 2019 being declared the warmest month since records began in 1880.[24]

According to the UN, this is now directly driving a rise in human conflict, land disputes and hunger.[25] Ice caps and glaciers are in retreat – one-third of Himalayan ice will disappear by 2100, with serious consequences for almost 2 billion people.[26] Devastating wildfires, from the Arctic to New South Wales to California, are now annual disasters that wantonly ruin homes and livelihoods.

Forests, including tropical and temperate rainforests, hold an astonishing 80 per cent of all the planet's terrestrial species.[27] Yet they are being destroyed at an alarming rate. According to Global Forest Watch, from 2002–19 368 million hectares of tree cover were lost – which is equivalent to a global decrease of 9.7 per cent since 2000. As testimony to the interconnectedness between environmental issues, that deforestation caused 105 gigatons of CO_2 to be emitted into the atmosphere.[28]

Scientists are warning with increasing alarm about such continued degradation of ecosystems. At some point, irreversible 'tipping points' will be triggered – a switch being flicked, where nature goes from being our protector to our opponent. A 2020 study, for example, showed that the rapidly warming Arctic is starting to cause vast methane deposits trapped deep within permafrost to be released into the atmosphere – which, as methane is many more times potent than CO_2, will develop into an exponential cycle of warming.[29] Or the great Amazon rainforest, being deforested at such a rate that if it loses 29 per cent of its tree cover large swathes could turn into a savannah – turning from a carbon sink into a net emitter.[30] Current deforestation is at 17 per cent.[31]

According to research published in *Nature*, the year 2020 also marked a very different, symbolic tipping point: human-made materials (such as concrete, metal, plastic and bricks) now exceed the total biomass of the natural world.[32]

On top of all of this, we are literally choking the life out of our marine environment: 34 per cent of the world's major commercial fish species are overfished[33], the ocean is set to contain more plastic than fish by 2050[34] and by 2070, coral reefs – which support an estimated 25 per cent of all marine biodiversity – could be gone altogether.[35] As any sea-lover will attest, such distant forecasts are now becoming cold facts, with an endless tide of plastic being washed up on every beach around the world, coral bleaching events becoming commonplace and ocean life disappearing.

Yet despite bold intentions such as the Paris Agreement signed in 2015, where 189 countries legally pledged to limit warming by well below two degrees above pre-industrial levels (through nations' pledges to hit net zero carbon emissions by 2050, or earlier), there has been precious little action. Global carbon emissions – ultimately the only metric that counts – have continued their inexorable rise. In 1995, the year of the first international climate convention in Berlin, Germany, humans emitted about 23 billion metric tonnes of carbon dioxide. By 2019, we were estimated to have produced 33 billion metric tonnes.[36] The clock is ticking.

Corporations are in a unique and powerful position to take this action – but are doing nowhere near enough. This is partly because the pervading thinking is still that the role of a business is to maximise shareholder profit. This relatively new paradigm is fundamentally wrong, constraining firms to a single narrow objective that has had wide-ranging and damaging consequences for the environment and society.

But it is also because business operates within a broken system.

Short-term thinking can be important when driving day-to-day tactical decision-making, yet it is the enemy of real, systemic change. Short-termism has disproportionally become the essence of business investment, with huge pressure put on corporate boards to be judged on their quarterly returns. There is also evidence that this is not all driven by the City of London, with some chief executives responding to self-imposed pressure from their own boards and executive colleagues.[37] So, this is also about corporate culture.

Government policy is also at odds with a healthy society and planet. Taxation systems should stop taxing things we want (like jobs) and prioritise taxing things we don't want (like waste and pollution). Policies should be designed to set 'demand signals' to the market, driving change faster while enacting stronger social equality and environmental action. Companies should be competing on the basis of how environmentally friendly and socially beneficial they are.

....

It is not difficult to understand *why* we should care about these issues. We live in a dramatically warming world with an alarming rate of nature depletion, and if we don't do something about it, immediately, then in the not-too-distant future we can look forward to untold human suffering – which will hit the poorest the hardest.

What should be done about it is easy: reduce carbon and restore nature, alongside creating greater social equality.

These debates were had a decade ago, and I'm frustrated that they haven't really moved on. I suppose it's easier to talk platitudes about why things must change, wring our hands and feel guilty, rather than focus on the specific actions that would actually deliver it.

How is hard – it involves transformation, tough choices and compromise.

I'm sick of being made to feel shocked and horrified about what's going on in our world. And eco-alarmism doesn't help anyway – when you become overwhelmed by an issue you feel powerless.

Despair and pessimism is also easy. What we now need is leadership, rather than finger-pointing. And leadership can come from anywhere – politicians, citizens and businesses, large or small. For all it is about taking action; it is about doing.

In fact, I passionately believe that we should feel positivity rather than helplessness. Action is now on an ever-increasing curve: from ambitious net zero carbon roadmaps announced by governments across both the developed and developing worlds, to businesses reimagining their role in society and standing up for climate and social justice, to a global movement of school children striking for a better future.

Mindsets are changing, and rapidly at that: climate and biodiversity is suddenly the top of political agendas, the protecting and rewilding of landscapes are becoming urgent priorities, and business and investors are enthusiastically embracing lower carbon futures. Total carbon emissions have finally stabilised in recent years, and a December 2020 report by the Climate Action Tracker suggested that the Paris Agreement's goals are finally coming within reach.[38]

People talk about 'saving the planet' – but the planet will be just fine, in the long term at least. What we really mean is 'saving ourselves', and when nature and climate issues are viewed through the lens of social justice, a whole new world of possibilities opens up.

At an individual level, this can mean affordable and accessible public transport for all, improved mental health, breathing clean air, alleviating winter fuel poverty and reducing household expenditure.

From a business perspective this means reviving left-behind local economies to restore pride in our overlooked communities, creating 'green collar' jobs in brand new industries fuelled by innovative technologies.

Politically, this means reclaiming our decision-making away from corrosive corporate lobbying and reimagining and redesigning our public infrastructure to create a fresh system that rewards good environmental outcomes and penalises bad behaviour. And at a time of leaving the EU, we have the opportunity to block harmful new trade deals and rewrite old ones.

This book attempts to move the agenda on, by focusing on what business and government can do about social and climate injustice, and how we can go about it. This is not a theory book written by an outside commentator: I draw upon my direct experiences to focus on how corporations can become more resilient, more successful and act as better social enterprises – benefitting the many not the few.

As I show from over 20 years of corporate activism by Iceland, I believe that maintaining healthy sales and profits, while also doing the right thing, need not be a zero-sum game.

At the end of each chapter I have pulled out some of the key lessons I've learned so far, or advice and recommendations I would give.

I draw both upon my own personal experiences and of those as Iceland's managing director. I also look into our long history of trying to make a mass-market value food retailer more environmentally conscious and socially progressive. I try to be honest – not just about our successes, but also about the huge scale of the challenges we've faced along the road towards a more sustainable form of business.

I examine the realities of how industries might change for the better, the responsibility that business has to do so and show examples of those leading lights who are doing just that.

I lay bare the commercial trade-offs between giving consumers what they want versus what they say they want; and of the tensions between being in business to make a profit versus being in business to do the right thing.

In 2020, our experiences on the front line of the Covid-19 nightmare saw heroic actions from colleagues, communities pulling together and unprecedented levels of industry and government collaboration. I consider what the constructive legacy could be for business, communities and sustainability – how we can, in actual practice, 'build back better'.

Over the decades, there have been many who have depicted capitalism as being at war with our planet. But we do not need to change the system; we need to change how we *do* the system. Ultimately, we have got to make positive social and environmental actions align with the making of money.

Crucially, those actions must come from a position of honesty, authenticity and integrity. Not only is this what consumers deserve: it is the only viable course of action now that digital empowerment through the internet makes insincerity easy for anyone to spot and call out.

I passionately believe that by understanding the true urgency of the situation in which we find ourselves, by bringing people together and, above all, by acting with empathy and kindness, businesses must be the catalyst for a better future.

CHAPTER 1
A WHISTLESTOP TOUR OF 'DOING IT RIGHT'

Iceland's quest to become a more responsible business

'NEVER, EVER, EVER, EVER GIVE UP.'

SIR MALCOLM WALKER[1]

Before I started at Iceland, I thought 'retail' merely consisted of putting something on a shelf and waiting for it to sell. Upon joining, I quickly learned that food retailing is infinitely more complex than that – involving deep analysis and a vast amount of minutiae. Product development and procurement, supply chain logistics, store operations, merchandising, customer insight and communication are all essential ingredients of the retail cocktail. I had also assumed that Iceland is in the business of selling frozen food ... which of course is partly true, as well as retailing other products sold in other ways, as I'll explain in a moment.

But the company is many other things too – an employer, an investor, a consumer, a producer, a supplier, a taxpayer, a community, an activist and a philanthropist. Like every corporation viewed in its entirety, Iceland is an extraordinary institution, which combines many different purposes and values for a multitude of stakeholders; not just its shareholders.

Viewing our business in this multi-stakeholder way gives me a profound sense of our responsibility, both to society and the planet. And it is the drawing upon each of these stakeholder responsibilities which informs the best strategic decision-making for the long-term health of our business.

Our business

We're a fairly small business by the standards of the market in which we operate. Although we now have an annual turnover of £4 billion, we are the smallest national food retailer in the UK, with a growing grocery market share of just over 2 per cent.

We have three distinct businesses within our group. There's the 850+ Iceland stores, traditionally smaller shops on high streets, in pretty much every town and city community across the UK and Ireland. Then, in 2014 we also started The Food Warehouse, which are much larger, destination supermarkets with a focus on bulk buys, located on 150 retail parks and expanding rapidly. And finally, our online business, where we pick from store before opening and deliver to more households than the digital supermarket specialist Ocado every week. Each business has a focus on frozen food but sells equally as many chilled and ambient groceries.

The last half a century has been a swashbuckling tale of constant evolution and adaptation for Iceland. Against the odds, facing goliath market incumbents such as Tesco or Sainsbury's, we've successfully grown the business for 50 years in what has to be one of the most competitive industries on the planet.[2] Indeed, one of my Dad's favourite quotes is by a management guru called Mori Shepman, who spoke to him at some business conference he attended decades ago. Dad can't remember anything about the speech, except for the pertinent line: '… if you guys still want to be in business in five years' time, then you better be in a different business.' A healthy dose of paranoia that it might all end tomorrow has served us well, because *nothing* is ever taken for granted.

But the one constant, and the only thing that hasn't changed over the last half a century, is our culture. It's been carefully crafted, curated and invested in since 1970. If perpetual evolution is how we've been able to grow and prosper, our rock-solid culture is why we've been able to do it.

We are something of an outlaw within the supermarket sector – family owned and operated, as opposed to our publicly listed competitors, which are run by faceless managerial careerists who will move on every three years. Being the smallest of the national food retailers, we're often seen as the 'say it how it is' underdog who punches well above its weight. Sometimes, I think that our larger competitors view us as the petulant kid at the back of the classroom. Indeed, many times over the last half century we have been able to lead our whole industry in new directions. Smallness can be beautiful in enabling businesses like ours to be agile and fast-moving – low on bureaucracy and high on impact.

We can stand up and publicly speak out on issues we really care about. I've done this numerous times, on shows such as BBC One's often-heated panel debate *Question Time*; or facing off against the often-outraged Piers Morgan on ITV's *Good Morning Britain*.

Because we are embedded within 1,000 communities around the UK, we see and hear many of the daily problems people struggle with today – and I feel like we have a duty to talk openly about it rather than hide away. In today's world business does not have enough of a face, which only makes society's low opinion of it worse.

Many employees are attracted to work for us precisely because of this unique and irreverent style. And it engenders fierce loyalty too. In terms of the UK public's perception of us, it's fair to say that we have traditionally been a 'Marmite' brand. As I mentioned in the Introduction, we serve well over 5 million customers a week, and around half the UK's population will shop with us in the course of a year. Some make a dedicated visit once a year at Christmas just for our famous party food offerings; many others are steadfast, regular shoppers.

On the flip side, around half the population absolutely loathes us – usually without having ever set foot in one of our stores. This negativity is driven by the false perception that we sell cheap, over-processed frozen food that is only bought by really poor people who can't afford anything better (and advertised by C-list celebrities like Kerry Katona). British snobbery at its worst.

Yet actually – and perhaps surprisingly – we've been leading the way on a range of ethical issues for decades. We've believed in 'Doing It Right' ever since my Dad picked up a book of matches from Marriott Hotels in the States in the 1970s. They were renowned for great customer service and their motto on the matchbook was 'We Do It Right'.

So, yes, he stole the idea. But then Dad, along with his business partner Peter Hinchcliffe, also stole the idea of selling loose frozen food – which was how we started in 1970 – from Lewis's department store in Leeds. There's no disgrace in borrowing someone else's idea so long as you execute it a little better than the person you took it from. Once Mum had thought of the name 'Iceland'[3], they were away.

Dad and Peter put in £60 between them to pay for the first month's rent, with Dad borrowing his £30 share from his Mum.[4] They managed to negotiate credit for everything else – from the food to the freezers.

They bought catering packs of fish fingers, burgers, peas and so on, and from a tiny shop in Oswestry, Shropshire, sold them by weight to customers looking for something to eat that day, who were buying frozen food to eat fresh.

Back in 1970, amazing though it seems today, many consumers did not even own a fridge, let alone a freezer, so they had nowhere to store a full pack of Birds Eye or Findus branded frozen food – and buying it loose and unbranded was also cheaper. With no pointless plastic packaging, selling loose frozen food is one of those old ideas that now looks like an up-to-the-minute, environmentally friendly dream.

Dad worked the stock and my Mum was on the checkout. It was exciting, but long hours, not helped by the fact that to hedge their bets they owned and ran a late-night fish and chip shop as well. After Iceland's first week Dad added up the takings, deducted the costs – and had turned a small profit. After the same result every week for six months, they realised they didn't need the chip shop any more.

I look back on those warm, yellow-toned photos of that first store. The window posters, the signage inside, all in that oversized 70s bubble writing advertising the pre-decimal prices per pound. Dad stood in front, wearing a huge toothy grin and an even bigger, kipper-style tie. And my Mum, with her long, straight dark hair, stood proudly next to him.

Fresh versus frozen

Back in the 1980s, 'Doing It Right' meant being the first UK supermarket to remove artificial colours, flavours and preservatives, monosodium glutamate and mechanically recovered meat from our own label food. Because the point that the snobs who look down on frozen food miss is that freezing is an entirely natural process – 'nature's pause button' – that locks in nutrients and minimises the need for the preservatives and other additives required to give 'fresh' food an economically viable shelf-life. It's nothing new – the Greeks and Romans stored food in special cellars containing compressed snow to preserve food naturally.

We relish busting 'fresh versus frozen' myths. Your more expensive 'fresh' Christmas turkey? – often slaughtered months earlier and kept in depot deep chillers until it's defrosted and sold as fresh in mid-December. What about premium priced 'fresh' fish, sold on a bed of ice from that lovely fishmonger's counter in your local supermarket? Well, that has also been previously frozen, defrosted in store and sold supposedly as fresh ... either that, or it really is fresh – has been transported via a high carbon supply chain and is nearing the end of its life at the point of sale.[5] Those aromatic hot cross buns at Easter – manufactured and frozen the previous year. Fresh pizza – previously frozen constituents that have been reassembled. Chilled soup – frozen. All con jobs, sold to an often-uninformed public for a premium.[6]

Corporate activism

In 1998 Iceland took a global lead on becoming the first retailer *anywhere in the world* to ban Genetically Modified ('GM') ingredients from our own label products. Something that everyone told us was completely unnecessary and technically impossible, but which we did anyway – driven by my Dad's personal conviction that it was wrong for consumers to have no choice but to eat what he coined 'Frankenstein food'.[7]

Segregating GM ingredients out of our supply chain was no small feat. At the time, 60 per cent of processed foods contained soya, mainly sourced from the US. The agrochemical companies had started to deliberately mix non-GM soya with GM products, making traceability difficult. Iceland tracked down suppliers outside the US who did not use the gene technology, and we introduced gene-testing measures to our supply chain. We relied heavily on the hard work and tenacity of our suppliers, and in turn the suppliers to our suppliers. But by sticking steadfastly with a clear end goal, and without giving way to compromise or political pressure, we were able to secure non-GM sourcing relatively quickly.

At the time, the GM debate had become symbolic of humans' ever-increasing domination over nature. On the one hand, multinationals such as the US agrochemical company Monsanto heralded their technological ability to provide drought-resistant crops supplemented with vitamins, which could reduce disease and feed the world.[8] On the other hand, environmental NGOs such as Greenpeace saw GM as an unacceptable crossing of the

Rubicon – one notable example being the transferring of Arctic fish genes into strawberries (in order to make them resistant to cold and frost, in case you wondered).[9]

Things started to get febrile. Two months after Iceland's announcement, the Prince of Wales called for a public debate on the merits of allowing GM crops to be grown in Britain.[10] The late Lord Melchett, the former boss of Greenpeace UK, was briefly incarcerated for his role in the NGO's direct action cutting down a field of GM maize in Norfolk[11] (and in a genius PR move, Dad sent him an Iceland Black Forest Gateau while in prison with a 10-inch file wedged inside). Hilary Berg, mastermind behind most of Iceland's corporate activism over the last 25 years, received a threatening legal letter from Monsanto – hand-delivered to her remote cottage in rural Cheshire. And the company's then CEO reacted to Iceland's announcement by ordering a worldwide advertising blitz – including spending millions on British press ads that unsuccessfully sought to convince the public of the technology's safety.[12]

My own opinion is that the frantic race through the late 1990s to introduce GM into food chains was much less about 'feeding the world', and much more about companies like Monsanto selling their GM crop-compatible weedkiller Roundup. The 'Roundup Ready' GM soybean, invented in 1996, was resistant to glyphosate, allowing farmers simply to spray their crops to eliminate weeds in place of much more expensive mechanical methods. Its appeal to both Monsanto and farmers was obvious; the benefit to consumers rather harder to discern. And to nature, well, once things are done, there is no undo.

In May 2019, over 20 years after Iceland's seminal campaign, news came that a US jury had awarded $2 billion of damages against Monsanto to a couple who successfully argued that use of the glyphosate-based weedkiller Roundup caused their cancers. A further 13,000 lawsuits related to the weedkiller have also been launched in the US.[13] The cases continue.[14]

Dad has always had a sincere passion for naturally produced food. It started when one day he noticed his gardener spraying weedkiller onto the vegetables he was growing ... and eating. Yet, not only was the gardener wearing a mask, but the spray had a distinct 'skull and crossbones' toxic symbol on the bottle. It spurred his life-long interest in growing low-input fruit and vegetables.

I remember as a kid coming home from school one day to discover four disabled hedgehogs trundling around the walled vegetable garden. Unable to be released into the wild, they were adopted by Dad to keep down pests – he named them after the other supermarket CEOs (Archie, Phil, Dino and Ken). He even founded a chain of London-based organic supermarkets 'As Nature Intended', which my sister Caroline successfully operated for almost 20 years.

Despite initially being ridiculed when we announced our GM campaign, within months every other UK supermarket had copied us, responding to overwhelming consumer demand. It's kept the country pretty much GM-free right up to the present day.

I am, of course, hugely proud of the part that Iceland played in the GM debate. And yet, to quote John Maynard Keynes, 'When the facts change, I change my mind.'

Given what we now know about the soil degradation that has resulted from the ever-increasing use of fertiliser to prop up crop yields, GM (or its less controversial, related technology 'genetic editing') is today seen by a minority of environmentalists – including myself – as a potential opportunity to restore nature within our agricultural environments. Man's manipulation of nature, which extends to 'geoengineering' techniques such as cloud seeding or fertilising the oceans with iron, remain highly controversial. Yet I believe that they now must be openly considered if we are to deploy our full armoury of potential solutions in our fight for the climate and nature.[15]

Another seminal campaign was Iceland's key role in scrapping industry's use of chlorofluorocarbons (CFCs). By the late 1990s, climate scientists had become utterly alarmed at the depletive effect these insidious gases, used in technologies such as refrigerants and aerosols, were having on the Earth's ozone layer. Back in those days not only did we sell frozen foods but were also the biggest retailer of fridges and freezers in the country. So, we felt compelled to step up and take action – becoming the first retailer to get serious about capturing, recycling and ultimately replacing CFCs with the now commonplace hydrofluorocarbons (HFCs).[16] In 1998 we launched the eco-friendly Kyoto range in partnership with Greenpeace, using natural gases. It was the first – and I think still the only – commercial product the campaign group ever endorsed.

We called on the domestic refrigeration industry to follow our lead and delisted Hotpoint (owned by the market dominant General Electric) as the only supplier that refused to comply. Iceland is now written into environmental history books as being pivotal in 'Greenfreeze' technology becoming commonplace within five or six years.[17]

Our corporate activism for causes that the Iceland community really cares about continues up to the present day. Sometimes it's not just about the big, disruptive campaigns; small tactical actions are also important.

During the Covid-19 lockdown of summer 2020, Chester Zoo was forced to close. Without any visitors they started to run out of money, fast – needing £1.6 million of funding per month just to survive.[18] A major north-west attraction, it was a big part of my childhood growing up and now my kids love going there too. This was also clearly the case for many of our customers and colleagues, as we began to receive concerned comments about it. By June, the situation had become critical. The issue was compounded by the fact that while attractions such as Kew Gardens were allowed to reopen, despite Chester Zoo having plenty of space to do so in a Covid-secure way, they were not being allowed to.

The team at the Zoo decided to take action and sent out a public call for help using the slogan #SaveOurZoo. We began to lobby the government. I wrote to the Prime Minister and cabinet members, as did my kids and some of our customers. The campaign really took off when we adopted the Zoo's entire rookery of Humboldt penguins – all 50 of them.[19] Suddenly, staff and store teams all around the country started to do so too. Very quickly we had enough exotic animals for our own Iceland Zoo, including lions, giraffes, orangutans (of course – see Chapter 4) and red pandas. We even donated the cash profits from our McVitie's Penguin bar sales to the Zoo.

Within a week, the government saw sense and the Zoo was allowed to reopen – safeguarding their 35,000 threatened and critically endangered animals, the jobs they support and allowing their world-renowned research and conservation work to continue. We were proud to play a small part in the Zoo's campaign to engage the public and help change the government's policy.

A business of families

Iceland is often described as a 'family business', but it's more than that. There are generations of families who work at every level of the business. From Peterhead to Penzance: we've got mums, sons, dads, daughters, grandparents and godparents. People who've been Icelanders for over 40 years, and those (like me) who grew up with the business and now work in the business.

This family culture makes us completely unique and sets us apart from the competition. When we embrace it and celebrate it, we can drive the business forward – and have fun doing it. I *always* try to be as accessible as possible to all of our staff – replying to emails and social media messages, dropping in on random stores around the country or wandering around the head office having a chat to whoever's about. It's amazing how many bosses hide away in their offices, not knowing the reality on the ground or the mood of the company.

The average distance that our staff and customers live from store is only 3 miles – 80 per cent of our staff live within walking distance of where they work. That means

30,000 of us, embedded within communities all over the UK, serving our 5 million neighbours, friends and family. It is something very different compared to any other retailer – such as those monolithic, sterile out-of-town supermarkets where people may travel for 10 or 20 miles to shop there.

Simply being there for each other is our secret weapon. When we get it right – like winning Best Big Companies to Work For, twice over the last decade – it means unparalleled levels of colleague engagement.[20] People are often surprised that a northern-based, discount food retailer can be voted the leading employer. But it's about how valued our colleagues feel. The first year we won, in 2012, one of the questions on the survey was 'How well do you think you're paid?' Our mostly modestly paid colleagues declared themselves more satisfied with their pay than the mega-bonused bankers at Goldman Sachs, who came in second place.[21]

As well as it being the right thing to try and keep our staff happy, there is, of course, a commercial reason too. Employee satisfaction translates directly into happy customers – such as in 2018, when we reached the top of the UK Customer Satisfaction Index for food retailers.[22] After a lifetime in retail, Dad knows that happiness pays, as his oft-repeated mantra attests: 'Happy staff means happy customers ... who put money in the till.'

Finding enough time to celebrate, have banter and fun along the way is critical in the tireless world of food retail. We've become known for our spectacular Store Manager Conferences, like in 2009 when we flew 800 Icelanders to Disneyworld in Florida to learn about unparalleled customer service – and have a party.[23]

This community feel spreads to our customers as well. We care about the high streets from which we operate and the communities we serve, and as I'll discuss in Chapter 6, the decline of bricks and mortar retail shops in our town centres needs to be urgently addressed if we are to maintain this unique fabric of our society.

We have a responsibility to our most vulnerable and lonely customers, with our staff potentially being the only person some of them see day to day. This issue came to the forefront during the early days of the Covid-19 lockdown, when many of the elderly and vulnerable were unable to get access to the goods they needed in store due to panic buying.[24] In response, driven by an idea from our West Belfast store we were the first to roll out accessible shopping hours for the elderly and vulnerable (more about this in Chapter 5).

Our store network can also form a powerful community campaign vehicle. On Boxing Day of 1996, two close friends Patrick Warren and David Spencer disappeared from their estate in Solihull, Birmingham. They were aged 11 and 13.[25] Around that time, as part of a wider radio discussion about kids who go missing, Dad happened to hear while driving to the office one day a distraught mother talking about the unfillable void that is left behind when your child vanishes. It really got to him. The lady described in heartbreaking detail how she still kept her son's room unchanged, some 15 years later, willing him to come home.

As soon as he got to the office, Dad called the National Missing Persons Helpline and offered to put photos of the two Solihull boys onto our milk cartons (an idea known as the 'Milk Carton Kids', which Dad had noticed the retailer Safeway doing on a trip to the US). Despite being on the shelves for over four weeks, the nationwide campaign yielded no leads.

But we did manage to deliver some successes. Between 1997 and 2006, we placed over 130 different missing person appeals on our milk carton packaging, of which over 40 were subsequently found.[26]

Reducing our impact

One of the great contradictions of the very concept of 'sustainable capitalism', is that businesses exist to produce stuff and encourage the consumption of it. If you think about it, no human economic activity is truly *sustainable* because it always takes more resources from the planet than it replaces. And yet every corporate noun nowadays seems to be prefixed with the word 'sustainable'. Apparently, we can have it all: 'sustainable consumption', 'sustainable flying'... even 'sustainable growth'.

Yvon Chouinard and Vincent Stanley set the record straight in their book *The responsible company: What We've Learned from Patagonia's First 40 Years*, 'A word about a word we've chosen to use as little as possible: *sustainability*. It's a legitimate term that calls us not to take more from nature than we give back. But we do take more than we give, we do harm nature more than we help it.'

Quite so. And for the record: Iceland is a long way from being a sustainable company, either. We are a mass market, high volume food retailer subject to many contradictions. We are *far* from perfect. But what we can do, however, is seek to minimise our footprint wherever possible.

As a food retailer the main way we can do this is by reducing food waste – in our supply chains, in our stores and in customers' homes. And at least in the first and second of those areas, food waste equals cost. Therefore, it's an easy sell internally to push to reduce it.

I hate it, because it's morally wrong to throw food in the bin – yet one-third of all the food produced in the world goes to waste.[27] But it is also a leading contributor to climate change: if food waste were a country it would be the third-biggest carbon emitter after the US and China.[28] Considering that the world is also on track to double its food supply by 2050 to feed the expected 9 billion on our planet[29], it is therefore essential that we start managing what we have in our supply chain first.

With food waste, not only are we wasting all the energy and water it took to grow, harvest, package and transport it; if it ends up in landfill it rots and produces methane – a greenhouse gas many times more potent than CO_2. It is unsurprising, therefore, that food waste contributes 8 per cent to all greenhouse emissions.[30] So never mind LED lightbulbs or electric cars – one of the most environmentally positive things you can do in your lives is simply not to waste food.

Our Finance Director, however, hates it even more ... considering that food waste also represents lost profits that are being chucked in the bin. Iceland currently wastes just 0.5 per cent of the food we sell – below industry average, but nevertheless that's a whopping £20 million of lost sales through the till.

And so, it's one of those perfect problems which

everyone is motivated to try and solve. The rub is that society is having food waste conversations at the wrong level. A series of celebrity chefs and other campaigners have lined up to castigate the British public for their reckless profligacy, and retailers and food manufacturers for pandering to these appalling habits.

But just let us pause to consider the reality of trying to feed a family on a really tight budget, perhaps dependent on the vagaries of Universal Credit. Are you really likely to be chucking edible food in the bin? No.

I attach much more weight to their insights than to those of comfortably off campaigners, and was particularly struck by one colleague, who works for us in the North West, who told me: 'If you're a family with only £25 a week to spend on food, you are not wasting food. In fact, you are an expert in providing good food for your family on a limited budget. If we want to learn about how to prevent food waste, these are the people we need to listen to.'

WRAP, the Waste and Resources Action Programme and the UK's 'circular economy and resource efficiency experts', conclude that the average British family wastes £70 a month on food[31], yet this is a clearly not a story I can recognise among Iceland customers. I would like to see a demographic breakdown of food waste so we can target messages more appropriately. Anecdotal evidence suggests that people who are cash rich and time poor (like me) are the main food waste culprits: not our average customer.

We also need to acknowledge the important role that freezing can play in cutting food waste, not just by freezing leftovers and batch cooking, but by buying more frozen food in the first place. Yes, I recognise that 'He would say that, wouldn't he?', but it is nonetheless true.

When Iceland ran a study with Manchester Metropolitan University early in 2020, working with 20 families for two weeks and switching them to frozen food, they ate healthily, saved the equivalent of £1,500 per year and literally halved their food waste.[32] These results have been echoed in wider UK and European research.[33]

We have been using wonky veg for the last 50 years, solving seasonality, ensuring value by freezing produce when it is most abundant, using ships not planes to transport it – and a few years ago our technical team extended the shelf life of many of our products from one to two years upon realising they can last perfectly safely for longer.

But while frozen food can really help any family on a tight budget, we also need to recognise that many of the poorest cannot afford a freezer. When we helped struggling families with frozen food recently, 80 per cent of the parents we spoke to had nowhere to store it – a good example of the intersection between environmental and social issues.

We also need to stamp on the idea that food waste giveaways somehow offer an answer to poverty. Private charity can never be a substitute for public welfare, and we need to get to a better place where people are given greater respect and security. Recently I met some of the clients at a food bank local to our head office and found brave, capable people who, despite the kindness of the volunteers, were stripped of their dignity by having to rely on handouts. A father who was out of work for the first time ever, had summoned up the courage to come in off the street, to be handed a carrier bag of pasta and canned food. He was in tears.

Food is a fundamental human right and there is no place for hungry children in our communities. I firmly believe this demands an overhaul of the welfare system, with an onus on the government to measure family food insecurity and coordinate a national strategy between departments.

Retailers are often painted as the villains, yet according to WRAP, a shameful 70 per cent of all food waste in the UK now occurs in the home. In 2018 that equated to 6.6 million tonnes – of which almost three-quarters was food that we could have eaten. The hospitality and food service sector accounts for 12 per cent of all food waste, manufacturing 16 per cent and retail only 3 per cent.[34] Campaigners' repeated calls for an end to wasteful 'buy one get one free' deals miss the point by failing to recognise the legion of real people who rely on these deals to feed their children.

Of course, none of us wants to waste food that could be put to good use. At Iceland, since 2017–18 we have reduced food waste in our own operations by 23.2 per cent.[35] And like other responsible retailers, we have been ensuring for years that none of our surplus food ends up in landfill, where the methane emissions from rotting food further contribute to global warming. Our backstop is anaerobic digestion to generate electricity and produce fertiliser, but we would much prefer edible food not to end up there either.[36]

We have set up systems to divert our depot surpluses

for use in the community through Company Shop and its Community Shop affiliate, and work with an amazing charity called The Bread and Butter Thing to help feed families across Greater Manchester and Lancashire.[37] Our retail teams have pioneered the collection of unsold bread and morning goods from our stores to be repurposed as animal feed. We are helping other, bigger supermarkets to do the same.[38] In 2018, we even took the unusual step of partnering with the Tiny Rebel brewery in Newport, South Wales, to make an award-winning craft beer from waste bread. Ten pence from every bottle of Bread Board was donated to the marine conservation charity Surfers Against Sewage (of which I am Chairman) to fund UK beach cleans.[39]

After years of struggling to think how we could efficiently repurpose the very limited, often random, items of food waste that our stores have left over each night, our CEO Tarsem Dhaliwal came up with a simple, yet disruptive idea: give it away to our colleagues. If that sounds obvious, consider the fact that in the past, some retailers have been so distrusting of their staff that they poured bleach on unsold food in order to stop internal theft. We trust our colleagues, who are embedded within the communities they serve, so are best placed to know how to redistribute food locally to those in need.[40]

There is ample business willpower to tackle food waste, but we need a policy framework that helps us. The US has introduced corporate tax relief on donated food.[41] Nine EU countries offer tax relief on food donations and French retailers that donate food surplus to charities receive a significant 60 per cent tax break.[42] None of which provides cures to poverty, but does provide easier ways for business to redistribute food and, therefore, alleviate the symptoms of hunger (while also being a better alternative than anaerobic digestion or landfill).

We also need more empathetic policy decisions on how we deal with the food that is inevitably wasted in the home, despite the best of intentions, even if that is confined to potato peelings and trimmings. More than 13.4 million English households are unable to recycle their leftover food, representing 57 per cent of all council collections.[43] Therefore the government's commitment to roll out separate food waste collections across the country by 2023 is welcome news.[44] Coupled with this, we need to create industrial composting at scale, to handle not only food waste but also the new generation of compostable packaging that is coming on stream to replace plastic.

Another type of waste business can seek to minimise is that of carbon. As climate change becomes the issue of our generation, carbon reduction is suddenly at the top of every business agenda. At Iceland, that has been the case for the last ten years – although I have to admit its early adoption was a consequence of the business's constant drive for efficiency rather than the output of an enlightened board.

The fact is, Iceland has a secret weapon in the war against carbon. Our Central Services team is led by the urbane Nick Jones, a veteran Iceland director, who epitomises the company's action-orientated approach. Nick leads our team of boffins – engineers and property and technical specialists who drive innovation and improvement and are immersed in the fabric of the business. They do this with quiet humility – no noise, no award entries, no self-congratulation, but it turns out their efforts are having a big impact.

In 2011, they set themselves targets to reduce our operational carbon footprint (known as Scope 1 and 2) by 30 per cent by 2020 and 60 per cent by 2030, with the aim of meeting the government's target of net zero by 2050. They then rolled up their sleeves and set to work.

Since then they have steadily switched our freezers to use greener gasses, with new models saving 30 per cent of energy. We have invested millions in new signage and salesfloor LED lighting, automatically synchronised with opening times. We even now turn off our store fascia signs at night – saving energy and nocturnal insects.[45]

In 2019 the team switched the entire business to 100 per cent renewable electricity. At the same time, they have worked with retail and depot colleagues to re-plan our HGV and van journeys, trained all of our drivers to use telematics, and are exploring the use of electric vehicles.[46]

Our quest to save energy has seen our carbon footprint drop from almost a quarter of a million tonnes of CO_2 in 2011 to just 46,257 tonnes in 2020: a 74 per cent reduction, despite having added a net 181 stores and grown sales by 36 per cent over the same nine-year period.[47] That also means we should reach zero carbon years ahead of our original target of 2050, which Nick Jones and team put down to 'just doing our job'.

An employer

Perhaps the most obvious way in which our business contributes to society, is our role as an employer. As I mentioned earlier, Iceland employs tens of thousands of people directly and provides jobs for many thousands more in our supply chain. I am always conscious that the business keeps roofs over their heads and food on their tables – and that I have a responsibility to ensure that anything we do to improve planetary sustainability does not detract from our ability to provide sustainable employment.

When I talk about democratising environmentalism and making it relevant to everyone, I am conscious that we must always maintain the right balance between our responsibilities to our own people, the communities we serve directly, wider society and the natural world.

'Doing It Right' for our people means paying them as well as we can and treating them like I would like to be treated myself. Following our return to private ownership in 2005 we consciously drove up our hourly pay rates so that we became almost the highest-paying retailer on the high street – in fact, second only to Tesco, and ahead of supposed 'blue chip' retailers like Marks & Spencer and John Lewis. Unlike many of our competitors, we have also always paid the same rate regardless of age and experience, refusing to take advantage of the loophole that still exists in minimum wage legislation, allowing lower rates of pay for those under 25.

The welcome introduction of the National Minimum (now National Living) Wage has driven up pay rates across the retail industry, and eroded our ability to pay a significant premium to it, particularly since the business model for our traditional high street stores means that wages are a considerably higher proportion of our costs than they are for the major supermarkets, and still more so when compared with our fast-growing discounter rivals. Nevertheless, we continue to work hard to keep our pay rates moving up ahead of the statutory minimum.[48]

An investor and taxpayer

Over our last three financial years Iceland has invested close to £200 million in the business, mainly in opening new stores and refurbishing existing ones to make them more appealing to consumers – and to provide a better working environment for my colleagues. Instead of taking money out of the company in the form of dividends, we plough it back into making the business better and stronger for the future.

We also believe that business has a duty to pay its fair share of fair taxes, to fund the public services on which we all rely. Since Iceland became a private company in 2005, we have paid more than £1.6 billion in UK taxes up to April 2020[49] – and we wouldn't want to have paid a penny less. I even welcome the exponential increase in environmental taxes that have come our way in recent years.

A philanthropist

Businesses can – and should – also be effective philanthropists. Our own Iceland Foods Charitable Foundation (IFCF) was established in 1973 and has given

£30 million to good causes to date.[50] This total was considerably boosted by the windfall generated by the introduction of a compulsory 5p charge for single-use plastic carrier bags, which is a neat example of turning a negative environmental consequence into a positive impact for society. In addition to carrier bag income, the Foundation typically raises money through two major events: an annual charity week in our stores, involving our colleagues and customers, and a charity golf day where we encourage the donation of the maximum amount possible from willing suppliers.

The IFCF has a clear mission: to make life better for people. Rather than place small amounts of money with a multitude of organisations (or as my Dad likes to put it, 'give fuck all to everyone'), we have historically focused on giving very large amounts of funding to charities where we can have a big impact. As of 2020, we have four core areas of focus: dementia, the environment, sepsis and child poverty – all important areas to the Iceland family for various reasons.

Child poverty, for example, is something that is very close to the hearts of many of our colleagues because they can clearly see the problem getting worse in the communities they serve. Following the economic damage caused by the Covid-19 pandemic, more than ever there are literally thousands of young people and families across the UK who will struggle to pay for the most basic of things, food being the most obvious one.

So, they were delighted when we announced in December 2020 that the IFCF became the lead partner with the Action for Children Secret Santa Campaign. We donated £10 on behalf of every colleague in the business, meaning that every member of the Iceland family became a Secret Santa to children in the UK – helping to provide hot meals, presents or a safe place to sleep during Christmas.

With my Mum's illness, clearly Dad and I have strong personal reasons for taking a keen interest in dementia research. But it is also an area of research that is much in need. Dementia is now officially recognised as the biggest killer in the UK[51], affecting 850,000 people and costing the economy more than £26 billion a year.[52] Yet it has never attracted the profile or funding – either from government or the charitable sector – of other terminal conditions like cancer or heart disease.[53] I am sure that this partly reflects the mistaken belief that it only affects the very elderly, who are going to die of something quite soon any way.

Dad was nervous when we first adopted Alzheimer's Research UK as our official charity partner in 2011. How would our colleagues react to being asked to raise money for this rather than, say, a children's hospital?[54] But he was pleasantly surprised to find that the response was overwhelmingly positive, because almost everyone in the business had direct experience of dementia within their family or circle of friends.

Shortly before the carrier bag charge was extended to England in 2015, my Dad went to a meeting about the construction of an urgently needed new UK Dementia Research Institute, to bring together all the leading scientific researchers working to find an effective treatment or preventive for the condition. He was told that there was a shortfall of £100 million in the funding needed to make it happen.

On the way home he had his own lightbulb moment: the money likely to be raised by the new carrier bag levy would be around £100 million a year, so if he could persuade all the UK's food retailers to pledge their money to dementia research – for just 12 months – they could make it happen.

He worked really hard to persuade our competitors to step up to the plate – as Asda, Waitrose and Morrisons all did. Despite being continually told that it was all too late, with the support of these rivals and some other, smaller retailers, we managed to raise a total of £20 million – of which Iceland itself gave half. And while this was well short of our original hopes, it proved to be enough to trigger other funding from government and charities ensuring that the building of the new Dementia Research Institute went ahead.[55]

For these charitable efforts, as well as all the other good that has come out of the business he founded and grew, Sir Dad was knighted in the Queen's Birthday Honours of 2017.

My own view on 21st-century philanthropy has developed out of Iceland's approach. It's no longer OK for a donor to write a big cheque and walk away – there needs to be a plan. Looking forward, the most effective donor relationships will be based on strategic investment and collaboration, by getting the right people together in order to make things happen. By maximising and measuring social impact, we can help to create solutions that make people's lives better and are sustainable over the long term.

. . . .

There was never a grand plan or end vision for Iceland. Through a combination of hard work and good luck (which often seem to go hand in hand), Iceland has grown into an extraordinarily successful business – far beyond what my Mum and Dad could have initially envisaged working from that first, tiny shop in 1970.

But there has always been a set of beliefs since our foundation. I came across an internal book we produced to celebrate the company's 20th anniversary in 1991 called *Doing It Right*. Long before concepts such as 'Corporate Social Responsibility' (CSR) became fashionable, the following statement struck me as something that must have been quite progressive for its time:

> *Iceland has a commitment to protect the environment and preserve the quality of life. We care about the planet, natural resources, family life, fair practices and community issues, and in all company business give them due consideration. The cornerstone to our success is, and will continue to be, linking efficiency with a social conscience and profitability with good business ethics.*[56]

From delving back through the company archives, late-night discussions with Dad over bottles of wine, and my last few years working within the company, I would summarise these principles as follows:

THE ICELAND PRINCIPLES

LOVE OUR CUSTOMERS
Because without them we wouldn't exist.

BE LONG-TERM GREEDY
Focus on doing it right, and the profits will follow.

CUT MINDLESS BUREAUCRACY
Something that can easily choke a business and hamper your
ability to stay agile and keep innovating.

STAND UP FOR OUR PEOPLE
Be that our customers, colleagues or the communities we serve.

STAY FOCUSED AND ACCEPT REALITY
Remember exactly what business you are in. Don't try to be
anything else.

KEEP IT SIMPLE
Easier said than done in today's multi-channel retail world.

... AND REMEMBER TO HAVE SOME FUN ALONG THE WAY
Rewarding and recognising success is so important. Sometimes
when you're in the trenches it's easy to forget that.

Looking back, these principles have formed a framework,
of sorts, that describes us when we're at our best; or 'how
we do things around here'. In a word, it's our *culture*.
Something that has been the bedrock for past successes,
and for certain our future survival.

CHAPTER 2
BEAUTIFUL CORPORATIONS

What businesses need to do

'THE BUSINESS OF BUSINESS SHOULD NOT BE ABOUT MONEY. IT SHOULD BE ABOUT RESPONSIBILITY. IT SHOULD BE ABOUT PUBLIC GOOD, NOT PRIVATE GREED.'

DAME ANITA RODDICK[1]

I remember watching media coverage of the Extinction Rebellion protests that multiplied across the UK throughout 2019. Boomer generation vicars were gluing themselves to gateposts. Bullnose-ringed millennials haphazardly attempted to spray the Treasury with fake blood from a fire engine. Capitalist mausoleums everywhere were under attack from decentralised, middle-class mobs.

One such unfortunate cohort had elected to unfurl a protest banner on the roof of a London Underground train carriage that had stopped at the station of the traditionally working class and ethnically diverse Canning Town – in the morning rush hour.[2] Big mistake.

'I've got to feed my kids!', screamed one exasperated commuter as the angry crowd surged to detach the protesters from the top of the train. The tension was palpable but fortunately the misguided eco-warriors were unharmed. I don't think I've seen a more powerful example of the dichotomy that can exist between some monotonal green activists and ordinary people just trying to provide for their families.

. . . .

It is of course essential to make people sit up and realise

what we are all doing to the planet. And it was ever thus – William Forster Lloyd's 1833 essay *Tragedy of the Commons* described how shared resources can become depleted or spoiled through the collective action of individuals acting out of self-interest. But as I have very quickly learned, evangelising on environmental issues to people who haven't got the luxury to prioritise such concerns above all else is wrong. We need to tell people, without telling them off.

And rather than capitalism itself being the scurrilous root cause of these problems (as some green protestors would see it), I think the private sector has a key role to play in working towards solutions. How and where businesses invest their capital, the supply chain choices they make, the products they sell and, crucially, how they communicate – to staff, suppliers and customers – can all strongly influence greener actions and agendas. Trailblazers such as Anita Roddick, who founded the cosmetics producer and retailer The Body Shop, led the way by shaping her business model around such ethical consumerism.[3]

Don't get me wrong – I'm supportive of the fact that a lot of climate activism from NGOs such as Greenpeace is directed towards big 'dirty' corporations: according to the Carbon Majors Report 2017, 100 of the active fossil fuel producers – companies such as ExxonMobil, Shell, BHP Billiton and Gazprom – were responsible for an astonishing 71 per cent of all greenhouse gas emissions since 1988.[4]

But we cannot simply say that this crisis is all about the oil and gas majors, any more than we can say that it isn't also about the rest of the business sector. Along with individual choice, corporations are the co-drivers of consumer behaviour – and consumerism is wrecking the planet. Business orchestrates what people buy, when and how they buy it – what type of car or water bottle, which mortgage product or holiday destination.

Even if a business does not deal with the end consumer – you and me – it directs how a particular product was sourced, designed, made and transported. All corporations, either directly or indirectly, shape our lives and lifestyles, so are complicit in the part we all personally play in contributing to environmental breakdown.

It follows from this that corporations are in a unique and powerful position to take action to put things right. It's simply a plain fact that every business needs to play a part in mitigating its impact and encouraging consumers to make the right choices. And above all, to be transparent so that consumers know what they are buying into behind any superficial marketing messages.

Granted, many corporations are not doing nearly enough – yet. But we will, whether it is through strategic choice, future government intervention or an upswelling of consumer demand.

A multi-stakeholder approach

The totally inadequate response from business over the last 50 years is at least partly based on the pervading, outdated and narrow-minded view that the role of a business is simply to maximise shareholder profit. Such 'shareholder primacy' is fundamentally wrong, constraining firms to a single narrow objective that has had wide-ranging and damaging consequences for the environment and society.

The Friedman Doctrine, as it's known (that shareholder profit should be the only pursuit of a business), has got a lot to answer for. First argued by the Nobel prize-winning economist Milton Friedman (described by *The Economist* magazine as 'the most influential economist of the second half of the 20th century ... possibly of all of it'[5]), who advised world leaders such as Ronald Reagan and Margaret Thatcher. His philosophy has been taught and preached in every business school and corporate handbook for the last 50 years: shareholders as sovereigns.

But as my friend John O'Brien explains in his excellent book *The Power of Purpose*, pursuing profit is not a strategy: it's a result. The reason why businesses exist is because of their purpose, not just to make money.[6] There is now a growing movement within business which believes that the Friedman Doctrine is not a law of nature and should not be the business paradigm of the 21st century.

The fact that faith and trust in business is currently at an all-time low[7] has much to do with shareholder primacy. It wasn't always the case – a century ago, great companies such as Guinness, Cadbury and Lever Brothers set up trusts and foundations at the forefront of their endeavours – their purpose was a paternalistic, benevolent capitalism. But from the 1950s the idea that enriching shareholders was the ultimate goal of any business really took hold, which has led to the exponential inequality we see today, with vast wealth concentrated among the very few.

I welcome the fact that there is a lot of discussion in business circles at the moment about whether 'purpose' should come before 'profit'. Do the right thing and the profits will follow ...? Or, be profitable to enable you to do the right thing ...? Of course, the choice is not that simple, or as binary.

Those adopting a more far-sighted view have come to realise that doing the right thing can be good for business, too. Marc Benioff, the founder, Chairman and CEO of the cloud-computing company Salesforce, correctly points out in his book *Trailblazer* that 'Over time, I've become convinced that there are two types of CEOs: those who believe that improving the state of the world is part of their mission, and those who don't feel they have any responsibility other than delivering results for their shareholders.'[8] Benioff has also reached the conclusion that Friedman was wrong, and that in addition to making a profit, business should serve to drive *stakeholder* – not just shareholder – value. The underlying point of course, is the realisation that in the long term this will be good for business.

Either way, if it follows the right path – one of consideration towards all stakeholders – then business is not the enemy ... it's the missing link within the social and environmental debate. We have the power to make a difference by following kinder, empathetic and more responsible practices; enabling the general public to see the issues and make the right choices. This chapter is a broad attempt to explain how that might happen.

The business of business

Having dealt with many different companies through my career across multiple sectors, the problem is that I don't think business genuinely sees *itself* as part of the solution. All too often it is easier for management to focus on maximising their existing business models, continue to look the other way and sell existing products to existing customers, without questioning how they can become part of the change we need. It's always tempting to side-step a difficult issue: shrug your shoulders, cross the road, put it in the 'too hard' folder, and say 'it's not my problem'. This inertia can of course be down to greed and ignorance; but from my experience it is more often the result of leaders not appreciating their power and influence on wider issues.

Because 'business' is not some segregated entity, operating within a vacuum. In fact, all that any business consists of is just a collection of individuals. Those individuals combine under a corporate structure to affect other people and the planet in positive and negative ways. Corporate entities are most definitely not things that are intransigent to change, because business is people and people are business. So, I have little time for business people who merely see themselves as passive players trapped within a status quo that they, alone, are unable to change. And if capitalism is to survive, change it must.

It's also true that, as far as the general public is concerned, business would not be front of mind as the key to unlocking a more equal society or greener future. Partly this is self-inflicted, with financial scandals such as BHS and Carillion doing so much harm, compounding the view of business as something that is corrosive to society, which needs to be treated with suspicion and disdain.[9]

Yet, while far from perfect, no other system has done more good than capitalism and the businesses that operate within it. From lifting billions out of poverty, to delivering happier and healthier lives, to giving people a sense of purpose and identity.

Our media narrative doesn't help either. I was struck by this when listening to the BBC's *Green Originals* podcast.[10] The series profiled activists, scientists, authors and politicians throughout history who had made a dramatic, positive change to environmental causes. Yet the podcast neglected to mention *anyone* from the business community. Why? Even when Microsoft made their extraordinary pledge to become carbon negative by 2030, it was met with doubt and derision in some quarters.[11] Why?! When did our healthy scepticism of business and business people turn into unbridled cynicism?

Even those enlightened operators from within the business world who recognise the problems, and realise they hold the power to engender positive change, often do not use it to full effect. This is particularly the case for smaller businesses. I often receive questions from people running small enterprises, who are concerned at the state of the world around them but feel powerless to do anything meaningful about it.

Yet no one should assume that their business is too small to make a difference. In fact, it's essential that small businesses do step up. There are almost 6 million businesses in the UK and 99 per cent of them are what are known as Small and Medium Enterprises (SMEs).[12] Globally, 95 per cent of businesses are SMEs and they contribute approximately 40 per cent to the world's aggregated gross domestic product (GDP).[13] They serve as key drivers for innovation, social impact and employment – representing 60 per cent of all private sector jobs.[14] Therefore, if we want to make a scalable impact, small businesses *must* act.

Fortunately, there are plenty of positive examples. Many micro businesses are highly socially responsible without using a CSR label – run by their founders, looking after their employees and contributing to the local community.

Iceland is a minnow by UK food retailing standards – yet as I discussed in the previous chapter, many times over the last half century we have been able to lead our whole industry in new directions. And OK, I admit we are a very big small business, with significant resources. But smallness can be beautiful in enabling businesses to be agile and fast-moving in assuming the role of a corporate activist.

And it's not just about the size of your cheque book – some of the companies having the biggest impact are on the small side. Businesses such as Responsible Travel, set up by my friend Justin Francis, which is not only seeking to change the way people think about and go on holiday, but is lobbying the government and aviation industry to think in the same way too. Or the Bristol-based Boston Tea Party, which in 2018 became the first coffee chain in the world to stop selling single-use coffee cups – a move that led to pretty much every coffee shop chain around the world taking action.

All businesses, regardless of size, have a platform and a responsibility to take a lead and make their voices heard. And if you feel that you are so small that you're not being heard ... then just shout louder.

Too many companies, from start-ups to multi-nationals, opt for generic, herd commitments on everything from climate goals, diversity and product standards. Ironically, it can be the case that the more ambitious companies can be held back through collaborative frameworks of existing agreements. Being bold and going above and beyond basic minimums sometimes means breaking rank and upsetting industry peers.[15]

Fear of failure can also hold people back, particularly in today's social media-led world where there is seemingly zero room for error. We operate within a system, particularly in the UK, where people and organisations are often ridiculed and publicly humiliated for failure. Or 'found out' in 'gotcha' exposés if 100 per cent of ambitious targets are not quite reached.

A good example is that of the drinks multinational Diageo, who in 2008 announced an ambitious set of environmental targets including a 50 per cent reduction in carbon emissions by 2015. These were entirely voluntary, and all accurately measured and transparently shared. They fell short on seven of their eight main goals and were lambasted.[16] Yet, the significant amount of terrible coverage missed the point that they had actually reduced carbon emissions by 33 per cent and wastewater by 45 per cent, which were admirable sector-leading successes. Other targets, like 'make packaging 100 per cent recyclable', were missed by just 1 per cent. The business said they wouldn't have achieved these results without stretching themselves.

Given such reputational risks, which can cause huge consumer and investor damage – even destroy smaller businesses – it's no wonder organisations are not doing as much as they could or should.

Yet two quotes come to mind. First, as Christiana Figueres and Tom Rivett-Carnac rather bluntly put it in their book *The Future We Choose*: 'We can no longer afford the indulgence of feeling powerless.'[17] And second, one of Winston Churchill's many pearls of wisdom that 'Success is stumbling from failure to failure with no loss of enthusiasm.'[18] We should not only recognise the power that we all have and our responsibility as business people to use it for positive change, but we should also embrace failure when doing so.

Failure is part of the process. Iceland hasn't always got it right. In fact, sometimes we've got 'Doing It Right' plain wrong. Our disastrous foray into organic food in the early 2000s was a classic example of over-ambition, which just wasn't right for our customers or suppliers. And, as I'll explain in Chapter 3, on our quest to completely eliminate plastic by the end of 2023, for every 10 trials we have about nine abject failures.

As I mentioned in Chapter 1, I don't think there is a business that exists which puts back more into nature than it takes away from it – including Iceland. But that shouldn't stop anyone involved in business from trying to use it as a platform to change things, do things better and advocate.

There are still things that I'm not happy about within Iceland's supply chains. Some of our fish comes from industrial trawlers. Some of our chicken is fed on soy that has probably been grown in the Cerrado region of Brazil, which is subject to an alarming rate of deforestation. Recognising the fact that neither Iceland nor capitalism is perfect, but that it can be a vehicle for change, is important. Not being perfect shouldn't be used as an excuse to do nothing. It's about doing what you can, where you can. You don't have to be *perfect* – you just have to do *something*.

Ultimately, it's down to leadership. And that can come from anyone.

Leadership can be uncomfortable, but leaders of businesses – large and small – must now become activists. They must stand up, speak out and, above all, take risks. And if they don't, leadership is beginning to bubble up from the other direction. In April 2019, over 8,000 Amazon employees released an open letter to the management board criticising the online retailer for its lack of action on climate change and cosiness to the oil and gas industry.[19] Within a year, the company's founder and CEO Jeff Bezos had pledged $10 billion of his own fortune to launch a global initiative to fight climate change (which, maddeningly, was also derided by some[20]).

Considering such businesses now have market capitalisations well in excess of many countries' GDPs around the world, more than ever corporations need to reassess their duty to society and the environment. Shareholder primacy has led to extraordinary wealth concentrations and social inequality. Such separations ultimately will not prove healthy for long-term success. Businesses need to respond by reassessment; moving towards stakeholder capitalism and looking equally at the needs of all.

People, planet, profit

So how should businesses be holding themselves to account? What is the measurement that will enable the management to adopt a multi-stakeholder approach? How can, as Yvon Chouinard and Vincent Stanley put it in their book *The responsible company*, 'business [...] see the economic and environmental equivalent of the astronomic truth that the Earth rotates around the sun?'

Indeed, any business is dependent on nature, and yet does not properly account for it. Standard accounting practices deem 'resources' as something that we can take from nature, at our disposal, cost-free. The vast bounty of the Amazon rainforest does not appear in any ledger book, yet Amazon, the e-commerce giant, is now one of the world's most valuable companies. And while this cost does not show up in the books, there is, of course, always a cost. This cost to nature can often, tragically, be borne by society rather than by the offending companies.[21]

Leading economists are now trying to put a number on nature – knowing that destroying it not only hurts the economy but also makes it harder to combat emission reductions. Yet, as Hank Paulson, former US Treasury Secretary and Goldman Sachs luminary, says, 'The problem is that people assume that natural capital is a free good, and if you don't put a value on it, they will value it at zero.'[22] His foundation, the Paulson Institute, issued a report suggesting that 30–50 per cent of the planet's species will vanish by the middle of this century without action – and that the bill to prevent this would be over $500 billion a year.[23] That's a lot, but also the same amount that people spend on fizzy drinks every year.[24]

As the United Nations Special Envoy for climate action and finance, the former Bank of England Governor Mark Carney is currently trying to work out exactly how the market can reflect its true cost of capital and risk premiums that are currently being paid for by society instead.[25] And in September 2020, the leaders of the UK's Big Four accounting firms came together to unveil a framework for Environmental and Social Governance (ESG) standards[26] – some 25 years after The Body Shop originally campaigned to move ESG into company accounts.

But I think John Elkington's Triple Bottom Line (TBL) – a management framework published in 1994 to examine companies' social, environmental and economic impacts – remains the best theory as to how to show the full cost involved of doing business. Not just financial value, but natural, social and human capital as well.

More than just a simple accounting tool, according to Elkington in his book *Green Swans*, the idea 'was supposed to provoke deeper thinking about capitalism and its future.'[27] It inspired a great deal of related concepts, from ESG to Biodiversity Net Gain and Environmental Profit and Loss accounting. There is no need for me in this book to further add to this extensive lexicon. The world is running out of time to do so anyway.

Because the problem is, of course, that since TBL and its variants arrived there has been very little formal adoption of them. This could be because, as Elkington goes on to put it, 'the sheer range of options, this Tower of Babel we have been building, provides business with yet another alibi for inaction.'[28] Indeed, words like 'sustainability' can often prove either divisive or meaningless for many.

Without a globally defined set of yardsticks and measurements, businesses' acceptance of any particular concept will always be hampered. It is interesting to note that Iceland is among those reluctant companies ... although that could be more to do with our generational division as to what constitutes worthwhile importance ('Why?' was my Dad's response when asked if we could adopt such an accounting charter).

Despite the global sustainability sector growing rapidly over the last 25 years (which as I'll go on to explain is more about managers following the money than finding enlightenment), it would not be unfair to conclude that such accounting measures have largely failed. In 2018 Elkington himself announced the first ever 'product recall' of his management concept due to its failure to move the needle. I think the reality is that many of these concepts fail to gain traction because they rely on the goodwill of companies to adopt such complicated charters.

However, an encouraging ray of light against this disappointing backdrop is the rapidly growing B Corp movement. The group measures companies on the impact and value they add to workers, community, environment and customers. Those who attain high enough marks become certified Benefit Corporations and are even required to make multi-stakeholderism a legal obligation by updating their Articles of Association (the document that governs a company's constitution and its directors' responsibilities). My friend and fellow surfer Tom Kay, founder of cold-water surf brand

Finisterre, has worked hard to achieve B Corp accreditation for his business. Douglas Lamont, the CEO of the fruit drink brand Innocent, is also a passionate advocate for the transparency, accountability and networking that the movement brings.

Yet once again, this is not a party that Iceland is willing or able to join. The reality is that for bigger businesses such as ourselves, our expansive supply chains would make B Corp accreditation very costly and time intensive. And while Tom has managed to realise genuine value from the scheme via a crowdfunding equity raise, I do not think most Iceland customers would know or care what a B Corp is – making the internal sell to do it all the more difficult.

Bywater Properties, however, is now on the road to becoming one of the UK's first B Corp commercial property developers. The value to both their tenants, wanting to lease space in buildings that have been responsibly built, and their investors, who want to place money with managers who are making a positive impact, is clear.

Iceland's plan is, and always has been, not to look for schemes or accreditations but simply to take what positive action we can. Or as the late, great founder of Southwest Airlines Herb Kelleher put it: 'We have a strategic plan. It's called doing things.'[29] Indeed, my Dad has always admired 'players' and loathed 'commentators' – probably a legacy of his experience running a public company where he was beholden to 'teenage scribblers' in the City – those young, 20-somethings straight from university, who had no idea of the real-world operational challenges of running a company.

I see a parallel with so many of the environmental books I have read by academics, climate scientists and naturalists and especially politicians. All without question experts in their fields, and people who are far better qualified than me to know what systemic changes need to happen to reverse climate and ecosystem decline.

But they always get stuck on mapping out exactly *how* this necessary change will be enacted. It is not enough to come out with bold statements about 'shifting away from our extractive, linear incumbent systems towards a more circular economy.' It is all very well to champion 'a more optimistic and regenerative mindset' as the solution – but the cold realities of customer and shareholder value often make such commentary redundant.

The power of collaboration

Paul Polman is the former Unilever CEO, and now founder of Imagine, a new type of business collaborator. I admire him hugely for his ability to adroitly navigate corporate politics and cynicism in order to drive systemic change. This is the guy who told City investors that if they didn't agree with Unilever's values, then they shouldn't invest.[30]

Paul is a fantastic advocate for the power of collaboration, having convinced both key stakeholders within Unilever and outside investors to follow a more responsible path. Paul is a super-passionate advocate for stakeholder capitalism. His eyes light up when discussing the need for collaboration to solve big category issues. But he is also commercially savvy about solving them in non-competitive spaces. As the Imagine website states: 'We believe no CEO wants people or planet to suffer because of their value chain. But if they try to raise the bar alone, they put themselves at risk competitively. We help increase the pre-competitive space, and raise industry norms over time.'[31]

The Imagine website goes on to say that 'When enough business leaders take a bold stand, political action is de-risked. Youth movements, civil society and NGOs move from adversaries to allies. Other companies join in a race to the top.'[32]

I couldn't agree more. I have perhaps experienced this most collectively through DEFRA's Council for Sustainable Business (CSB), which I helped Michael Gove, then Secretary of State for the Environment, set up in 2018.[33] Bringing together 15 business leaders from a diverse range of sectors and locations, our CSB meetings and resulting action plans are dedicated to tackling three key environmental challenges: carbon and climate change; biodiversity loss; and plastic pollution. As well as being businessmen and women who run medium and large-scale companies, we are also citizens who are as concerned about the destruction of the natural world as anyone else. We advise DEFRA ministers and policy teams on the role that businesses can play in achieving the goals of the UK's 25 Year Environment Plan[34], and how government can support them to do so.

Our logic invariably proceeds as follows: 'This problem is terrible .... we have the ability to do something about it ... so what should we do ... and how should we do it?' Our hypothesis always tries to be action-orientated, because we all know by now that our house is on fire.

That's old news. What we need to do is act collectively and play our part and do something about it. It's about using business to provide simple actions based on powerful insights.

In June 2020, driven by our endlessly energetic and irrepressible CEO Liv Garfield (who also manages to juggle being CEO of the water utility Severn Trent), the CSB hosted a virtual event to kick-off business action in the run-up to the UK's hosting of COP26 (the UN climate change conference), in November 2021. We managed to convene over 200 business leaders – including chief executives and chairs from nearly half the FTSE 100 companies – employing 5 million people between them, with a joint market cap of over £1.3 trillion.

They were asked to make bold commitments to drive a 'decade of difference' for climate change and nature. Forget about platitudes, we wanted action. As I write, nearly half of those businesses have already started to make promises on carbon reduction and biodiversity. Over 40 have committed to carbon neutrality by 2040 or before, and over 20 have committed to biodiversity net gain.[35] Their response is evidence of the ability to accelerate action by corporates when they are convened together in the right way.

Do what's right for the customer

But at the end of the day, does the customer actually care? I suppose that depends on who the customer is. Sure, Patagonia and Whole Foods customers care. They were bought in before they even walked through the door. But do customers care in the real world, away from middle-class virtue-signallers? Many recent surveys can be used as evidence of modern consumers showing a preference for ethical brands. The 2018 Deloitte Millennial Survey showed that millennials believe that businesses should be measured by more than just profits – everything from planetary impact to inclusivity and diversity to improving peoples' lives.[36] And the 2019 Edelman Trust Barometer evidenced that 75 per cent of consumers said that they wouldn't buy from unethical companies.[37]

All of which sounds promising on the face of it. But at Iceland, the reality that we face time and time again is that customers do not want to be lectured to about environmentalism. They've got enough on their plates. They care about all of these issues, but just haven't got the time for first-world indulgences.

For example, take our 30-store trial replacing plastic carrier bags with paper bags. I quickly learned the useful lesson that above all else our customers want to get in, buy what they need and get out ... quickly. They certainly do not want to be barraged with a load of CSR messages about the state of our oceans; or be told to think really hard about paying more money for the more sustainable paper bag. Because they won't. (And they didn't.)

Ultimately, for any business it has to be customer first. Without customers, there is no business. And if they aren't interested in your particular initiative ... then it was never a sustainable initiative. Real sustainability is the ability to keep going. It's about weaving the right choices into the heart of day-to-day decision-making.

Too often, driven by the personal mission or messianic tendencies of a CEO, businesses can confuse PR vanity projects for sustainability initiatives. I've certainly succumbed to a few of those over recent years. But if you're not putting the customer first in any purpose-led campaign, considering whether it's right for them and if they actually want it … then it's doomed to failure. Believe me, I've learned the hard way!

So, my role as a leader is to take off any personal hats and do what's right for our customer and right for sales … not to shoehorn sustainability messages onto our customers if they do not want to hear them.

At Iceland, operating as we do in the cut-throat industry of UK food retail, many of our more recent sustainability initiatives that I talk about over the following chapters have not directly driven sales – well, at least not yet. Although, as I like to point out, who knows where sales would be if we hadn't undertaken them? We have certainly found ourselves on the radar of a whole new generation and demographic of shoppers who otherwise wouldn't have tried us. And there is no question that both our palm oil and plastics campaigns drove brand and employee value, as evidenced in many surveys over recent years.[38] This, of course, also helps our equity value.

As one of the main shareholders in a privately held, family-owned business, I can be a little more patient in waiting for the sales line to tick up than perhaps some publicly listed companies. But no business can tolerate something that is detrimental to sales. And I am acutely aware that Iceland is a wide ecosystem with many depending on us to do well.

People power

But ultimately, even with the customers on board, any boss's declaration of wanting to pursue such sustainability goals is irrelevant, really. As I have found out at Iceland, the most essential thing – above supplier or even customer engagement – is first and foremost to engage your employees. It galvanises a sense of purpose.

Sell them the vision as to why *this* is the approach that needs to be taken. Explain *how* it can be achieved, and what the part is that *they* have to play is in helping to deliver it. Constantly communicate updates of your shared journey – by conference, video, newsletters, or just stopping by their desk. Because without employee engagement, without your people believing in the mission and wanting you to lead them ... you simply cannot deliver it.

And often, it is actually the employees not the leaders who have the best ideas and answers. Our Backyard Nature campaign, which seeks to reconnect kids from the poorest urban communities with nature, came from staff feedback. In the middle of the Covid-induced panic buying and product shortages of March 2020, it was a store manager who came up with the idea of having a dedicated opening hour for the vulnerable; as was an NHS worker hour. A myriad of other ideas – such as removing plastic from till rolls to switching to eco-friendly cleaning materials – also came from stores. One store colleague who heard us talk about deforestation made a change to a single piece of paperwork that, when replicated across every store, now saves 200 trees a year.

Green: the new greed

Even with both happy customers and engaged staff, businesses won't get very far unless they have the right investor capital alongside it. Transforming business models away from shareholder primacy towards a multi-stakeholder approach costs money (in the short-term), and so those controlling the capital that is the fuel for corporate engines to drive sustainability need to be bought in. Although if you're bold enough, like Paul Polman was, you can always respectfully tell investors not to be investors if they don't share your company's values (those that left must have rued the day – he achieved a market-beating shareholder return in excess of 300 per cent during his decade at the helm, which he put down in no small part to his sustainability focus).[39]

If your company's values are not aligned to your outside investors, it can be a hugely distracting time sink. When Iceland was on that treadmill of being a publicly listed company for 21 years from 1984, we were constantly trying to satisfy investors' demands for short-term growth. Our share price was as strong or as weak as our last reported like-for-like sales. (To get away from short-termist investors, on his first day as Unilever's CEO in 2009 Polman scrapped quarterly reporting – controversial at the time but now commonplace.[40])

Fund managers and the companies in which they invest are both judged by their performance quarter on quarter, and this drives a relentlessly myopic thinking that can only be detrimental to the long-term wellbeing of any business.

This is a fundamental flaw of our public markets,

often driving short-termism to the detriment of the wider ecosystems that companies serve. That's why ExxonMobil, for example, were planning on pumping 25 per cent more oil and gas by 2025 than in 2017.[41] It may have dire consequences for the planet, but it helped their market capitalisation at the time.

I realise what I'm saying may sound contradictory or – even worse – self-serving: in order to benefit the many, company ownership needs to be concentrated on the few. But some experts do believe this to be the case. In his book *Prosperity*, Professor Colin Mayer recognised that the UK has a particularly extreme form of ownership, with most of it dispersed among a large number of institutional investors – few of whom have a significant controlling shareholding in our largest companies. The argument being that such shareholder fragmentation invariably leads to a lack of purposeful leadership.

I don't actually think that's the case, I just think whatever type of capital companies employ it needs to be long-term in nature in order to engender long-term thinking. That can be true whether you're a public or a private company. But when it has been alleged that the average length of time a stock is held for is only 22 seconds[42], I don't think the average shareholder – or much more likely nowadays, a computer – really cares about the long-term strategy and corporate responsibility of the company in which they are investing.[43]

But shift is happening in the capital markets. In January of 2020, Larry Fink (Chairman and CEO of the global investment manager BlackRock) used his annual letter to CEOs to warn that the climate crisis would bring about a 'fundamental reshaping of finance' with the reallocation of capital set to take place 'sooner than most anticipate.'[44] As a result, BlackRock is now focusing more on companies with sustainability credentials. Other major investors are dumping investments in firms that explore for oil and gas, such as Norway's $1 trillion sovereign wealth fund (ironic, given the fact that the country made its money from offshore oil). Others, including the Church of England, have gone a step further by divesting from oil and gas investments altogether.

And it doesn't have to be just the multibillion-dollar money managers making a difference – we all can. In the UK, there is a jaw-dropping £3 trillion under pension fund management, which constitutes the well-earned savings of about 21 million adults.[45] And yet for many of us, this money is hidden. We don't really think about how it is put to use by the investors who run our pensions. Obviously, we would all want this money to go to the fairest, most diverse, greenest companies ... yet the reality can be very different. Many people are often horrified to learn that their money is funding harmful industries, such as tobacco, arms, fossil fuels, gambling and deforestation.

Pensions are powerful – according to Nordea Invest, focusing on where you invest your money is an astonishing 27 *times* more effective than any other actions you can take on climate change.[46] The Make My Money Matter campaign, launched by film director and campaigner Richard Curtis in July 2020, has tapped into the enormous power that individuals have via their pension savings and is urging the UK public to check where their money is going. If we don't like the answer, Curtis says we should simply ask our pension provider to switch to a more sustainable fund.[47]

At the same time, Mark Carney is working on clear carbon labelling for pensions, in order for savers to be able to switch to less environmentally destructive portfolios if they wish. Working in a sector that adopts labelling systems for shoppers to navigate things like salt and sugar content, I see this as a really positive idea, which puts power back to the consumer.

Even companies themselves are taking note of this new investor sentiment. In June 2020, following a demand slump initiated by Covid-19, BP wrote down the value of its oil and gas reserves by $17.5 billion.[48] While this move was quite prosaically about protecting shareholder value, I hope that it also signalled a first, tentative step by the oil and gas company towards recognising its associated climate obligations.

The green finance industry – covering everything from direct investments to sustainability-linked bonds – is indeed booming. I once did a talk on plastics and the oceans to the investment bank Goldman Sachs. As the glass elevator silently whisked me up to the 25th floor of their London headquarters, I pondered how odd it was that the 'vampire squid' (as it's known) had suddenly found a green conscience. However, upon entering the conference room and surveying those razor-sharp-suited bankers, I realised why – they could smell the money.

By the dawn of 2020, at the annual meeting of the World Economic Forum in Davos, there had become something of a sustainability arms race. Companies and investors across the Swiss Alps were making bold pledges about becoming carbon negative, resource positive and everything else in between.[49]

That's because the private sector has woken up to the fact that 'corporate purpose' is starting to serve profits ... and, rather than being cynical about it, that's totally fine by me. If green is the new greed, then in fact I'm very supportive. With the might of big business and investors behind the green movement, things should start to move a lot quicker. It's also clear that fear of being left behind in this environmental race is starting to encourage wider action. And with the fossil fuel sector being the worst performer in the benchmark US stock market the S&P 500 during the 2010s[50], business models and associated investor incentives are starting to be realigned.

Innovation nation

Now aged a sprightly 100, the scientist, environmentalist and futurist James Lovelock (proposer of the Gaia Hypothesis, which postulates that the Earth functions as a self-regulating system) phlegmatically said in 2019 that 'We have all the things needed to stop global warming – we're just not using them.'[51]

As we look to the decade ahead, this has never been more accurate. Promising innovations that can make our world a fairer, greener place are set to make the transition into commercial reality as markets scale their applications. In aviation, for example, electric planes and synthetic sustainable aviation fuels are subject to huge research and development as the sector seeks to secure its longevity by decarbonising – and to make it more accessible, given the likelihood of future carbon taxes (currently, only about 6 per cent of the world's population flies in a single year[52]).

According to Project Drawdown, another technology set for huge transformation is electricity, as efficiency and transmission is enhanced, and production is moved away from fossil fuels. Currently electricity accounts for 25 per cent of heat-trapping emissions globally[53]; the key as we move to electrify everything from cars to home heating is to focus on renewable generation to ensure this does not increase. Yet 840 million people across developing countries are still without this basic human need.[54] Once niche technologies such as green hydrogen, microgrids and waste-to-energy will not only clean up how electricity is generated, distributed and used, but also democratise its access.[55]

The speed of change will only accelerate. In order to survive, business models must keep pace with that change in an increasingly customer-centric world. Disintermediation – a fancy word for 'taking out the middleman' – is inevitable. Even in my own fairly prosaic industry, we are starting to offer more personalisation through our digital platforms. Strategic decisions are increasingly becoming data-driven, and communications geo-targeted. Customers want heightened levels of user experience and enhanced localisation, in their rejection of ubiquity. Purchasing activity is now 'omni-channel': spread across multiple platforms.

While this may all sound discombobulating, it is also an exciting opportunity for those more purpose-led businesses. Some people still use 'millennials' as the reference point for the upcoming, younger generation. But I'm a millennial (just) – and we're getting on a bit now. It's Gen-Z, those 18-year-olds who are applying for their first jobs and starting to shop at our checkouts who are really the ones to watch. They instinctively understand hyper-personalisation and their power as a consumer in the digital age. They may not have much money yet – in fact, given the generational wealth gap they may not ever have much money. But they do want to associate themselves with brands who stand for something that make a difference. And any business that ignores them does so at its peril.

In the future, whole new industries borne out of the green revolution will emerge that are barely conceivable today. Once carbon taxation and pricing start to bite – but before we have fully developed all industries to be zero-emission – just imagine the potential for carbon removal. Technologies currently being developed, such as carbon capture and storage, could be developed on a global scale – symmetrically replacing the oil and gas industry of today.

Or more ominously, consider how technology could be used to track all our carbon emissions. It is not beyond the realm of possibility to think about how phone apps, satellites and online purchases could give rise to a giant form of carbon surveillance, as governments enact their obligations to hit net zero emissions by 2050.[56]

Systemic change

But most deep-rooted social and environmental problems will not be fixed by a technological solution alone. Lovelock's point of course, was that we must not sit around, cross our fingers and hope that somebody somewhere invents something clever in the future that means we don't have to change our ways today.

The private and public sectors need to set about urgently rethinking and redesigning entire systems. Across a whole array of industries, such systemic change is the only way we will truly shift towards a more sustainable future.

Take plastic pollution, which I talk about in the next chapter. It's all too easy to simplistically brand it as 'the retailers' fault'. Whereas what we really need is an honest conversation about the role that communities and government must play alongside industry in fixing the problem. From the litter bugs oblivious to the consequences of their actions; to the retailers forcing unnecessary plastic onto consumers; to the manufacturers who have become addicted to the material; to the oil companies profiteering from petrochemical production; to successive governments who have under-invested in our recycling infrastructure and struggled to develop a taxation system that discourages over-use.

The same goes for the built environment, which accounts for a staggering 40 per cent of the UK's total carbon footprint.[57] This needs to be squared against the reality that we have nowhere near enough housing in the UK. Yet that presupposes that what we need is more houses; whereas what we actually need are more homes. As the traditional retail high street declines, town centres could be reimagined to provide affordable, convenient and vibrant communities that would appeal to a new generation of homeowners who currently struggle to set foot on the housing ladder.

The public debate seems exclusively focused on constructing new-build, more energy-efficient homes and retrofitting the home insulation of old houses. This, of course, is hugely important – but we need some joined-up thinking about the full lifecycle of buildings. It's essential that we ensure buildings are built to last, as opposed to concrete blocks that might survive less than a lifetime. The planning system needs to be freed up and the taxation system modernised in order to better enable the repurposing of old buildings and encourage new ways to use them.[58]

Much greater consideration should also be given to the greenhouse gas emissions that come from furniture – which account for 30 per cent of the carbon footprint of a commercial building over its entire life.[59] According to the sustainable office furniture company Rype, there is a disgraceful 300 tonnes of office furniture going to landfill every working day in the UK.[60] We need to be remanufacturing more furniture than we buy new: a simple, but high-impact solution.

Most importantly, we need to focus way more on the high levels of embedded carbon within building materials such as steel and concrete, and rapidly move towards more timber-framed construction, as countries such as France and Norway are doing.

The biggest systemic change required of all, in my opinion, is within our global food and agricultural sector. Over the previous generation we have become encased within an ever-increasing industrialised agricultural system, which has led to a devaluation of food and a dramatic under-estimation of its true cost – to both nature and society.

According to the Office for National Statistics (ONS), for the year ending March 2019 the average UK household spent £56.60 per week on food.[61] That's the second lowest out of the OECD (the Organisation for Economic Co-operation and Development) countries. This represented less than 10 per cent of total household expenditure. Back in 2006, the ONS calculated that the average household spent 15 per cent of their income on food. At the time of their first ever survey in 1957 it was 33 per cent.[62]

So, where has this disappearing cost gone? After all, people are eating more not less.

Well, I can tell you that some of it has been the result of a lowering of supermarket margins. I look back with a wry smile at the larger profits Iceland made 10 years ago on much lower sales. That's competition for you.

Coupled with that, modern agricultural systems have, of course, enhanced productivity and yields significantly. Yet, as a result, we have also seen a large element of that cost simply transfer onto the environment. It is the depletion of our soils, for example, which bears the brunt of increasing fertiliser use. And through extensive pesticide spraying, UK farming has undertaken a war with nature that has been the chief culprit in the halving of Britain's wildlife over the last 50 years.[63] Even a seemingly positive trend such as the growth of free-range egg production is causing trouble, given the amount of land it uses. In the Wye Valley, for example, the proliferation of egg farms and associated effluent is causing a deadening of the River Wye.[64]

Indeed, John Sauven, the Executive Director of Greenpeace UK, estimates that food should be at least twice as expensive given the externalised costs to society and the environment. However, the government says that food cannot pay its way, because some people cannot afford it. So, instead, we pay with our poor health and our degraded environment. Cheap food should not be a substitute for proper welfare policy.[65]

The Covid-19 pandemic shone a light on just how weak and compartmentalised our food system has become. Supermarkets' just-in-time supply chains were blown to pieces when faced with unprecedented panic buying. We struggled to fill our supply chain with enough toilet roll, for example, and so as soon as they were replenished onto our store shelves, they were stripped bare within an hour.

For several weeks in April 2020, flour became a rare find in any supermarket, driven by the rise in home baking during lockdown. Millers couldn't redirect the vast quantities of flour they produced for shuttered wholesale markets, as they struggled to adjust line speeds and packaging formats to retail. In the south of England, strawberry growers were forced to let their crops rot following the cancellation of events such as Wimbledon. In the US, farmers in Montana and Idaho were left with no choice but to bury billions of tonnes of potatoes following the forced closure of restaurants and wholesalers who accounted for more than half of their market. And without the ability to fly in migrant farm workers, across Europe the summer fruit and salad crops grew redundant without anyone to pick them.

Of course, it's not just the food sector's fault – consumers have a role to play too. It is interesting to note that the UK could move to high welfare egg farming much quicker if only consumers would buy white-shelled eggs.[66] As it stands, customers tend to shun them in supermarkets, and therefore their only destination is for catering and restaurants. When Covid-19 struck and the dining-out sector was forced into hibernation, a lot of white eggs went to waste.

As Henry Dimbleby, the government's food tsar, has stressed, we need to look holistically at how we can join up our food system to make it more sustainable – not just for when the next pandemic comes along, causing another demand side shock – but also to make it more resilient against climate change. Indeed, the next large-scale shock to our food system could well come from the supply side, such as simultaneous crop failures across multiple continents. The result of which, is invariably human conflict.[67]

Not only is our current food system ill-prepared for climate change; it is a massive contributor towards it. Every stage of food production releases carbon and other greenhouses gases – from the energy used to produce fertiliser, to the methane belched out by ruminants, to the transporting of the end product to consumers. Indeed, it is estimated that globally, food is responsible for 26 per cent of all greenhouse gas emissions.[68]

A systemic shift would move towards a more diverse, flexible and therefore resilient food system. One that is both lower in carbon and encourages nature restoration, which in turn is our best defence in our fight against climate change: foods that are part of the solution instead of the problem and agricultural systems that enable investment in both biodiversity and soil rehabilitation.

Encouragingly, we are starting to see much more focus and investment in agricultural science and innovation, from lab-grown meat, to insect protein feedstocks, to weed-picking robots. Across the world, a range of businesses from start-ups to established multinationals are harnessing the power of new technology, and rediscovering the benefits of old.

Companies such as Plenty in the US and GrowUP Urban Farms in the UK are pioneering indoor, vertical farming techniques. Their produce, such as leaf salads, kale, tomatoes and strawberries, are of impressive premium grading and consistency. Low human intervention (such as weeding or harvesting) means there's no need for chlorine washing, resulting in longer shelf lives. This is done inside warehouse units with produce grown on high vertical walls, photosynthesised by intelligent LED lighting, using zero pesticides, less than 5 per cent of the water and less than 1 per cent of the land compared to outdoor farming techniques. The result is high-technology, sustainable farming that provides well-paid jobs. Such 'farms' can be located in city conurbations, close to the end consumer. And once the practice becomes more commonplace, theoretically surplus land from outdoor farming could be used to rewild.

At the other end of the technology scale, my all-time favourite company Patagonia has branched out into the food business to focus on the lost farming method of 'regenerative agriculture'. Patagonia Provisions is the personal pet project of founder Yvon Chouinard, who sees reform of the world's food system as quite simply a matter of human survival. A friend of mine, the surf photographer Al Mackinnon, tells a great story of visiting Yvon at his cliff-top estancia overlooking the

Californian surf a few years ago. Spread all over his kitchen table were numerous high-nutrition, organic foods, such as buffalo meat and smoked salmon. Al was enthusiastically invited to join in the taste test as the octogenarian's personal passion and commitment to the project shone through.

The idea, starting to be rediscovered by farmers all around the world, is a move against the modern agricultural system that seeks to maximise yield and profit – without consideration for the long-term consequences.[69] According to the UN Food and Agriculture Organization, repeated soil disturbance from monoculture practices, such as tilling and intensive fertiliser use, has degraded roughly 25 per cent of the Earth's surface – to the extent that there could only be about 60 harvests left.[70] And then what?

Regenerative agriculture harnesses age-old, respectful land techniques, such as crop rotation, compost application, cover crops and no-tilling – with the ultimate aim to build healthier soil, which is an essential carbon store.

Of course, I'm acutely aware that Iceland often perpetuates the industrialised farming system, with our globalised sourcing of volume commodities produced on a large scale. It's the ultimate corporate cop-out to say that 'we operate within the confines of our market', and we are, therefore, constantly searching for more respectfully grown products. In September 2021, for example, we are planning to launch our first vertically farmed produce range.

Through our fast-growing, stand-alone business No Meat we are developing the largest plant-based frozen food range in the world, encouraging lower meat consumption, without compromising variety, taste, and importantly, price. Made from European soy, wheat and pea protein, our range includes ready meals, pizzas, No Porkies sausages, No Bull burgers, No Fish fingers and No Chick nuggets. The brand is now being sold by other UK supermarkets, and internationally.[71] (Although my Dad loves to question: if vegans are anti-meat, why do they like to eat imitations of it?)

As previously mentioned, 20 years ago we had a move to try to sell organic produce from our stores – which we continue to do on a small number of lines. Our family even set up a chain of organic supermarkets in London as a sideline, which my sister Caroline ran and developed over two decades, before successfully selling in early 2020.

But there is so much more to be done. And yet, ultimately, operating as we do in some of the most deprived communities in the UK, I am very conscious that price will always be a primary consideration for many of our customers. Looking at the products for sale on the Patagonia Provisions website, I cannot see many of our customers forking out $7.89 for a 30oz bag of organic basmati rice.

To be scalable, and therefore truly impactful, we need to find cost-neutral solutions for the end consumer. As Iceland is discovering, advances in technology and productivity are starting to make this possible. Price parity could also come from businesses lowering their profit expectations – but unless mandatorily imposed this simply will not happen. Which is why, as I discuss in Chapter 6, governments need to be more interventionist to nudge the market towards better practices.

Our food system is just one sector – albeit perhaps the most important – that is in desperate need of systemic change to reduce carbon and enhance nature. I have deliberately focused on food, given that is the industry in which I operate ... and the disproportionate size of the sector's contribution to global carbon emissions.

Yet, of course, there are many others, from aviation to fashion, that also require the same reassessment and lateral thinking in order for us to find a more sustainable future.

Changing entire systems is, of course, damn hard. It requires unparalleled levels of industry collaboration and government support. Often, the greatest and most immediate impact that any particular business can have is to look at what skeletons lurk within their own closets.

Over the course of the next two chapters, I'll take a deeper look at how Iceland investigated and took action on two very specific issues. One that was hiding high up within our supply chains, and the other, an all-too-ubiquitous part of the products that we sell.

. . . .

This chapter has covered a broad sweep of issues, which businesses both large and small should consider if they are to adapt to the needs of all the stakeholders they serve. However, when trying to summarise particular recommendations, it really depends on the specifics of your business – what type of people or capital you employ, the products or services you sell, and who your competitors are.

Therefore, on our journey as corporate activists, I'm going to riff off Daniel Goleman's simple advice in his book *Ecological Intelligence*, when he provides a creed for how I believe all business people should act: 'Know your impacts, favour improvement, share what you learn.'[72]

THE KEY THINGS FOR ANY BUSINESS

TAKE A MULTI-STAKEHOLDER APPROACH
Map out your responsibilities to all your stakeholders.

UNDERSTAND YOUR IMPACT ON COMMUNITIES AND SOCIETY
Whatever the size of your business, you are in a unique and powerful position to change people's lives for the better.

UNDERSTAND YOUR ENVIRONMENTAL IMPACT
Ninety per cent of a product's environmental impact is determined at the design stage.[73] A full lifecycle analysis for all your products can be very costly and time-consuming, so if you are a small business with many lines then focus on the Pareto Principle – those 20 per cent of your products or services which generate 80 per cent of your sales.

ADVOCATE
Share what you learn with your employees, your customers, your investors and even your competitors – some issues are more important and can be solved much quicker with collaboration.

CHAPTER 3
MISSION IMPOSSIBLE
Eliminating plastic

'HOW CAN I DESCRIBE MY EMOTIONS AT THIS CATASTROPHE, OR HOW DELINEATE THE WRETCH WHOM WITH SUCH INFINITE PAINS AND CARE I HAD ENDEAVOURED TO FORM?'

VICTOR FRANKENSTEIN[1]

A few years ago, I had never heard of a nurdle. Who had?

And then, one freezing cold day in 2017 I found myself at New Brighton beach on the Wirral. The wind howling from the north, with long plumes of sand swirling in its wake, made my eyes stream. I was there to join a community beach clean with the BBC's environmental reporter Lucy Siegle and John Sauven, the boss of Greenpeace UK, looking at the scourge of plastic pollution and meeting some of the many local heroes dealing with it.

A month beforehand, one of my colleagues when out walking her dog, had been intrigued by a bunch of locals turning up at the beach in fancy dress. She ended up in conversation with a tall, friendly guy in a Superman outfit. He turned out to be Dave Peddie. He and his wife Jan belong to the New Brighteners, a group of community activists who campaign against plastic pollution. They were running the day's activity and Dave introduced me to Chris Cureton, another hard-working activist from the charity British Divers Marine Life Rescue.

I mentioned that the windswept beach looked remarkably clean. 'You really think so?' said Chris and then crouched down to pick up a handful of tiny plastic spheres. 'These are mermaids' tears – also called nurdles. They are the raw material for everything made from plastic. And as they look exactly like fish eggs, the birds eat them.' Now I had seen them I couldn't un-see them: they were literally everywhere I looked – long lines of multicoloured dots endlessly stretching out across each tideline. A visceral signpost of systemic failure.

The moment was captured on film by Sam, one of the two awesome filmmakers who works for us at Iceland, and ended up being shared on social media in January 2018, when Iceland became the first major retailer anywhere in the world to commit to eliminating plastic packaging from all our own label products – and to achieve it by the end of 2023.

Taking action

It was a watershed moment. Yes, public awareness had already been raised by the moving scenes of marine life and seabirds dying as the result of marine plastic pollution in Sir David Attenborough's landmark *Blue Planet II* TV series, broadcast three months earlier.

But it was our announcement that really caught the imagination of the media and the public, raising their expectations of business, and prompting a string of pledges to take action on plastic from all the other retailers and a wide range of organisations as diverse as the Royal Palaces to the BBC. Suddenly, the war against plastic was everywhere. By the end of 2018, the Collins

English Dictionary announced that its word of the year was 'single-use'.

The British Plastics Federation were less than impressed[2] and Bernard Chase (then special advisor to packaging charity WRAP) stood up at our supplier conference and said our plan was 'moral folly'. We were, however, praised by the then prime minister Theresa May[3] and Environment Secretary Michael Gove[4], and by more than 200 MPs.[5] Though the endorsement I valued most was a personal letter of congratulations from Sir David Attenborough himself.

There was certainly a great deal of positive brand sentiment. While we were planning our announcement we polled 5,000 consumers, and 81 per cent told us they supported the idea of our pledge. According to a YouGov poll in the week before and week after our launch, there was a 429 per cent increase in the number of people who saw Iceland as the leading retailer for reducing plastic.

In May 2018 *The Grocer* magazine put me – the bloke who didn't even sit GCSE Chemistry – top of their Packaging Power List, saying I was 'masterminding the industry's boldest and most pioneering move to tackle plastic pollution.'[6] And by the end of 2018, Iceland's Brand Buzz score (a measure of trust, consideration, and perceptions of quality and value among consumers) was the highest for a decade. If this had been conceived as a PR stunt, it would have to be considered a spectacular success by any standards.

But it wasn't. It was motivated by an entirely genuine belief that this was the right thing to do. The planet's oceans are both immense carbon sinks and oxygen producers ... vast, silent ecosystems upon which all life on Earth ultimately depends. The oceans are our critical ally – the more diverse, the better.

Yet they are being swamped by plastic waste, with a truckload of the stuff dumped into the seas every single minute of every day.[7] The UK supermarket sector alone accounts for almost 1 million tonnes of plastic waste a year.[8] The soft drinks industry churns out 500 billion plastic bottles every single year.[9] A dog-eared plastic bag has even been found 10km down at the bottom of the deep ocean[10]... our last, great unexplored habitats, home to wondrous creatures such as the yeti lobster or the leafy sea dragon, no longer beyond the reach of the plastic plague.

Plastic is literally choking the life out of our oceans. Most of plastic's impact on our marine wildlife goes unseen, hidden beneath the water, out of sight and mind. But occasionally nature serves us a visceral reminder: a dead sperm whale washed up on a beach, its stomach hopelessly blocked full with plastic bags. Or a rescued sea turtle, unable to breathe properly because a plastic straw has worked its way up into its nostril. In a stark warning, the Ellen MacArthur Foundation has forecast that by weight there will be more plastic than fish in the seas by 2050.[11]

The very qualities that make plastic so fantastic – indestructible, versatile, colourful, lightweight and above all cheap – also make it so harmful when it escapes into the environment. Plastic has revolutionised design, such as lightweighting cars (thereby reducing their emissions), and our wellbeing, such as 3D printing used for healthcare (quickly and economically creating things like heart valves and prosthetics). It has enabled us to travel to the outer reaches of our home planet and beyond.[12]

But the problems start with our abuse of this miracle material. My issue is solely aimed at our over-reliance on 'frivolous' plastics – single-use, throwaway plastic that is so recklessly at odds with how we should be using something so special. We have become completely addicted to it – the supermarkets in particular, who lazily coat, bag, seal and wrap it around almost all products. Something that provides consumers with momentary convenience, which once discarded can last for 500 years.

Humanity has already produced more plastic since the turn of the millennium than in the whole of the previous century[13] – and, unless it had been incinerated, every bit of plastic ever made is still around, and likely to remain so for several hundred years to come. The writer Robert Macfarlane evokes the terrifying legacy we are leaving in this Anthropocene age, with plastics working their way into our geological strata creating future fossils like shampoo bottles and deodorant caps.[14]

Worse still, as global reliance on fossil fuels declines, in order to prop up business models the petrochemical and plastics industries are planning a massive expansion in production. According to the Center for International Environmental Law (CIEL), if these growth rates proceed as planned, by 2050 the annual emissions from plastic's production and incineration are set to reach 2.8 gigatons – that's 2.8 x one billion metric tonnes, or the equivalent of 615 new 500-megawatt coal-fired power plants. Then compare this to the 850 million metric tonnes of greenhouse gases added into the atmosphere by plastics in 2019, and you get a sense of the planned acceleration in plastic production over the coming decades.[15] Needless to say, our dwindling carbon budget simply cannot afford such reckless expansion.

Recent research has also revealed a previously hidden dimension that plastic's downstream emissions are having on our climate. Looking beyond the carbon emitted from the fossil fuel extraction, refining and manufacturing of plastics, CIEL are now considering the impact that both managed and unmanaged plastic waste is having on our atmosphere. Not only does landfilling, recycling or incinerating produce greenhouse gases, but plastic that is unmanaged continues to have climate impacts as it degrades in our oceans, waterways and landscape. In a ground-breaking study in August 2018, a team led by Sarah-Jeanne Royer of the University of Hawaii found that not only does ocean plastic continually release methane, but it also interferes with the ocean's capacity to absorb carbon dioxide.[16]

Unfortunately, there is a final reason to be concerned.

Back when I was a teenager in 1996, three scientific commentators, Theo Colborn, John Peterson Myers and Dianne Dumanoski, published a book called *Our Stolen Future*. At the time it was described as the biggest scientific and PR bombshell to hit the chemical industry since Rachel Carson's 1962 classic, *The Silent Spring*. The book warned about how manmade chemicals cause hormone disruption, with implications for future human health. These included PCBs (used in plastics and banned in the 1970s) and Bisphenol A (BPA), now banned in baby bottles but still widely used to harden plastics.

Over 20 years later we failed to take enough notice, and according to the team at CIEL, plastics and their toxins are also having a pervasive effect on human health.[17] Those nurdles I saw on New Brighton beach are just one example of microplastics. All plastic in the environment eventually breaks down into microplastics, and then tiny nanoplastics. Plymouth University have found that one single acrylic garment can shed upwards of 700,000 microfibres when machine washed[18], generating a growing source of nanoplastics heading straight into our water systems as synthetic clothing becomes more popular.

Scientists are now learning that such nanoplastics and their by-products have slowly entered our food chains ... and insidiously worked their way into our own bodies. The average European shellfish consumer is said to have an uptake of 6,400 microplastics per year.[19] And according to research by the charity WWF (World Wide Fund for Nature), we're now ingesting the equivalent of a credit card of plastic every week.[20]

We are yet to fully understand the consequences, but research into plastic and health is now showing that exposure to such plastics and their related toxins may lead to a wide variety of health complications. A 2015 review set out possible links between some chemicals used in plastics and Alzheimer's disease – but concluded that more research is needed.[21]

Endocrine-disrupting chemicals such as BPA, for example, are still commonly found in things like plastic containers and till receipts. Yet it has been dubbed a 'gender-bending chemical' due to its mimicking of the female sex hormone oestrogen, with links to low sperm counts, infertility, breast and prostate cancers.[22] The most recent scare is around PFAs, known as 'forever chemicals' because they don't break down.[23]

I wanted to find out exactly what was going on inside my own body, and so organised a toxic non-metal chemical profile through the Biolab Clinic in London. As I had suspected, my urine sample clearly showed that my body had burdens of toxic compounds, such as monoethyl phthalate, phenylglyoxylic acid and diphenyl phosphate. These markers are the result of exposure to particular tracer chemicals like phthalates, styrene and triphenyl phosphate – all used in a wide range of plastic products.

While disappointing, these results were not a surprise: I am a surfer who loves spending time in the ocean. Such chemicals are now ubiquitous and impossible to avoid. They have been found in 80 per cent of teenagers' bloodstreams and even in human breast milk.[24]

Impossible

Getting rid of plastic is a lot more difficult than people realise – some say impossible. The scale of what we need to achieve is enormous, working across 1,400 product lines with 300 different suppliers – it is a truly collaborative approach. Every step along the way requires hard choices and trade-offs that are fraught with jeopardy.

Our primary challenge is ensuring that we adopt alternatives to plastic that do an equally effective job, and don't lead to unintended consequences. These include a growth in food waste, creating new problems in packaging disposal or unsustainable increases in demand for alternatives to plastic's fossil fuel feedstock.

Take those infamous plastic-wrapped cucumbers for example. Superficially, it seems absurd (although not as mindless as shrink-wrapped coconuts, which still baffles me). But by wrapping a cucumber in plastic, moisture is retained, and the shelf life is dramatically increased – thus cutting down on food waste in both the store and the home.[25] The packaging alternatives we've seen are either more expensive or technically inferior. Increasing frequency of cucumber deliveries to our stores (to hold less stock and therefore sell unwrapped cucumbers more quickly), would increase both cost and emissions. And so, the mystery of how to sell an unwrapped cucumber remains unsolved, for now.

In searching for a technological holy grail, we initially spent the best part of a year staring down the superficially attractive rabbit hole of biomaterials. Compostable biomaterials sound great, but they won't break down effectively in your garden compost heap, assuming that you are lucky enough to have a garden. They require industrial composting along with domestic food waste, and we concluded that it would be wrong to foist these on the public at a time when (as discussed in Chapter 1) the infrastructure to deal with them is simply not in place. So, we have strongly lobbied the government to introduce consistent household food waste collections and to combine these with industrial composting.

Another type of bioplastic behaves just like traditional plastic – one that isn't compostable but is made from things like corn starch. Such materials are a false solution: while not derived from fossil fuels they are, technically and legally speaking, still plastic and therefore suffer the same issue of indestructability. Just like oil plastic, they will not fully degrade in the oceans and will thereby contribute to the continuing problem of microplastic pollutants entering the marine and, therefore, ultimately the human food chain.

We have to consider, in addition, whether it can be responsible to contemplate devoting millions of acres of farmland to growing crops as feedstock for biomaterials, when they could be producing food, or indeed rewilded – acting to both sequester carbon and restore nature.

I am more sympathetic to the idea of using waste materials from food crops, such as corn husks, and there are also some interesting experiments in farming seaweed for use as a raw material – subject to the inevitable caveat that, if it takes off, large-scale seaweed farming may yet prove to wreak as much ecological damage as the surge in global demand for palm oil.

Finally – and crucially – we must also ensure that our products remain cost neutral to our customers, many of whom have very little cash to spare. This is essential if we are to make environmentalism accessible to everyone, and is the only way we can make solutions really scalable.

After years of research and trials, we have come to the conclusion that in most cases the best alternative to plastics does not in fact lie in some miracle new material. The best solution is probably in fact the oldest material known to man, used by our ancient cave-dwelling ancestors: trees. And by trees, I don't mean wood – I mean materials derived from wood such as paper board, pulp and so on. And yes, the irony of going back to a material that plastic replaced because of environmental concerns about chopping down too many trees has not escaped me.

Normally a managing director of a food business wouldn't personally involve themselves in the nitty-gritty of packaging supply chains, relying instead on their food suppliers and in-house teams to source the appropriate packaging. But because we are taking such an industry lead, I felt that it was incumbent on me to see with my own eyes every part of the process, right up to the ultimate source of our sustainable timber in Scandinavia and check that we really were doing it right.

So I have personally visited not just the packaging factory in Belgium where our paper-based meal trays are made, but the paper mill that supplies it, and even the sustainably managed forests of south-east Finland from which the timber for the mill is sourced ....

In a forest camp, a local ranger cooked sausages over a fire as he explained how generations of Finnish families own small pockets of trees, which they grow and harvest with great care to sustain the local environment. These forests stretch on for thousands of miles across the nearby Russian border, with my inbound flight reviving memories of the view from my Trans-Siberian Railway carriage when I made that journey as a backpacker fresh out of university 20 years ago.

Nearby, the trees were used by renewable materials specialist Stora Enso. I was struck not just by the business's very public corporate commitment to good sustainability practices, but also by the great care with which their forest stewardship is exercised on the ground – for example, by visually inspecting every tree scheduled for felling to ensure that it contains no nests.

Most importantly, being certified by the Forest Stewardship Council, for every tree that is chopped down, four are planted – making this a reforestation project. You could even argue that materials derived from sustainable forests are in fact 'carbon negative', because more trees are planted than were growing before and therefore incremental carbon is sequestered thanks to the end product being produced.

My property company took the learnings from Iceland's research into wood and has now secured planning for the UK's first commercially developed carbon negative building. On the site of the former Costa roastery in Vauxhall, London, Bywater Properties are preparing to build a 60,000 sq. ft office building constructed almost entirely of Cross Laminated Timber (CLT).[26]

CLT is a miracle new building material derived from perhaps the oldest. Layered in a specific way to provide equivalent strength to concrete, CLT could become the environmental building material of the future. And let's hope so – the concrete, steel and cement industries are among the most pollutive on the planet, with concrete alone being responsible for up to 8 per cent of the world's CO_2.[27]

Back in south-east Finland, the vast lakes provide a natural gateway for the export of timber that is denied to more geographically challenging parts of Scandinavia, and the quantities of timber piled up waiting for export at the railhead are astonishing.

Even more mind-blowing, though, are the world-leading research and development laboratories that Stora Enso has developed deep within the forest, pushing the uses and applications of the age-old tree to the extreme. I saw but was not allowed to photograph scientists in crisp, white lab coats working to create completely transparent paper, which could replace the flexible plastics used to seal the top of ready meal trays, for example. And by breaking down the wood fibre into microfibrils, they are even developing a new source of carbon fibre that one day will allow us to make aeroplanes and racing cars out of trees.

The Stora Enso paper mill I visited, also in Finland, was a vast, cathedral-like structure representing hundreds of millions of pounds of investment, where mind-boggling statistics abounded; our guide assured me that one fast-whirring machine – large, but small in the context its surroundings – had produced the card for almost every Christmas card posted since the 1960s.

Meanwhile in Belgium, in late 2019, I visited a factory using the Finnish card to make cutting-edge packaging which we are now trialling to wrap and display a wide range of fresh produce without plastic. I felt great empathy with this entrepreneurial, family-run business that had taken the risk of investing in machinery to produce a novel design for which there was no identified customer – and was delighted to be able to fill that role. And our initial trial results are promising – sales are up almost 20 per cent as customers respond positively to the aesthetic paper packaging. Given the fact that it cost us almost double the plastic equivalent, our next challenge is to work out how to scale it up across our estate at a cost-neutral price to the customer, without losing a fortune.

In answer to the inevitable question of why we need to wrap our produce at all (cucumbers aside), Iceland is a limited range store that our customers look to for convenience and value. We trialled loose fresh produce in one of our larger The Food Warehouse stores for three months in 2019: sales fell by 30 per cent. So, investing millions in scales and new tills to permit the sale of loose produce more widely was never going to be a viable option for us; though it may well be for some other retailers.

Within our business, plastic removal was preceded by a painful process of trial and error. Our first two ready meal ranges launched in board trays – Mexicana street food and Hungry Heroes meals for kids – did not last long because customers did not take to them (the food, I firmly believe, rather than the trays). Because we only carry a limited range, we cannot afford to devote cabinet space to slow-moving lines: we move on through relentless innovation in the hope of creating food that our customers will want to buy again and again.

Similarly, we launched the UK's first plastic-free chewing gum in August 2018 – an entirely natural product that is also completely biodegradable, eliminating those hard-to-shift chewing gum deposits that plaster 95 per cent of British pavements and cost our hard-pressed councils around £60 million a year to clean up.[28] It's fair to say that the average chewing gum user was pretty horrified to find that the stuff they had been putting in their mouth for years was based on plastic and chemicals – but evidently not as horrified as they were at the concept of paying a bit more for a non-plastic alternative. We had to delist it a year later because of poor sales.

We introduced paper bands to hold together bunches of five bananas, hoping to replace the ten million plastic bags a year we were wrapping them in. But the bands weren't strong enough to hold the bunches together: wastage increased, sales fell and we had to revert to bags in many stores. Undeterred, we're now running a trial that combines the bands with a merchandising fixture specifically designed to improve the presentation of the product, which does seem to be working.

The introduction of a UK-wide 5p plastic bag charge in October 2015 reduced demand across the industry by a massive 86 per cent, saved the business $10 million that we were spending on giving them away for free, and raised many millions for charity – a triple win. And clear recognition that nothing humanity creates (least of all the estimated one trillion plastic bags used globally every single year[29]) has zero cost to the environment.

Along with other retailers, we then stopped selling 5p single-use plastic bags altogether from October 2018 and replaced them with 10p 'bags for life' made from recycled post-consumer waste. This seemed like an improvement on the virgin plastic used in the 5p bags. We reasoned that the doubling of price, and the fact that the new bags were clearly designed for multiple re-use, would curb demand. Only it didn't. In fact this attempt to reduce the industry's plastic footprint actually led to all supermarkets selling a greater weight of plastic, because the new bags were thicker and stronger than the ones they had replaced.[30]

So, we looked for a less environmentally damaging alternative. An initial trial of 10p brown paper bags in place of plastic in May 2019 proved a failure (the bags weren't strong enough and customers didn't like them). In July 2019 we tried again, making our Hackney store in London the UK's first completely plastic bag-free supermarket. Here we offered extra-strong 15p white paper carrier bags together with lighter weight paper carrier bags and jute bags. We also launched a trial of the 15p paper carrier bags alongside 15p plastic bags for life (increased in price from 10p) in 40 stores across the north-west of England.

And finally, we found a system that worked. Customer acceptance of the 15p paper carrier bags has been excellent and we will be looking to roll these out across the business as our long-term replacement for plastic.

As our brilliant Head of Packaging Stuart Lendrum says, 'The maddening thing of course is that no one wakes up in the morning wanting more carrier bags in their life – plastic or otherwise.' And so in 2021, Stuart is planning to try some form of carrier bag rental scheme from an Iceland shop, where customers can loan and return their bags as and when they need them – just like a pair of bowling shoes.

In some product categories we are awaiting the delivery of completely new technologies to achieve optimum solutions. The single biggest challenge is likely to be in milk, for example – also, as it happens, our single biggest-selling line – where retail supply is in the hands of an effective duopoly that has invested hundreds of millions of pounds in dairies where raw milk and plastic pellets go in at one end, and pasteurised milk in HDPE (high-density polyethylene) bottles comes out at the other.

We have also yet to see a technical solution to replace gas-flushed plastic packs to prolong the life of meat products, and there will doubtless be a few other lines where the cost of switching out of plastic packaging will be prohibitive, bearing in mind our commitment to deliver the change at no cost to our customers.

The process of trying, failing and iterating is crucial in our quest to find viable solutions to replace plastic. If we were to give up at the first hurdle, we wouldn't have made much headway. But steadily we are making progress – and in March 2020 I was delighted to announce that two years into our mission Iceland reduced its plastic packaging usage by 29 per cent, totalling 3,794 tonnes annually.[31] Using the comparison deployed by Lucy Siegle in her book *Turning the Tide on Plastic*[32], that's the weight of 542 elephants.

The myth of recycling

Meanwhile, Big Plastic has dedicated much time over recent years trying to hoodwink the public that the way to allay any concerns they may have about plastic is simply to improve recycling, rather than reduce production. Or to put it another way: the problems of plastic can be answered by creating yet more plastic. I supposed it should come as no surprise – it is in their interest to say that, after all.

But I was genuinely shocked when the head of sustainability at a major – one might even say iconic – UK retailer told me that the answer was indeed more plastic, just of better quality than the stuff we have been using up to now, in order to recycle more of it.

This is what I call the 'myth of recycling': a misdirection away from the real issue of excessive production. It's much easier for Big Plastic to spend money on advertising campaigns lecturing the public to recycle more, while knowing full well that most plastic will never be recycled.

Recycling as the golden-bullet solution to the plastic pandemic is wrong on a number of levels.

First, the snag is that actually there is no such thing – you can't recycle plastic indefinitely (unlike aluminium). Plastic was never meant to be recycled and in trying to do so the polymers are degraded; so typically, you can only 'downcycle' it into an inferior product. Plastic food trays in their second incarnation might become plastic pipes, then car mats, and ultimately you reach an end point where the only thing you can do with the product is incinerate it, send it to landfill, or dump it in the ocean. Less of a 'circular economy' and more of a 'downward spiral economy'.

Second, even if they were recyclable, plastics are not actually being recycled. Globally, a pitiful 9 per cent of plastics are recycled.[33] This is the result of poor consumer behaviour, hard-to-recycle plastics and under-invested recycling infrastructure.

It's important to note that littering is without exception worse in areas of high deprivation, from the rivers of Kathmandu to the retail parks of Byker. But this is not because people in those areas are coincidentally all uncaring of their environment – I've seen plenty of mindless idiots driving posh cars chucking something from their window. The reasons are truly systemic, with worse access to waste management infrastructure and an over-reliance on highly packaged goods.

In the UK we are doing better than the global average, with 32 per cent of our plastic either recycled or composted – but not as efficient as Sweden who are at 50 per cent (these figures exclude 'energy recovery' – which is code for burning plastic).[34] Yet the average UK citizen produces a shameful 77kg of plastic waste per person per year, compared to the conscientious Swedes' 18kg per capita.[35] Therefore simple maths show us that when using the UK as an example, reducing our plastic consumption down to Sweden's levels would have *three-and-a-half times* the impact than improving our recycling infrastructure up to their standards. Globally, the stats differ but the reality is the same: using less, rather than recycling more, has to be our focus if we want to make meaningful progress.

The final myth of recycling is what can actually happen to the material once it is sent into the waste stream. Late in 2017 I visited a MURF (a mixed use recycling facility) in Leicestershire. It was an utterly depressing day. Millions had been invested in state-of-the-art mechanical, optical and magnetic automated sorting, but pretty much everything still ended up being picked by thickly gloved human hands on fast-moving conveyor belts.

Despite the fact that this was a facility dealing with paper, plastic, glass and other dry recyclables, the place smelled awful – because clearly people do not obey the instructions to rinse food containers before putting them in their bin. It was handling mixed recyclables, predominantly and bizarrely trucked all the way across the country from councils in Wales. Even after all their sorting efforts one could still see that the success rate was way less than 100 per cent – batteries lodged among shattered glass, paper mixed up with the plastic and so on. This also resulted in waste – so, for example, textiles were destined for incineration rather than recycling because of the risk that they could be contaminated with broken glass.

Out in the yard stood large cubic bales of imperfect-looking mixed plastics. I asked where they would go next, knowing that China had just barred the import of plastic waste.[36] 'Oh, that's no problem,' came the reply, 'we'll be sending them either to India or the Philippines instead.'

It is hard to overstate the sheer immorality of exporting our waste to ill-equipped developing countries, which hits the poor the hardest. According to Inger Andersen, Executive Director of the United Nations Environment Programme, in low-income countries 93 per cent of waste goes into open dumps.[37] A series of journalistic exposés have shown it blighting the environment as well as the lives of communities living close to facilities that deal with rubbish (which is the case even in rich countries). What can actually happen to that yogurt pot you diligently wash out and put in the correct recycling bin might be very different to what you presumed.

I've heard many in the West try and shift the blame for plastic pollution onto the rest of the world. And research has indeed found that most of the plastic in the ocean today flows from only a handful of Asian rivers.[38] So, the logic is that, rather than us taking the inconvenience to change our ways, it is really up to people in Asia to do something about it.

But we have been exporting our plastic waste to Asia for 'recycling' for years, so we have no moral high ground on which to stand. Ultimately, we in the UK led the process of industrialisation and its associated environmental degradation, and our per capita carbon emissions and plastic waste remain vastly higher than those of citizens in poorer countries. Hence the onus is very much on us to lead by example.

After years of growing other people's plastic mountains, one by one developing countries are now bravely standing up to the West and banning imported foreign waste. So now that the UK is losing the option to offshore its used plastic, we are going to have to deal with our own problems. Except that after years of dumping trash around the world, our neglected internal waste management infrastructure is in a pitiful state. Decades of under-investment have led to a disjointed system, where every council has different collection rules and capabilities. Nothing is harmonised or scaled up to create the efficient, modern recycling infrastructure we so desperately need.

Don't get me wrong – recycling, if it actually happens and is done correctly, is a good thing because it keeps plastics in circulation for longer. We should try and do more of it. But we must not accept the greenwash being fed to us from companies who want to produce ever-more plastic, because in itself recycling is not the answer, nor will it go anywhere near far enough to turn the tide on plastic pollution.

One area of recycling we have been pushing for is a

nationwide deposit return scheme (DRS) of PET plastic bottles. When put in a separate waste stream, the resulting high quality recyclate can actually be made back into more plastic bottles, thus providing an exception to the 'downcycling' rule. We have proven this through our own industry-leading trial of reverse vending machines in Iceland stores in England, Scotland, Wales and Northern Ireland. In just over a year we collected more than a million bottles through the five participating stores, trucked them back to our depots and sent them off for recycling into new bottles. Customers benefited with a 10p shopping voucher for every bottle bought from Iceland that they returned, and our research showed 96 per cent customer approval for extending a deposit return scheme to every retailer.

Common in many countries around the world, DRS works[39]. The deposit also provides an incentive not to litter, as well as income for those who are struggling by collecting bottles which others have discarded. Westminster and the devolved administrations have been talking about introducing a DRS for years – and they should just get on with it.

Plastic heroes

In the meantime, communities around the UK have been taking matters into their own hands. Surfers Against Sewage has more recently been focusing on battling the new sewage – plastic pollution. Not just on coastlines, but along rivers and in towns as well. Through national campaigns such as Plastic Free Communities and the Big Spring Beach Clean (sponsored by the IFCF) they focus on empowering communities to take action on plastic. As their charismatic CEO, my good friend Hugo Tagholm often says, 'Every piece of plastic picked up is a victory for the ocean.' In late 2019, Hugo and I developed the inaugural Plastic Free Awards in Bristol, to celebrate and bring together the very best of the UK's community activism and entrepreneurship.[40]

New, disruptive campaigners have emerged in the fight against plastic as well, such as Sian Sutherland, the effervescent co-founder of campaign group A Plastic Planet. I've partnered on some of Sian's high-energy and high-impact campaigns such as 'One Plastic Free Day' and 'Sack the Sachet', which challenge both big business and our own behaviours.

Rowbacks and progress

But unfortunately, events of 2020 provided a set-back for the positive momentum that has been created around changing attitudes towards single-use plastic. As well as its hugely damaging social and economic impacts, Covid-19 also saw a boost in pandemic plastics. If 2018 saw plastic go from hero to villain, 2020 saw its previous status resurrected. Personal Protective Equipment such as face masks and latex gloves became key symbols of the pandemic.

At the height of the coronavirus, fearful consumers (myself included) coveted the sterile, pre-packaged convenience that plastic enables. Customers certainly didn't want to root through loose produce displays in a supermarket, nor use refill stations. Coffee shops, once they were allowed to reopen, suspended the use of reusable 'keep-cups'.

Retailers (Iceland especially) also saw a massive shift to online grocery shopping, attracting more new shoppers in 2020 than the previous five years put together.[41] E-commerce adds more layers of packaging than a shop. At the same time, locked-down families were consuming record numbers of restaurant deliveries and takeaways, meaning more plastic waste.

Lockdown and its aftermath also saw a crash in the oil price. And because petroleum is a major constituent of plastics, this meant a production boom as well as less of an incentive for businesses to recycle. Big Plastic seized the opportunity, with the American Chemistry Council exposed at the height of the pandemic for lobbying the Trump administration to push plastics across Africa (despite knowing full well that many countries on the continent do not have the waste management infrastructure to deal with it).[42]

Maddeningly, governments around the world also rowed back on anti-plastic legislation, such as suspending the taxation of single-use carrier bags, and the UK government delaying the ban on plastic straws, stirrers and cotton buds.[43]

However, in the longterm I remain optimistic that sustainability efforts won't be stymied. Team Iceland, despite being locked down at home, continued undaunted with our plastics mission. The orchestration, development and retail trials of plastic reduction and removal carried on. We even held a 200-supplier virtual conference, updating them on our progress and setting goals for the year ahead. Indeed, based on our supplier working groups, we are now estimating a further reduction of 20 per cent by mid-2021.

As I will discuss in Chapter 5, one silver lining, of course, is that the enforced lockdown showed us that the world breathes easier when we slow down. Despite these short-term setbacks, I firmly believe that Covid-19 will give tailwind to the environmental movement, of which plastic is a key gateway issue for many.

A tax on virgin plastics would be an excellent way to discourage its use and to incentivise increases in recycled content. The UK government's announcement of a packaging tax on plastics with less than 30 per cent recycled content (despite significant lobbying from the British Plastics Federation[44]) is a step in the right direction. Revenues could usefully be hypothecated to fund much-needed investment in the UK's recycling infrastructure, to end the scandal of exporting our waste and bring uniformity and certainty to the currently haphazard pattern of local authority recycling.

Mandating nationwide waste food collections would be useful in the fight against climate change and would also facilitate the establishment of an industrial composting infrastructure that might make viable the greater use of bio-based packaging materials.

Planned reform of the existing Packaging Recovery Note (PRN) system will in any case create a powerful incentive for retailers and manufacturers to get out of plastic, by pushing 100 per cent of the onus away from consumers and onto producers by 2023. These notes are a form of tradeable currency, providing evidence that the producers and sellers of packaging have fulfilled their legal obligations to recycle or otherwise recover a specified proportion of the materials involved. The prices of plastic PRNs, in particular, have been rising sharply as overseas export markets for UK plastic waste have been closed. It is estimated that, in the absence of action to cut usage, Iceland's bill of around £700,000 for PRNs in 2019 could reach nearly £10 million by 2023.

These are the sorts of numbers that really cut through with the people who hold the purse strings in any business. And this matters, because however strong the moral, social and environmental case for any course of action may be, the sustainability champion in any organisation also has to convince their finance director that what they are proposing makes sound business sense. My plastics pledge now makes perfect sense to our Finance Director – vindication at last.

Yet by September 2020 I was getting frustrated with the rate of industry progress, and so we decided to do something really radical – tell the truth. In a first-of-its-kind for any supermarket, we fully disclosed our entire plastic footprint: not just the volume that goes through our customers' hands at the front of store, but also all the plastic we use in our operations at the back of store, further up our supply chains as well as in our international business.

There is an old adage in business, usually attributed to the management guru Peter Drucker, that 'You can't manage what you can't measure.' Indeed, the problem by the end of 2020 was that, while all of the supermarkets had finally set themselves plastic reduction targets, they were all taking different approaches, setting non-comparable targets, and reporting progress in inconsistent and often externally unverifiable ways.

There was no measurable context for systemic change.

Take the 2019 annual plastics survey of supermarkets by Greenpeace UK and the Environmental Investigation Agency, for example. It relied on unaudited and self-selected submissions from retailers, which saw the likes of Marks and Spencer and Waitrose only deciding to include 500ml plastic bottles in their data, while Tesco submitted their own-label plastic bottles but ignored the rest. Sainsbury's and Asda chose not to provide any data.

The amount of plastic we disclosed in our transparency announcement was nothing short of horrific: in the single year 2019 we generated more than 1.8 billion items using primary plastic, and over 100 million items of secondary and tertiary plastic.[45] Even more terrifying is the context that we are a relatively small player in UK food retailing, with a fraction of the national grocery market. Do the maths and scale up our plastic waste for the food retail industry as a whole, then add non-food retailing and all the other businesses in every sector that are using plastic to protect and package their goods: the total amount will be almost unimaginably mind-boggling.

The honesty of our announcement was applauded, and (unusually) backed by all of the leading plastic campaign groups. We urged all the other retailers to follow, and change happened almost instantly: Lidl published their full plastic footprint on the day of our announcement[46], following enquiries from *The Grocer*. A month later, we were in discussions with two other supermarkets who were planning to do the same.

If everyone adopts a consistent, nationwide approach that we all share, it will not only allow all of us to see who is genuinely making progress towards solving the plastic problem, but also finally enable us to fully comprehend the scale of the challenge ahead. The good news is that finding out all the information we published was relatively cheap and painless. Like every other business with a turnover of over £2 million and handling more than 50 tonnes of packaging a year, we have to report our packaging waste figures to the government under the PRN scheme anyway.

We are also urging the government to make such public reporting for all businesses mandatory, through an amendment to the Environment Bill, which should sit alongside bold and clear national plastic reduction targets.[47]

Notwithstanding the above, over the last three years a shift towards action on plastics is finally happening by business. According to the business sustainability website edie, '2018 will most likely be remembered with fondness by sustainability and CSR professionals as the year business action on plastics reached a tipping point. Triggered by Iceland's five-year plan to remove plastic from its own brand packaging, the sheer breadth of bold pledges made by businesses to phase-out plastic packaging and scale up innovation was truly incredible.'[48]

Since our announcement in 2018, every major supermarket has now moved towards our position and set themselves dramatic (albeit inconsistent) plastic reduction targets. Tesco have pledged to remove one billion pieces of plastic, Sainsbury's will halve their plastic footprint by 2025 and Waitrose will eliminate unnecessary plastic by 2023. They are all to be applauded. And, in turn, this will help to make Iceland's hugely ambitious 2023 own-label plastic removal target more deliverable.

But it's not the big companies who are leading the charge. The issue has been firmly picked up by a wide range of start-ups, who can see both the environmental benefits as well as new business opportunities. The Boex twins, surfing brothers from Porthleven, Cornwall, are teaching the global packaging industry a thing or two with their sustainable, plastic-free sleeve design company Flexi-Hex. They've developed a range of products for the transportation of consumer and industrial goods.

I personally wear sunglasses made from discarded 'ghost' fishing gear designed by the start-up Waterhaul, who are literally turning waste into profit. And my comfiest pair of shoes are from the scale-up WAES footwear company, producers of the world's first zero plastic trainer.

A refill packaging company, Loop, are creating new shopping platforms to enable direct delivery to customers' homes of reusable containers from big brands, such as Heinz, Coca-Cola and Persil, via a dedicated website. Vegware (a manufacturer of plant-based, compostable foodservice packaging) is growing rapidly, distributing and collecting their products in a closed-loop system across 70 countries.

I think that what such innovative companies are really showing us, is that as a society we urgently need a reassessment of the relationship between material design and consumer usage. According to the UN, globally 50 per cent of consumer plastics are single-use[49] – but the same issues of a failing linear economy and planned obsolescence can be found across many other products and materials too, from iPhones to T-shirts.

We need a greater focus, not just on low-impact materials, but also on building things to last and then repurposing them (when Bywater Properties' wooden office building reaches the end of its life, the component parts can find new life in other buildings, be composted or used as fuel).

Ultimately, it is critical that we eliminate wasteful design and change consumer habits. So, in 2019 Iceland introduced an additional commitment to simply have 10 per cent less packaging *overall* – plastics or otherwise – also by the end of 2023.

. . . .

Some say the task we've set ourselves of eliminating plastic entirely is impossible. But I don't care what the naysayers think. Twenty years ago, my Dad was told that removing GM ingredients was both unnecessary and technically impossible. No supermarket had even attempted to remove palm oil by 2018 either, assuming its ubiquity and cheapness made it unavoidable.

With people like Stuart Lendrum setting clear, deliverable steps for our buyers and 11 supplier working groups, the landing strip of our final destination is starting to come into view.

In only a few short years, we have improved the recyclability of the packaging of over 400 products and introduced clear labelling as to what is recyclable on all products.

We have fully removed the worst types of plastic (black plastic, PVC and polystyrene). Every year, we are delivering a growing range of plastic-free Christmas products to our stores.

Thanks to the enthusiastic engagement of our suppliers, we are set to deliver a reduction of over 50 per cent by 2021 and 60 per cent the following year, based off our 2018 tonnage starting point.

But the remaining road to 100 per cent is far from certain. Most of our reductions are coming from light-weighting, down-spec'ing and reducing plastic, rather than complete elimination. Often, the hard yards we have achieved are not visually apparent to the consumer. It's also difficult to say how the Covid-19 pandemic, and its long-term impacts on both consumer behaviour and our sales volume, will ultimately affect our overall progress.

Am I worried that we won't meet our target? Of course. Am I worried that I'll be dragged through the media and accused of not fulfilling my promise? Yes. But will that fear stop me from giving it everything I've got? No way.

I would much rather have our colleagues galvanised around this clear 'impossible' goal, pointing in exactly the right direction and being certain that what we are trying to achieve is the right thing for our business, the communities we serve and our planet.

THE KEY THINGS I'VE LEARNED

FIND THE PEOPLE ON THE FRONT LINE
Whether it's beach cleaners, customers or cashiers, the people experiencing the issue at first hand generally know the most about it.

TRANSFER YOUR THINKING
A solution designed for one issue or industry can be adapted and expanded for greater good.

NEVER BE AFRAID TO MAKE THE FIRST MOVE
If it's the right thing to do, others will follow.

WHEN YOU LEAD FROM THE FRONT YOU WILL INEVITABLY SUFFER MANY FAILURES
Be prepared for them, and be ready to dust yourself off and keep trying. Never give up.

REMEMBER THAT THERE WILL ALWAYS BE PEOPLE WILLING YOU TO FAIL
Assuming the worst about your motives and seeking to trip you up at every opportunity. Don't let this discourage you!

GETTING YOUR FINANCE DIRECTOR ONSIDE IS KEY TO DELIVERY
Sustainability initiatives that also make clear financial sense are the easiest to implement, so always look out for the business case for action as well as the moral, social and environmental one.

YOU DON'T HAVE TO BE A BIG BUSINESS TO LEAD CHANGE
Often the most disruptive and effective ideas come from start-ups.

CHAPTER 4
HOW A CARTOON ORANGUTAN HELPED TO CHANGE THE WORLD

Eliminating palm oil

'A NATION THAT DESTROYS ITS SOILS DESTROYS ITSELF. FORESTS ARE THE LUNGS OF OUR LAND, PURIFYING THE AIR AND GIVING FRESH STRENGTH TO OUR PEOPLE.'

FRANKLIN D. ROOSEVELT[1]

Some issues just aren't as tangible or as obvious to consumers as plastic. A lack of public awareness, and therefore engagement, means that urgent problems are often hidden from view. Improvement is slow and tragedies go unchecked.

These types of issues lurk within supply chains, out of sight and mind. Sometimes they might be hiding in plain sight – such as those Leicester textile factories producing dirt cheap garments for online fast fashion companies, which in July 2020 were allegedly found to be paying their workers as little as £3 an hour, far below the minimum wage.[2]

At other times, such controversies occur silently, on the other side of the planet. In remote places, enforcing modern slavery laws or policing overfishing within Marine Protected Areas can be exceptionally difficult. As a western-based retailer, rather than send out armies of auditors on a wild goose chase across the globe, we must rely on high industry and regulatory standards, robust supplier agreements, work alongside trade service providers and, ultimately, hope that no one cuts corners that we can't look around.

Yet just because such problems cannot be seen does

not mean they do not exist. And sometimes, it is easier simply to look the other way. As consumers, we may have read disturbing accounts of incidents of child labour and appalling working conditions in the cobalt mines of the Democratic Republic of Congo. But it doesn't stop our insatiable desire for the latest lithium-ion rechargeable phone or car – and the booming trade in what are now called 'blood batteries'.[3]

Unearthing these issues, understanding where the politics of supply chains might lead and confronting our own complicity can be nothing short of epiphanic.

When I decided to investigate one such concealed issue, I started on a journey that took me high up our own value chain, to a world far removed from the orderly retail shops of the UK's high streets. A place where not only was I confronted with the stark environmental reality of our ignorant sourcing decisions, but the social injustice they were causing too. And little did I know when I started thinking about palm oil that I would eventually be taken on a collision course with hostile media outlets around the world, and even some governments, protective of their nation's interests.

The palm oil problem

Our campaign against tropical deforestation, primarily caused by the illegal growth of unsustainable palm oil production, was one of the highest profile corporate environmental initiatives of recent years. And despite being fiercely contested by the governments of Malaysia and Indonesia, and wilfully misinterpreted by some commentators in the UK and Asia, it was also one of the most effective – because it made people see the issue for the first time.

As a long-standing supporter of Greenpeace, I had naturally been aware of the growing environmental concerns about palm oil for some years. The huge forest fires in Sumatra and Borneo in 2015 that covered much of South East Asia in a toxic haze for months, and killed 100,000 people, were a very clear warning signal that clearance was running out of control. The map of tropical rainforest coverage in Borneo, showing its devastating, progressive attrition since 1950, told a similarly depressing story.[4]

In early 2017 I sat down with John Hutchin, Greenpeace UK's Head of Key Relationships, to discuss just how urgent the problem of tropical deforestation, particularly in Indonesia, really was. It turned out that the issue ranked among the most concerning of all the environmental ills overfilling Greenpeace's inbox. Rainforest clearance in South East Asia was and is happening at an unprecedented rate to make way for monoculture palm tree plantations, from which the vegetable oil is derived from its fruit.

Rainforests matter on a number of levels. They are vitally important as a carbon sink, absorbing vast quantities of CO_2 from the atmosphere. When trees, plants and the animals they support die, they add carbon to the soil as leaf litter and other dead matter. Deforestation interrupts this carbon cycle and re-releases the sequestered carbon, accounting for about one-fifth of greenhouse gas emissions caused by human activities – even exceeding global transportation. Indeed, simply halting deforestation and restoring forests as a natural carbon sink could provide us with one-third of all the action we need to combat climate change.[5]

In return, healthy rainforests emit most of the oxygen to which we all owe our very existence. But their free services to humanity don't stop there – from regulating global rainfall, to protecting soils, reducing floods, to providing medicines, fuel, and paper – forests (and particularly the turbo-charged rainforests of the tropics) are essential ecosystem regulators and providers.

We ignore such interconnectedness at our peril. I discussed this with businessman and co-founder of the rainforest charity Cool Earth, Johan Eliasch. He explained to me with utter conviction how he believed tropical rainforest deforestation had caused Brexit. His theory went that the exponential growth throughout the early 2010s in logging and mining in central Africa had affected that region's rainfall patterns, which in turn had been a major causal factor in the severe droughts experienced across east Africa in 2011. That had then led to multiple humanitarian crises and civil unrest, spreading north to countries such as Egypt, Libya and Sudan. As a result, the EU was hit with a wave of migrant refugees in 2015. Against this backdrop, the UK's febrile referendum debate of 2016 saw issues such as border control and the immigration system at its heart.

There is another, more intrinsic reason to care about rainforests. They are the absolute crown jewels of global biodiversity – covering only 2 per cent of the planet's surface, yet containing around 50 per cent of its known plant and animal species (not to mention the myriad of as yet undiscovered species), according to the Nature Conservancy.[6] Looking beyond what they do for us as humans, rainforest biomes are simply stunning in their own right. From slithering anacondas to fluttering blue morpho butterflies, from exquisite orchids to spongy, green blanketing mosses, these precious ecosystems are home to a jaw-dropping array of beautiful flora and fauna. They showcase the pinnacle of 4 billion years of evolution.[7]

And all this evolution – which interestingly is defined by words such as *progress* and *development* – is now being wiped out to make way for vast new palm oil plantations. Our runaway demand for palm oil, to provide a cheap vegetable oil for consumer products like shampoo, soap, biscuits, chocolate and ice cream, is causing rainforests to be ruthlessly cleared – chopped down or simply (more cheaply, and of course illegally) burnt, incinerating everything along with them.

Western demand for palm oil began in the 19th century when industrialists like William Lever discovered its benefits – in his case for soap production. In a shocking example of the impact of colonialism, Lever Brothers exploited the Congo for palm oil supplies, at enormous human cost and in stark contrast to his reputation for philanthropy.[8]

However, the market really took off in the early part of this century with widespread concerns over partially hydrogenated vegetable trans fats. Hydrogenation is a process by which a liquid unsaturated fat is turned into a solid fat by adding hydrogen. During this process trans fats are created – which were found to upset the balance between good and bad cholesterol levels in the body. Once this issue became clear everyone sought to eliminate trans fats from their supply chains. Palm oil, being solid at room temperature, was the perfect replacement.

Today, palm oil is used as an ingredient or a derivative in an endless variety of consumer products – far beyond the more obvious ones mentioned above, and in food and non-food items as diverse as lipstick, detergent, sausages, bread and pastries. According to the charity WWF, by 2015 it was finding its way into almost 50 per cent of all supermarket products. Just like plastics, it's the manufacturing and retail industries' lazy over-reliance on this 'gold oil' that is the problem.

Worse still, to help the EU meet its fossil fuel reduction targets, palm oil is even being used in European biofuels, something I find so idiotic it is worth saying again: we are chopping down rainforest, to cultivate palm oil in order to stick into the fuel tanks of our vehicles and burn – and calling that a greener alternative.

Like the UK's environmentally disastrous encouragement of motorists to switch from petrol to diesel cars up until the 2010s, this is an absolutely classic example of the law of unintended consequences in operation. The areas in South East Asia's rainforests being cleared for palm oil are particularly rich in carbon, owing to their peaty soil (far more so than in the Amazon). The net result of this lunacy is that the greenhouse gas emissions from every litre of palm oil biodiesel are three times worse than those from the fossil diesel to which it was billed as an environmentally friendly alternative.[9] It is therefore impossible to drive a biofuel car for long enough in order to offset the lost rainforest from where it came.

This great biofuel greenwash has culminated in the egregious reality that now over half of EU palm oil imports are destined for fuel tanks. In 2018, 65 per cent of all the palm oil imported into the EU was burned for energy (with 12 per cent used to generate electricity and heating, and 53 for transportation biofuel).[10] According to the research group Transport & Environment, in 2020 European drivers were burning 100 times more palm oil in their tanks than is used in the 40 billion Oreo cookies consumed worldwide every year.[11] They go on to frame it in an even blunter way: 'If the world were to follow Europe's current thirst for palm oil biodiesel, 4,300,000 hectares of land in the tropics would be needed to quench it. That area is equal to the remaining rainforests and peatlands of Borneo, Sumatra and peninsular Malaysia.'[12] After increasing consumer outrage, in June 2018 the EU announced that it would phase out palm oil's use in biofuels – but only starting in 2023, with a ban set to take effect by 2030. The rainforests simply cannot wait that long.

Again – just like plastics, our world had become hopelessly addicted to palm oil. But also, like plastics, palm oil is not in itself some demonic substance. It is, in fact, very versatile, easy for manufacturers to handle (being able to tolerate a variety of temperatures) ... and above all cheap. This cheapness comes from the fact that oil palms are over five times higher yielding than other vegetable oil crops[13] – a statistic often used by the palm oil lobby groups to defend its increasing use, but one which entirely misses the point that the crop is almost exclusively grown within fragile areas of tropical rainforest. Indeed, according to a study by the European

Commission, palm oil has by far the highest share of expansion into forestland at 70 per cent, as opposed to all the other alternatives (including corn and soybeans) at 4 per cent or less.[14]

Such runaway demand has led to an explosion of palm tree plantations in the tropical regions where it can be grown, particularly on a few islands in Malaysia and Indonesia, which account for around 90 per cent of global production. Originally a west African subsistence crop, global palm oil production reached 73.5 million tonnes in 2018–19 – an astonishing quantity considering its fractional use in many products as a trace ingredient.[15]

With only 20–25 years' worth of fruit-bearing, more and more palm trees are required as old trees become redundant. Therefore, exponential amounts of land have to be cleared to make way for further plantations. In Indonesia alone, in early 2018 an area the size of 146 football pitches of rainforest was destroyed *every hour* – or one every 25 seconds, Indonesian Ministry of Forestry statistics reveal. And emerging producers are creating worrying hotspots – Papua New Guinea production increased by nearly 20 per cent between 2011 and 2016. The Global Forest Watch reports that the nation experienced '70 per cent more tree cover loss in 2015 than in any [other] year on record.'[16]

According to Greenpeace, when compared to levels in 2000 demand for palm oil is predicted to more than double by 2030 and to triple by 2050. The urgency of this crisis cannot be overstated.

Taking action

Iceland first started thinking seriously about palm oil in 2015, when we resigned our membership of the certification body, the RSPO (Roundtable on Sustainable Palm Oil) because we weren't convinced that it was proving effective in bringing genuinely sustainable palm oil to the mass market. At the same time, we asked our suppliers to switch to alternative vegetable oils where possible, and to continue to use certified and segregated palm oil where they found it impractical to switch.

By late 2016 we were a small user of only around 1,000 tonnes of palm oil a year, none of which we were buying directly. It was being sourced for our products by several hundred suppliers, many of them multinational companies for which we were a relatively unimportant customer. We considered what we should do next ... and identified three possible options.

First, we could re-join the RSPO and lobby for change. But as one voice among 4,000 – and an insignificant consumer at that – we believed that our influence from within would be minimal.

Second, we could – in theory – have tried to establish a certified sustainable palm oil supply chain for ourselves, through an organisation such as the Palm Oil Innovation Group (POIG), seen as the 'gold standard' in production. However, at the time there were just two POIG plantations, both in South America, and two things argued strongly against this: the complexity of our global supply chain and the fact that we are a value retailer, serving customers who simply cannot afford to pay more for their food. Whatever we chose to do had to add not a penny to the selling price of our products, and that ruled out an expensive, artisan solution.

The third option was to take an eye-catching and disruptive stand that would raise public awareness of the issues around palm oil and – we hoped – encourage the industry to get a lot more serious about delivering its promises on sustainability. As we knew from our activism on GM ingredients in the late 1990s, little old Iceland had the capacity to generate a great deal of publicity – and so exercise significant influence on the public debate. We decided to do the one thing that everyone said was impossible – to take palm oil out of our own label food – as a shock tactic to get the industry and major brands to take notice, and to apply pressure on them to move towards a truly sustainable supply.

Time was also of the essence if we were to make a difference. The RSPO was holding a well-publicised consultation on its future principles during 2018, and the Greenpeace campaign pressurising major brands to meet their 2020 deforestation commitments was gaining pace.

So, we began work to assess the practicality of removing the remaining palm oil from our own label food. Unsurprisingly, since the global food industry had come to be designed around palm oil, many people told us that getting rid of it simply wouldn't be possible. Not only would it require redesigning recipes, but also completely changing the manufacturing lines on which they were produced – further echoes of our GM experience from 20 years earlier.

Our chefs and technicians worked tirelessly with our suppliers on product reformulation for 18 months before we were ready to make our announcement in April 2018 that we would stop using palm oil as an ingredient in the manufacture of all Iceland own label food by the end of the year.

By then – after two supplier conferences, many trials and a long series of tough discussions – we were convinced that we could replace palm oil without affecting the quality or taste of our products. It wasn't easy, but it was certainly interesting – almost a voyage of discovery where we had to re-imagine volume food production. I remember in one of the supplier conferences, a cheesecake manufacturer was thoroughly stuck trying to come up with an alternative to using palm oil in the crumb base of his product. Only after some intense brainstorming did a rival supplier hit upon a suitable alternative – water.

The more obvious replacements for palm oil were vegetable oils such as olive, rapeseed and sunflower oil. What was less obvious was how to replicate the semi-solid state of palm oil at room temperature, which is particularly helpful in the manufacturing process of some products.

After much debate, we found and dusted off one of the last remaining hydrogenation machines in the UK – a relic of a world before mass palm oil, which had been well and truly mothballed. Our plan was to *fully* hydrogenate the replacement oils to create a solid substance, which would then be diluted back down to a palm oil-like, semi-solid state. This bypassed the need to *partially* hydrogenate, which is what caused those deadly trans fats. Full hydrogenation had no such consequences. Nevertheless, I was particularly nervous about what the consumer reaction might be to words such as 'hydrogenation', given its analogy with trans fats. But as it turned out, we had no adverse reactions.

The huge work streams that had been set up to focus on removing palm oil were ruffling a few feathers within Iceland – some rather close to home. I remember while sat in a strategy meeting planning the communications around our announcement, Dad burst into my office and said exasperatedly 'Not *another* monkey meeting?!' It had certainly started to consume a great deal of my time, and while he could see the environmental reasons behind our efforts, Dad was much keener for me to 'focus on the shops and stop saving the world.' He is definitely a businessman from the 'purpose *after* profits' school of thought.

An added internal pressure was that we were doing all of this work knowing that we couldn't charge more for our palm oil free products. Like our products in plastic-free packaging, they would simply not sell if we tried to charge our hard-pressed customers more for the privilege. This was despite the fact that all the alternatives to palm oil are more expensive. (That, after all, is why it had come to be so widely used in the first place.) So, all the time, effort and cost invested were unlikely to show a return – unless sales sky-rocketed and we brought in a load of new customers.

Yet we ploughed on, and by the time we made our announcement we had already quietly eliminated palm oil as an ingredient from half our own label range, and were on track to remove the remainder by the end of December.

Doing our homework

The mission had become personal. As well as visiting our domestic suppliers and their food facilities, I had to check the facts around palm oil production and its consequences for myself. By now I was so deep into this debate that I needed to get out of my comfort zone and see the reality on the ground. I decided that I must head out to Borneo, a vast island and one of the most biologically diverse places on the planet, which is also the epicentre of the booming palm oil industry. I wanted to see those vast monoculture palm plantations that I had read about, and witness first-hand what effect they were having on the diminishing rainforests and wildlife.

But most of all, before making such a big decision, I had to test the views of those who were going to be affected by it. According to the Indonesian Palm Oil Association, 50 million Indonesians depend directly or indirectly on palm oil and its derivatives. How did they feel about the potential withdrawal of the hand that feeds them?

With some trepidation, I flew out to a remote area of West Kalimantan in Indonesian Borneo, in November 2017 – on a commercial flight, not the private jet that subsequently became the fantasy of a PR campaign seemingly driven by Malaysian smallholders ... though actually funded by their government. These 'astroturf campaigners' (a phrase used for fake grassroot organisations) sought to portray me as 'Trust Fund Richard', a new generation of white colonialist driving around in a Rolls-Royce (they only missed an image of me lighting a cigar with a £50 note), while driving poor farmers in the tropics to the wall.[17]

On my visit I saw little evidence of any such smallholders on the ground. And those I met talked about the many land ownership disputes impacting their community. What I did see was an environmental disaster zone involving the replacement of vibrant, diverse rainforest with sterile palm monocultures. Forests and human settlements had been replaced with 'green deserts', containing virtually no wildlife or people. The associated ills of illegal deforestation, industrial scale draining of peat swamps, the devastation wreaked by forest fires, displaced communities and animals being killed and brutalised were all plainly evident.

The psychological trauma from previous forest fires lingered in the minds of locals. In 2015 the biggest forest fires of the century tore through Indonesia, which as a result temporarily surpassed the US for greenhouse gas emissions that year. They reduced millions of hectares of lush tropical rainforest to ash – and with it, some of the last habitat for Indonesian orangutans. A noxious haze blanketed the region for several months and spread as far as Bangkok. More than 28 million people in Indonesia alone were affected by the crisis, and more than 140,000 reported respiratory illnesses as a result.[18]

I heard stories from indigenous communities who had inhabited and protected their forest home for generations, only to be brutally driven from their land. In Indonesia, more than 700 land conflicts are related to the palm oil industry.[19]

There are also many sad examples of the exploitation of workers, child labour and slavery. According to the US Department of Labor, such practices are prevalent in the palm oil sector[20], with palm oil from Malaysia and

Indonesia failing to reach their minimum standards for eliminating trafficking (but they are at least 'making efforts to do so').[21]

The current reality is that palm oil production only meaningfully benefits a small proportion of those involved in the farming process, mostly foreign owned agribusinesses, while most smallholders struggle to meet their basic needs.[22] Their low margins and lack of resources actually discourage them from working sustainably.[23] They struggle with land tenure challenges, poor agricultural practices and a lack of finance for replanting and certification.[24]

Yet I do believe that long-term benefits of palm oil can trickle down to communities, but only from a supply chain that is truly sustainable. And the future livelihoods of smallholders can only be ensured by a sustainable industry, not one that destroys the environment.

My lasting memory of the trip was travelling far into some of the remaining rainforest with local people. After several hours, moving slowly through swamp water by boat and on foot, we came to a break in the dense vegetation ... only to be faced with a scene of complete, apocalyptic devastation. Acres of jungle and the wildlife within it had been razed to the ground by illegal fires, leaving just charred stumps of trees and, in contrast to the forest behind us, a deep and enveloping silence, interrupted only by the falling rain. As we looked out on the scene one of the Dayak people guiding us turned to me and, via his translator, said; 'So, are you going to do something about this?'

We also undertook research among the British public, most of whom proved to have little awareness of palm oil or its associated environmental issues. When we surveyed 5,000 consumers, 35 per cent proved to be completely unaware of palm oil; but, when informed about what it is, and its effects on the environment, 85 per cent of them said that they did not want palm oil in their products.

Until we made our pledge, customers had effectively had no choice but to consume palm oil in many types of food. Again, as with GM ingredients in the 1990s, Iceland offered consumers shopping in a UK supermarket a choice for the first time.

The media and public reaction was extraordinary. Our announcement on 10 April 2018 generated more than 1,000 pieces of media coverage, and reached more than 90 million people through social media. Our accompanying video was viewed more than four million times. Overall, if you understand marketing-speak, there were over 6 billion earned 'opportunities to see': the reactions were overwhelmingly positive.

Backlash

Of course, not everyone was pleased. As I noted earlier, an organisation emerged, claiming to represent small farmers. Faces of Palm Oil was in fact set up by several Malaysian groups, including two Malaysian government agencies. With the help of western PR and lobbying firms, they launched a notably vicious and personal paid campaign against me on social media in the UK.[25]

Another obscure outfit, supposedly representing subsistence palm oil farmers from Nigeria, somehow managed to negotiate and pay for full-page press ads in

UK newspapers, using a rather menacing headshot of me taken on the streets of London without my permission and deeming me a 'colonialist'.

Diplomatic pressure was also applied on the government in London to rein in Iceland, with the threat that Malaysian orders for fighter jets would be cancelled if they failed to comply.[26] I had been warned by various environmental groups that there might be repercussions, but I simply couldn't believe the knock-on consequences that our little protest was having.

Despite all of this negativity, I had quite enjoyed the heated debate that we had kicked off. The tipping point, however, came after I had been warned by a campaign group that I was almost certainly being followed by people 'with long lenses'. That week, my wife was approached by a complete stranger while sitting alone in a café in Chester. A woman marched up to her with a camera, snapped a photo and then left without saying a word. For the first time, we became quite scared. I was told by an NGO working on the ground in Indonesia that I should not try to return to the country.

I felt like I had inadvertently, perhaps naively, stepped into a geo-political drama – as the main protagonist. Indonesia, now the world's largest exporter of crude palm oil, produced over 47 million tonnes of palm oil in 2019.[27] This is an industry worth tens of billions of dollars to the country, and therefore vital to their national economy and security. I was learning that defending that income, and in turn palm oil's reputation, is seen by the world's fourth most populous country as paramount.

Our opponents were making much of the environmental arguments in favour of palm oil – which, as I've noted, is a very high-yielding crop. Yet the tone of their debate was always a level too personal and insulting. The once progressive environmentalist Sir Jonathan Porritt published condescending and fairly rude articles about me and Greenpeace, which were then amplified by the Indonesian and Malaysian press. In one, entitled 'Iceland, Palm Oil and Empty PR Stunts' he called me 'intellectually lazy', among other things.[28] When I finally met Jonathan over canapés and champagne at a Buckingham Palace do months later, I noted the hypocrisy of this accusation – given the fact that he failed to disclose his paid role as an advisor to Sime Darby, one of the world's biggest palm oil producers. Our tête-à-tête was only saved from escalating further by Prince Charles, as we took our turn in the royal procession.

When seeking palm oil alternatives, we were extremely conscious that we didn't just want to shift the consequences elsewhere, as people like Porritt were arguing. That is precisely why we steered clear of other oils produced in the tropics, such as coconut or shea, because our objection was never to palm oil itself, but to the deforestation that growing demand for it was driving. And I think most of us can accept that a hectare of virgin tropical rainforest is of greater environmental value, and more in need of protection, than 7 hectares of well-established farmland growing rapeseed oil in Lincolnshire.

We always acknowledged that there could be a role for palm oil – but contended that the rate of growth in demand, the unquestioned use of it in so many products, and the seeming inability of the industry to regulate itself was unsustainable. Our action was designed to prove that it did not necessarily have to be used, and so show that it would be possible to reduce the current runaway demand, while creating public debate with the aim of persuading the industry to clean up its act.

Our closest relatives

In May 2018 the BBC aired a moving documentary called 'Red Ape', about the plight of the critically endangered orangutan, which helped to keep the issue of palm oil squarely in the minds of the British public.[29] It showed how the unchecked expansion of palm oil plantations and logging directly threatened the survival of our closest relative on the planet – whose name literally translates as the 'human of the forest'.

These gentle, sentient animals have exceptionally high intellect and are capable of showing unusual levels of emotion. They can quickly learn how to use human tools, such as saws and hammers, and mourn the loss of others within their congress. Orangutan mothers stay with their offspring for six to eight years, who in return are known to 'visit' their mothers until the age of about 16. This is one of the strongest mother–infant bonds in nature.

Yet despite such an affinity to humans, it is not a case of a species that has been in slow decline over a long period of time – in less than 20 years the Bornean orangutan population had halved to perhaps only 70,000 by 2018, according to a study by an international team of conservationists.[30]

That banned ad

Two months later, I saw for the first time a Greenpeace animated film called *Rang-Tan*, with a voiceover by the Oscar-winning actress Emma Thompson. The poignant, 90-second cartoon showed an orangutan explaining to a young girl why the destruction of her forest home and loss of her family had forced her to take refuge in the girl's bedroom. It moved me to tears.

I showed it to some of the team at the head office, and we thought it so powerful that if we could 'borrow' it for our Iceland Christmas advertisement, we would be in a position to blow the traditional seasonal highlight from John Lewis out of the water – and provide a huge boost to the Greenpeace campaign to put pressure on big brands.

In August we shared *Rang-Tan* with our 2.4 million online customer base, to promote Greenpeace's campaign against 'dirty' unsustainable palm oil, and thousands of these customers were moved to sign the Greenpeace petition on the subject.

After some rather tense persuasion, I managed to convince the rest of the Iceland board that we would devote our Christmas advertising airtime to *Rang-Tan*. After a four-way negotiation, Greenpeace, their advertising agency Mother and *Rang-Tan*'s animators Passion Pictures, all kindly gave us their permission to adapt the ad for our use. Mother then began discussions with Clearcast, the industry body that approves adverts for commercial TV, about approving it for our use.

These conversations went on for some weeks, and while I knew that it wasn't going to be a straightforward approval process, I genuinely thought we would get it passed by Clearcast. I actually became more encouraged as our negotiations went on – to me it looked like if we made a few tweaks here and there we would get approval. So I was pretty shocked to be given their eventual decision that it could not be shown on TV because it contravened the UK's ban on political advertising. Not because of its actual content, but simply because it had originally been made by Greenpeace (which is deemed to be a political advertiser).

I was pretty upset – especially considering that I now had to explain to the board that because of my insistence on pursuing *Rang-Tan*, we were now without a showcase 2018 Christmas ad. We had even pre-booked over £600,000 worth of airtime on primetime TV to showcase it. Thinking all was lost, I even started to question my own conviction ... was I allowing my personal environmental concerns to blind my commercial judgement, ultimately affecting the business?

While stuck in the middle of this malaise, it was suggested to me that the unintended situation we found ourselves in might actually be an even bigger opportunity. I wanted to tell the world what had happened ... and I needed to tell as many people as possible, and fast. So, on 9 November I tweeted out a message with a link to our 'banned Christmas ad' ...

It was immediately clear that the public were genuinely shocked that such an urgent and important issue hadn't been allowed on TV. By the end of the day, the video had hundreds of thousands of views. By the end of the week, millions. Celebrities like Stephen Fry, Ricky Gervais and James Corden began sharing the ad with their enormous fan bases, who in turn started retweeting and posting to their own followers. It quickly ranked among the highest trending topics across most social media platforms, and within a few weeks our banned cartoon ad had been viewed across the world, tens of millions of times.

A month earlier, palm oil was still a fairly specialist environmental issue limited to those who really cared and understood about tropical deforestation. Suddenly, *everyone* seemed to be talking about it – debating the pros and cons, the alternatives, and what action they could take as consumers.

Keen as ever to please their concerned constituents, I was contacted by politicians and even a senior cabinet member offering their personal help. Outraged protestors picketed the Clearcast offices, and well over a million people ended up signing a petition set up by a care worker called Mark Topps to 'un-ban' our ad.

TUI travel company stated that *Rang-Tan* had led to a 900 per cent increase in gap year students wanting to work in orangutan sanctuaries.[31] Over a thousand schools got in contact with Iceland and Greenpeace about the issue, and Google searches of the phrase 'palm oil' increased 10,000 per cent.[32]

A tidal wave of feeling and awareness had been unleashed – and we proudly considered that a job well and truly done.

The unintended consequence of *Rang-Tan* being banned has now made it the most watched Christmas ad of all time according to the *Daily Mail*, being viewed well over 80 million times. Its online viral success has even led many in the industry to question the value of terrestrial TV ad spend. It's been shown and discussed on TV, radio, websites and newspapers globally, and I regularly hear of it being used by consultancies and universities as a case study.

However, rather than being part of some genius Machiavellian PR plan, it was a genuine case of serendipity.

Most importantly, we had contributed to the global pressure that led the RSPO in November 2018 to announce its commitment to achieving zero deforestation within two years.[33] And to Wilmar, the world's largest palm oil trader, who, according to Greenpeace, made a 'breakthrough pledge' at the end of 2018 to map and monitor all of its suppliers.[34]

Since then, the Malaysian government has promised to cap the country's oil palm plantations areas at about 6.5 million hectares by 2023.[35] It has started work on forest restoration and wildlife conservation, and has promised to stop planting palm trees on peat land and in forest reserves. Early in 2019, the *Financial Times* ran a special report on Iceland's efforts on both plastics and palm oil, and the impacts they had.[36]

Backlash 2

However, there was a downside. As we all know, any person, business or cause that has achieved public acclaim must inevitably be knocked down. In particular, many in the UK media harbour a depressingly negative desire to expose corporate wrongdoing and show up any attempts to take positive action on the environment as a sham. Naturally a 'cheap' store like Iceland caring about the tropical rainforest became a prime target for investigation.

Early in January 2019 a BBC reporter visited one of our stores and our website and reported – shock, horror – that we still had products containing palm oil on sale. The reasons proved to be the usual mixture of avoidable cock-up and wilful misunderstanding.

First, we had failed to update the ingredients listed on our website so that some of our own label lines were shown there as still containing palm oil, when the actual products in the stores did not. Not reality, but our mistake nevertheless: this was a fair cop.

Second, we were continuing to sell a number of frozen Iceland own label lines, produced before our deadline of 31 December 2018, because the only alternative to selling them was to throw them away, which would have invited another exposé about Iceland causing needless food waste. (And no, we couldn't have given it away to food banks because at the time they simply would not accept bulk donations of frozen food.)

Finally, it was highlighted that we also had 'hundreds' of other lines containing palm oil on sale, because it is contained in such a wide range of branded foods. And surely this was rank hypocrisy when we had just gained so much free publicity for our palm oil removal? The reality is that it was not, because we had never, ever suggested that we would stop selling brands containing palm oil, merely pledged to stop using it as an ingredient in our own label food.

As I explained to an irate Piers Morgan on a live TV grilling one morning, it would be commercial suicide for any retailer to announce to its customers that it would no longer stock many of the leading brands they want to buy, and we had never implied that we would.

I have to acknowledge that we did make one other big mistake. We had come nail-bitingly close to meeting our pledge of reformulating all our own label products to eliminate palm oil as an ingredient by 31 December 2018, but as the deadline approached we found that there were 17 lines for which the suppliers simply could not make the necessary changes to recipes and methods of production on time.

We didn't want to put a supplier under so much pressure that it endangered their business, simply to meet an arbitrary and self-imposed deadline. So, we decided to meet our pledge not by removing palm oil from this small number of products, but by temporarily removing our name from the label – only for a matter of weeks until the supplier had time to catch up. Our thinking being that the message for customers was simple: if the product says Iceland, you can be assured it does not contain palm oil.

The furore when this was 'spotted' by an investigative journalist was tremendous, and I learned an important lesson about transparency. We could and should have communicated what we did to those 17 lines when we made the decision to do it in September, rather than waiting for someone to 'uncover' it. Hindsight is a wonderful thing.[37]

Driven by misleading headlines, some of the public became outraged at our seeming hypocrisy and greenwash. Social media began to light up again, but for all the wrong reasons. I felt so frustrated that our triumphant palm oil story was being tarnished with a controversial epilogue.

A growing indignation started to take hold of me for what I saw as a twisted half-truth, driven by institutional snobbery by some in the media. In a heated exchange on *BBC Breakfast*, I pointed out that rather than focusing on the 97 per cent – those 450 lines that Iceland had reformulated or launched without palm oil – vitriolic reporters were highlighting the fact that we had 'failed' because 17 products had temporarily been removed from our own label.

The tone of our exchange sharpening, I chose not to wait for the next question, and pointedly went on:

We are sleepwalking into an environmental disaster, and corporations are doing nowhere near enough – but is it any wonder? Rather than celebrating this effort [...] we're being tripped up by journalists. Yet I think what my staff and suppliers have achieved is nothing short of incredible.

The back and forth continued for a while longer; but it was clear that I'd done enough to set the record straight. As I emerged from the cavernous basement of Broadcasting House and out into the daylight of Portland Place, my phone began lighting up with messages of congratulations. I took some long, deep breaths. Before any such big interview or important speech, for some reason I always think of my Mum – and that morning, I knew she would have been proud. In the cold, January air, I could feel my eyes starting to brim.

. . . .

By April 2019 we had relaunched nearly all those lines back under our own label, and also made a considerable investment to ensure that any remaining Iceland own label or temporarily unbranded stock containing palm oil ingredients was cleared from all our stores.

The other untruth that kept being recycled was that we deliberately set out to have our Christmas ad banned as a cynical attempt to gain free publicity and so boost sales (which as I explained we didn't – primarily because I am not that clever).

In fact, despite all the amazing publicity around *Rang-Tan*, Iceland did not enjoy a record-breaking Christmas in 2018. There is no evidence that we derived any sales benefit at all from our efforts – but then that was never the point. What we did achieve was what we had hoped for: a move by the global palm oil industry to clean up its act.

What we also saw was an enormous improvement in perceptions of Iceland as an ethical business, which can surely only enhance our long-term prospects ... particularly among younger and more purpose-led consumers. Yet again, many in the established mainstream media seemed to entirely miss this point.

In May 2019 the UK's *Sunday Telegraph* published a comment piece declaring that our palm oil campaign had 'failed' because it did not translate into sales. The 'communications specialist' James Frayne opined that 'It's no good companies being "woke" when their customers are all Brexiteer Tories.' Iceland's customers were 'urban, poorer, working class' and so indifferent to palm oil and the fate of the orangutan. So what was the point?[38]

Such snobbish prejudice really infuriated me, along with the suggestion that we do not understand who our customers are, or what they care about. Iceland has been in business for 50 years and, as one of the largest and most successful private companies in Britain and a genuine community retailer, I feel pretty confident that we understand our customers very well indeed.

It is also very clear to me that environmentalism can only succeed if it engages the whole of society, and makes the threat from climate change, plastic pollution, deforestation and the loss of biodiversity real and relevant to each and every one of us – not just those with university degrees and comfortable incomes.

The removal of palm oil from all Iceland products was an amazing piece of corporate activism, helping to push the industry towards major new zero deforestation pledges. I am damn proud of what our colleagues achieved, and I know very well from my email inbox that they are too. In an August 2020 interview, the boss of Greenpeace UK John Sauven (not one to normally praise a corporate), reflected on our campaign 'I think they did more than any other company.'[39]

The fact that our initiative didn't boost our sales was of absolutely no consequence – and I write that as one of Iceland's shareholders. Unparalleled levels of colleague engagement, an enhanced brand reputation and a win for the environment: for a business fit for the 2020s, all of this trumps simply turning a short-term profit. I think it serves as a good example of how businesses can create far more value when serving all of their stakeholders and move beyond Friedman's monotonal concept of shareholder primacy.

The lessons for environmental activism are clear, too. Environmentalism is democratising, and nowadays many people – rich or poor, young or old, southern or northern – care about these issues. Perhaps that's why, when surveyed, 82 per cent of Iceland customers agreed with our stance on palm oil. I certainly don't find that statistic suggestive of indifference.

While I noted earlier in this chapter that there are some similarities between plastics and palm oil, it is important also to acknowledge some important differences in the nuance of the message between the two campaigns.

On plastics, we very deliberately took a stand that we hoped that other companies would follow: indeed, as I discussed in the previous chapter, some of the challenges of finding replacement materials can only be met if our whole industry adopts a collaborative approach to changing its supply chains. On palm oil, we were careful never to suggest that others should follow us, or to call for a boycott or ban. We know very well that all the alternatives to palm oil have environmental downsides of their own. Genuinely sustainable palm oil is a good thing and, if the RSPO can deliver it in quantity to the mass market, we will welcome that.

Alongside highlighting the severity of deforestation that palm oil is causing, we also wanted to be part of the solution and take positive action on the ground in South East Asia. So, the IFCF has also funded the planting of a 1-million-tree mangrove forest located on the south-west coast of Yapen Island in remote West Papua, Indonesia. Not only will this restore an essential natural habitat, and mitigate 187,000 tonnes of carbon dioxide, importantly it will also support the local economy by providing 25 local people with full time jobs.[40]

Problems elsewhere

Even as the palm oil industry in South East Asia starts to show signs of reform, I cannot claim that my conscience is now clear – far from it. Other everyday commodities are causing tragedies elsewhere around the world. Regions such as the Brazilian Amazon and Cerrado are under threat as never before, due to unsustainable soy production – another crop that goes unseen but on which we are utterly reliant.

As Greenpeace UK stated, 'Spurred on by Brazil's President Jair Bolsonaro, the Amazon and other precious forests are being slashed, burned and replaced by beef farms and soya plantations to produce industrial meat and dairy that's sold in the UK by supermarkets and fast food chains. The destruction of forests for industrial meat is releasing millions of tonnes of CO_2, accelerating climate change, threatening indigenous communities and increasing the risk of future pandemics.'[41]

Iceland, along with all the other UK supermarkets and restaurant chains, is complicit in this devastation. We have looked at 'doing a palm oil' and dropping all of the Brazilian soy that is used as a feedstock for the chicken and pork we sell. But the development of sustainable soy is in its very first stages and the reality is that, unlike palm oil, we do not think the circumstances are right for us to take such action alone – and nor could we, given traceability issues.

However, we are now working with a key supplier to develop the first-ever soy-free fed British chicken. Farmers are so reliant on soybean meal to feed their chickens because it is packed full of protein. Historically in the UK (and still used in other parts of the world) chickens were fed bone meal – clearly not an option we can consider today. Rather, there is now a range of alternative feed proteins being developed such as insect meal, algae and grain legumes. I am really excited about these new innovations, and the proof-point that Iceland launching a genuinely sustainably fed chicken should provide to industry.

In tandem, we also believe that cross-industry collaboration is key to the soy problem. In December 2019, Iceland co-signed a letter with 87 other companies, urging Bolsonaro to stop further deforestation of the Amazon for soy production, and we have lobbied individual businesses for change. Working groups, such as the Round Table for Responsible Soy and the Cerrado Manifesto, are trying their best.

Yet putting the best efforts of industry to one side, what we really need to see are diplomatic solutions in the name of higher import standards that demand both zero deforestation and better traceability. These could now genuinely be delivered via post-Brexit trade deals with countries such as Brazil.[42]

Technology may also come to our rescue in the not-too-distant future. Several biotech firms are developing a synthetic alternative to palm oil, for example, made by fermenting genetically modified microbes, converting food waste and industrial by-products into a substance that one day may dramatically reduce the need for traditional plantations. An interesting example of how, 20 years on from original concerns about 'Frankenstein foods', we may need to revisit the acceptability of GM technology in order to help tackle some of our biggest environmental problems.[43]

Ultimately, my hope is that one day the world will see a fundamental switch in the economics of rainforests. Rather than the double-dip (but short-term) windfall of logging and monoculture, we need a system that reinforces that the highest value is attained from forest preservation and nature restoration ... and that value is protected for local communities. Market-based solutions, such as REDD+ financing (Reducing Emissions from Deforestation and Degradation) rewards custodians of a forest area in return for a measurable reduction in the rate of deforestation. Although such schemes are still in their infancy, and far too reliant upon carbon credits[43], they should nevertheless form part of our toolkit of solutions.

The global fight against deforestation and its consequences continues.

THE KEY THINGS I'VE LEARNED

ESTABLISH CLEAR OBJECTIVES

What are you actually trying to achieve? Environmental improvement, a better image for yourself or your business, or higher sales and profits? We were very clear from Day 1 that our palm oil campaign was all about stopping tropical deforestation.

BE AMBITIOUS AND DISRUPTIVE

We were a relatively small company seeking to change the approach of a major global industry – and of national governments. And we succeeded.

MAKE IT PERSONAL
Check the facts yourself. Be prepared to make that long and arduous journey to see the realities on the ground, do proper research and seek out the experts.

PAY ATTENTION TO DETAIL
Small errors will be pounced upon by the sceptics – and can easily end up obscuring your whole message.

BE TOTALLY TRANSPARENT
No matter how irrelevant some details may seem.

ACKNOWLEDGE THE OTHER POINT OF VIEW
Palm oil does offer some environmental benefits – we never sought to deny it.

BRACE YOURSELF FOR PERSONAL CRITICISM
And don't take it to heart or let it deflect you from your purpose.

DON'T EXPECT THE MEDIA TO BE ON YOUR SIDE
There will always be those who suspect your motives and try to bring you down, even if you are simply trying to do good.

CHAPTER 5
BIOPHILIC BRITAIN

**Learning the lessons
from Covid-19**

'THE ONLY THING THAT KEEPS ME AWAKE AT NIGHT IS THE THOUGHT OF A PANDEMIC.'

BILL GATES, FEBRUARY 2019[1]

We should have listened to Bill.

In late April 2020, at the height of the pandemic in western Europe and America, a group of the world's leading biodiversity experts published an article where they established that 'Rampant deforestation, uncontrolled expansion of agriculture, intensive farming, mining and infrastructure development, as well as the exploitation of wild species have created a "perfect storm" for the spillover of diseases.'[2]

In a chilling warning, they pointed out that the potential for future pandemics is vast. Animal-to-human diseases could spread much faster, with more ferocity and greater impact on economies and human health. I suppose this is plain logic – we rely on nature's finely tuned life support machine, yet we continue our ever-increasing exploitation and encroachment upon the natural world.

Our destruction of the natural world has indeed been relentless.

According to the UN Convention on Biological Diversity, of the estimated 8 million species on Earth, 1 million are now threatened with extinction. And it's not just magnificent species such as the white rhino or Bornean orangutan that find themselves critically endangered: 41 per cent of all known amphibians, 34 per cent of conifers and 28 per cent of crustaceans are now on the IUCN (International Union for Conservation of Nature) Red List of Threatened Species.[3]

A potential catastrophic decline of insects (ominously termed Insectageddon), is particularly concerning given that they are deemed to be the glue that holds the environment together.[4]

We now cut down over 15 billion trees each year[5] and according to the Royal Botanic Gardens, Kew, two in five plants are estimated to be threatened with extinction.[6]

All living organisms are of equal importance in the web of life and therefore all deserve protection – not least for our own protection. Yet overall, the global biomass of wild mammals has fallen by 82 per cent.[7] In his book *The Nature of Nature*, the conservationist Enric Sala points out that humans, along with our domesticated livestock, now account for 96 per cent of the weight of all mammals on earth. 'Only 4 per cent is everything else, from elephants to bison to panda bears.'[8]

Nature is simply not being given enough space to thrive, and this of course is due to human development. Since 1970, the global human population has doubled, and the world economy has grown fourfold. As a consequence, between 1980 and 2000, *100 million* hectares of tropical forest were lost (equivalent to over four times the size of the UK ... in just 20 years). Only 13 per cent of wetlands remain since the start of the Industrial Age. Half of the fertile land on Earth is now farmland, and urban areas globally have doubled in size since 1992.[9]

Now we are facing up to the consequences of this diminishment – not just increased likelihood of future pandemics, but also the impacts to our social foundations too. From the destruction of wetlands and forests that affects water supplies, the desertification of arable lands, to the decline in bees that pollinate our crops – if we don't act now, nature will impose solutions upon us. Covid-19, in my opinion, has been a warning shot from natural world ... and we must take note.

It is now glaringly obvious that we need stronger and better-enforced environmental and nature regulations to help protect and restore forests, grasslands, peatlands, oceans and freshwater habitats. While the catastrophic impacts of climate change have been firmly on our radar for some time, thankfully there is now growing realisation that we have also been taking nature for granted – and that we must urgently focus on the renewal of our ecosystems and the rewilding of our planet.

In September 2020 a charity of which I am a trustee, Fauna & Flora International, launched a major campaign called Our One Home which made a global call to both governments and the private sector to commit an initial $500 billion in funding to protect nature and biodiversity, and put it into the hands of those who are best placed to use it – local conservation organisations who have a deep understanding of the challenges we face and how to tackle them.

I also sit on Greenpeace UK's Ocean Advisory Board, a group of philanthropists and influencers who are helping the NGO campaign to establish a network of Marine Protected Areas covering 30 per cent of international waters, also by 2030, through the negotiation of a UN Global Ocean Treaty. At the moment, there are no enforceable protections from over-fishing of international waters, which cover 50 per cent of the planet's surface area and over two-thirds of the ocean.

And at a domestic level, The Wildlife Trusts (a charity for which I am an ambassador), launched in September 2020 a £30 million appeal to kickstart nature's recovery across 30 per cent of the UK land and sea, also by 2030: known as 30 by 30. Currently, only 10 per cent of the UK is actually protected and much of that is in poor condition ... the need to protect, restore and join up more land for nature is vital.

As described in Chapter 2, we must set about working on systemic change to our food system to embrace more regenerative approaches to agriculture with less use of pesticides and fertilisers. From a city planning perspective, we should embrace 'urban greening' – the process of making more space for nature in the towns and cities where almost three-quarters of humanity lives. One of the most innovative trends I have seen recently are 'tiny forests': a concept from Japan which focuses on the dense planting of local, fast-growing saplings on plots as small as a tennis court. The benefits to both biodiversity and local communities is almost immediate.

Nature protection and restoration aren't just intrinsically important. Through methods such as natural capital accounting, there is now serious work underway in both the private and public sectors to value the 'ecosystem services' that nature provides to humanity. From carbon capture and sequestration, air purification, weather stability, storm and flood protection, nutrient recycling, crop pollination, pest control, water filtration, food sources and outdoor resources – nature provides us with a multitude of critical and complex services.

The management consultancy McKinsey have quantified that doubling nature conservation on land and water by 2030 could reduce atmospheric carbon by 2.6 gigatons annually, support around 30 million jobs and provide $500 billion of GDP in ecotourism and sustainable fishing ... not to mention reducing the risk of future zoonotic diseases such as Covid-19.[10] The World Economic Forum has guesstimated that over half of the global economy – some $44 trillion – is dependent on natural capital.[11] Another consultancy, BCG, estimate the total value of the world's forests to be as much as $150 trillion (nearly double the value of global stock markets), mainly thanks to carbon storage.[12]

And, above all, we also need a paradigm shift in our thinking towards what is known as a One Health approach. Rather than the belief that the needs and welfare of humanity are somehow superior to all else, we need to reconnect with our rightful place as only part of a much wider planetary ecosystem. I do not think this is a radical idea – take one look at the famous Earthrise photograph taken during the Apollo 8 mission in 1968, and it becomes entirely obvious.

In their 2020 report, the Intergovernmental Science-Policy Platform on Biodiversity and Ecosystem Services (IPBES) biodiversity experts concluded by saying: 'We can emerge from the current crisis stronger and more resilient than ever, [by] choosing actions that protect nature, so that nature can help protect us.'[13]

. . . .

As we all now know, the UK government planned for a public health disaster, but not the sort that actually turned up: a conventional flu epidemic rather than a coronavirus. It is easy to be critical of officialdom always planning for the last war or crisis, rather than the one that is waiting around the corner, but other western governments were similarly wrong-footed. Those in Asia, with experience of the more analogous SARS pandemic and perhaps with populations more used to taking official advice, fared better in controlling transmission and reducing death rates.

At Iceland we began discussing what we would need to do as soon as the bad news started to emerge from China in early 2020. At that early stage, though, it seemed like a sci-fi fantasy when our HR Director started presenting contingency plans for closing our head office and running the whole business remotely. Little did we know.

Panic buying

The first time I really appreciated the severity of the impact was in mid-March 2020. I dropped in to a few of our London stores to see for myself what I'd been hearing. These stores are well-run by some of our most experienced teams and managers. But when I walked in, I couldn't believe my eyes. In anticipation of the expected lockdown announcement, the British public were going on an unprecedented panic-buying spree. Most shelves were stripped bare as soon as our colleagues filled them. The deputy manager of one store was close to tears as she described to me the pressures of frenzied customers, colleagues starting to go off sick and nowhere near enough stock.

Over the coming week, one by one, different high street shops were shuttered until the food retailers were the only businesses left trading. The world was going into hibernation. It felt like the end of days.

Toilet rolls inexplicably became symbolic of the national urge to stockpile. No one could really understand or explain this. Covid-19 is a respiratory disease, of course, unlikely to increase anyone's need to visit the lavatory. Toilet roll manufacturers were at pains to point out that they made the things in the UK, and that there really was no threat to supply. Nevertheless, shoppers continued to pile them into their trolleys along with rice, pasta, and canned and frozen food, prepping for a prolonged siege. I think it was a way of trying to gain control over a situation of which they had none.

We were experiencing a level of demand that we would normally only expect to see at Christmas – with the critical difference that we spend months preparing for that expected surge by building stocks. As I pointed out at the time, this stockpiling was inherently socially divisive: it was only an option for those who could afford it and clearing the supermarket shelves denied poorer and more vulnerable people the chance to buy the things they needed. Many of our customers, waiting desperately for a pension or Universal Credit payment, walked into store a week later to find empty shelves.

Normally we spend every waking hour trying to persuade more people to come into our shops; now I was doing the opposite. We reduced our store opening hours in order to give both our stock and our colleagues a chance to catch up. I publicly urged people to calm down and shop responsibly, revert to their normal buying habits and allow the supply chains chance to fill up again.

Our store colleagues did their utmost to help those people who were being disadvantaged by the shopping madness, sometimes being literally elbowed aside in the stockpiling rush.

As always, the best ideas come from people on the front line. In our store within the Belfast Kennedy Shopping Centre, senior supervisor Paul McTasney came up with the idea of a 'silver hour' – reserving the first hour of trading in his store for elderly and vulnerable customers. Paul's suggestion was championed by the store manager Daniel Burke and swiftly taken up across our business, and by virtually all the other UK food retailers. Similar priority hours for NHS staff and care workers followed. We were pleased to donate £150,000 to Age UK to aid their efforts in supporting the elderly through the crisis, and when customers asked how to help, we partnered with the National Emergencies Trust to raise money to be used in the hardest hit communities.

We also saw numerous acts of kindness by our colleagues and customers. In Letchworth, our team actually went around other outlets buying toilet rolls so that they could give one to each elderly customer with their shopping. Individual colleagues used their own initiative, cars and money to help customers unable to secure home deliveries. A fifth of our colleagues are under 21, and they also did us proud. There were countless examples of our young people making an extraordinary difference in their communities. In fact, stories of individual acts of kindness were so numerous that we set up a #NewsWeNeed feed to share them across the business and raise everyone's spirits.

This was much needed, because while the onset of the pandemic brought out the best in many people, it also revealed the worst side in others. We sadly recorded hundreds of instances of our store colleagues being abused and even physically assaulted by angry customers: usually enraged about stock shortages, or resentful of efforts to impose limits on their purchases to ensure that lines in high demand were available to as many people as possible. At a time when online deliveries were in unprecedented demand, we also witnessed the sickening destruction of two of our delivery vans, torched in a night of disturbances in Southmead, Bristol.

At our head office in North Wales, our customer care team worked round the clock to deal with thousands of calls, emails and social media messages from customers. Due to the volume of calls, scores of colleagues from teams across the business rallied to help answer them, into the night and over weekends. Many were simply calls for help. Just down the corridor from my office a colleague comforted a woman who said she had no support and was going to take her own life; another called a friend in Kent to get help to an elderly man, unable to walk, with no food in his flat.

We have always called our store teams 'front-line colleagues', but in those mad weeks throughout March and April it really felt like that they were on the front line in a war. Yet adversity can be galvanising. A firm sense of purpose developed throughout the business, as we worked tirelessly to help feed the nation. Our colleagues were nothing short of heroic.

Once people realised that they only needed so much toilet roll in their lives, slowly but surely the panic buying subsided. As the new social distancing rules were introduced throughout April, our next challenge was to adjust to the strange 'new normal'. On many high streets we were the only shop open for business. We did our very best to protect everyone by enforcing the new social distancing rules: limiting the number of customers allowed in each store, putting down tape to enforce the recommended 2-m separation, and installing protective screens for every till in every store.

Along with the rest of the world, we also ordered vast quantities of hand sanitisers, face masks and gloves, which took far too long to materialise. We were forced to think laterally and seek help from unusual places – I even asked the boss of McDonald's if they could let us have the disposable gloves normally worn by staff in their shuttered restaurants.

In fact, the willingness to help other businesses was one of the most heartening features of this time, as retailers who are normally the deadliest of competitors united – talking freely to each other, sharing information and ideas, standing shoulder to shoulder in a combined effort. I began regular communication with CEOs of competitors with whom I would normally be tight-lipped. In an unprecedented move, the government helped to achieve such collaboration by temporarily relaxing some of the normal industry competition rules, allowing retailers to share data with each other on stock levels and share distribution resource.[14] DEFRA and the British Retail Consortium (BRC) promoted industry co-ordination and co-operation on a scale never seen before.

While panic buying was leaving retailers short of stock, the sudden shutdown of the hospitality sector meant that many farmers, producers and wholesalers had no outlet for their goods and services. We were relieved to bump up our stock levels by offering our customers some stock from foodservice companies like Brakes and 3663.

With more than 2.2 million people across the UK advised by the governments that they should 'shield' in their homes for 12 weeks, and the Prime Minister in his lockdown announcement urging everyone to use home delivery services whenever possible, demand for grocery deliveries sky-rocketed and online slots became almost unobtainable. We faced our next challenge of quickly having to ramp up online capacity in order to meet this unprecedented demand.

Initially, we used the sticking plaster of appealing to people's better nature and placed a banner on our website asking only those who were elderly and vulnerable to place online orders. I also went public in urging those who were fit and well to ignore the Prime Minister's advice and go out to shop in store, thereby leaving delivery slots for those who needed them most.[15] With just 7 per cent of UK groceries bought online pre-Covid, it was never going to be feasible to increase delivery capacity on the scale that his speech seemed to envisage.

The government's move to share details of people needing support with us and other supermarkets meant we were able to cross-reference the list against our existing online customers and offer priority delivery slots to them. This also highlighted Iceland's unique place in the community, as a far greater proportion were already our customers than those registered with our competitors.

Behind the scenes we moved swiftly. We quickly grew our online delivery capacity fourfold from the 100,000 deliveries a week we had been making pre-Covid. We greatly expanded our delivery fleet, mobilising some additional vehicles from shuttered businesses to help prop up our own distribution operations. We also needed to recruit a lot more staff, and quickly – not only thousands more pickers and drivers, but also to temporarily back-fill in order to cover for those on our own team who were self-isolating.

We placed a simple ad online appealing for new recruits to help feed the nation. In just three days, we received more than 50,000 applications. While having such a deep pool of labour to choose from was helpful, it also made me feel a little queasy: swathes of the workforce had been sent home or simply lost their jobs.

We already have a brilliant and eclectic group of people working alongside us, especially our delivery drivers. I have met people who are semi-retired, ex-forces and who are community activists – men and women sharing a passion for helping customers. The latest recruits were no different. I spoke to one new colleague who described a common feeling: being without a purpose had affected his mental health. He merely wanted to help out and to play his part, despite already being paid on furlough. In June, customers around Manchester were amazed to find their groceries being delivered by comedian Jason Manford, who wanted to support the community and was offered a job by Iceland after his application was turned down by Tesco.

While I and the great bulk of my head office colleagues were working remotely from home, our front-line colleagues were dealing face to face with worried and often difficult customers every day. We paid them a bonus – which some refused to take because they stood to lose more in benefits than they gained in pay. A reminder that many of our colleagues and customers alike come from communities where every penny counts, and where the sometimes illogical Universal Credit system adds to their challenges.

Natural inequality

For my family and me, lockdown was an opportunity to reflect on our privilege in living in a house with a garden, surrounded by beautiful countryside. I remember watching a tree bumblebee, busily feeding on the stunning early spring blossoms. It struck me that she was getting on regardless; and that nature was getting on regardless. The world had stopped spinning for humanity, not for nature: underlining both our interconnectedness with nature and our detachment from it.

It seemed of note that the British weather was stunning during the first weeks of lockdown – with bright blue skies and warm days. It felt like a message from Mother Nature that she was healing. The skies were clear of airplanes and jet trails. News reports from Venice showed the water clear again and the fish returning.[16] The smog lifted over northern Italy[17] and satellite imagery showed a dramatic fall in emissions over China (which unfortunately came straight back as soon as their lockdown was lifted).[18] My favourite was a video of wild goats from the Great Orme marauding around the deserted centre of Llandudno, like some apocalyptic movie where the animals reclaim the streets.[19]

Of course, for many, lockdown was far from idyllic. Millions of people on furlough knew that they faced unemployment when the scheme ended. Some had built careers in sectors like tourism or the creative industries, which were seemingly obsolete overnight. Yet for months on end, with strict rules in place around how far you could venture from your home, the tonic of accessing nature was denied to many.

This inaccessibility of nature really brings into focus the problem that our eco-alienated society faces – 2.7 million people in the UK do not live within easy walking distance of a green space, according to the charity Fields in Trust.[20] This is particularly the case among the poorest in society. With underfunded rural transport links, there simply aren't the options for the urban poor to get out of the cities and into the countryside – let alone pay the steep entry and parking fees often involved. Others, particularly from minority backgrounds, simply feel unwelcome in natural environments according to Beth Collier, Director of Wild in the City.[21]

Such disconnect causes us problems. As the author Lucy Jones said when reflecting on lockdown life for the BBC's *Rethink* podcast, connection to nature is essential to our mental health. Yet sadly for many – during and even out of lockdown – the ability to do this just simply isn't an option. She went on to say that 'Inequality of access to nature must be a political priority.'[22]

According to WWF, the UK is one of the most nature-depleted countries on the planet. And so, simultaneously, our affinity to the natural world (known as biophilia) is on the wane.

This is especially the case among the young. Four out of five British kids now can't recognise a bumblebee and less than half know what a stinging nettle is.[23] Indeed, nature in our language is rapidly facing endangered status; an increasing number of nature-based words are being removed year-on-year from our dictionaries as they become less commonly used. As nature is removed from children's language it disappears from their imagination.[24]

According to government-funded research published in 2016, more than one in nine British children had literally no exposure to the natural world over the previous year. They had never even been to a local park, let alone a farm, a forest or a beach. As might be expected, children from low-income families, and from black, Asian and minority ethnic households, were the least likely to visit wild places.[25]

This alarming trend of nature disconnection among the young is little mentioned but needs to be urgently addressed. As the environmentalist and writer George Monbiot has observed: 'Most of those I know who fight for nature are people who spent their childhoods immersed in it. Without a feel for the texture and function of the natural world, without an intensity of engagement almost impossible in the absence of early experience, people will not devote their lives to its protection'.[26] Against this backdrop where will our future nature guardians come from?

Backyard nature

Discussing the issue with our Iceland store colleagues, and hearing first-hand stories of this nature disconnect among the kids from the very communities we serve, it became clear to me that as a business we must try to do something constructive to help.

The key is to inspire kids from *any* background – as with all forms of environmentalism, this cannot just be about middle-class families. For solutions to be scalable, we must inspire *all* children regardless of where and how they have grown up.

And given the enormity of the environmental challenges that the next generation will face, I sincerely hope that there will be a strong proportion of future activists who come from challenging backgrounds.

We need those with the tenacity and will to win that can often come from those who have had to fight their way out: kids from the real world, outside the establishment, with solutions that are rooted in pragmatism. I became very keen to launch a nature engagement campaign for kids whose families are our customers.

As usual, our wonderful Iceland Talking Shop representatives provided the impetus I needed to inspire some action. At our Talking Shop conference in 2018, Sally-Ann Morgan from our Newport store stood up and respectfully said: 'We care about the rainforest and we care about plastic – and we're proud of what we're doing. But the thing we care most about are the kids who are struggling in our neighbourhoods because we see them every week. We all want Richard to help us do something for them.'

My other great motivator was a wonderful group of kids from All Saints Catholic Primary School in Anfield – one of the most deprived wards in Liverpool. Calling themselves the Eco Emeralds, they bowled me over when they got in touch with their ideas for reconnecting children with nature and directly inspired the Backyard Nature campaign that was launched with the support of our Charitable Foundation in 2019.

The children came to our head office and gave us a lively presentation on how we should be 'seedbombing Britain' by giving away seed balls through our stores to improve habitats for bees, and turn our delivery vans into giant bees to help get the message across. So – we did exactly as the Eco Emeralds advised.

In July 2019 we took the Eco Emeralds to London to meet some of the UK's most senior environmentalists and to launch the campaign. Amazingly, they gained the support not just of 25 household-name charities, but from HRH the Duchess of Cambridge. At the event, there was huge applause when tiny nine-year-old Nell walked to the front of the stage and simply said: 'If you adults don't stop sitting around like lemons we will never solve climate change!'

In September, we launched a Save The Bees initiative that gave away 330,000 seed balls, containing over 15 million wildflower seeds. While we couldn't afford to turn all our vans into giant bees, we did livery two of them. We filled one with ice cream and strawberries and drove it up to Anfield to surprise the delighted kids.

Since our first campaign, Backyard Nature has run other activations, such as giving away kits for bug hotels, feeding birds, connecting kids with local activities in their neighbourhoods and suggesting ideas of how to protect their patch in lockdown. HRH the Duke of Cambridge even paid a surprise private visit to All Saints School to meet the Eco Emeralds and find out how they had inspired the campaign, later appearing with them in a television documentary shown as far afield as Australia and the US. The ultimate goal of Backyard Nature is to inspire 1 million hours of nature engagement from kids across the UK – and in early 2021 we are well on track.

School children should not just be encouraged to spend time outdoors, but direct experience of wildlife and wild places should be a compulsory part of a child's education, to enable them to understand concepts such as rewilding and natural climate solutions. Of course, such trips are possible for children from any background; but many would need to be subsidised. And while the government's budget may well be tight, I would consider it a significantly better investment in our future than the current level of state aid the oil and gas industry enjoys.

The government urgently needs to reverse the removal of climate change from the national curriculum that was one of the biggest mistakes committed by Michael Gove in his stint as Secretary of State for Education.[27] Recent calls for a new GCSE in Natural History are a welcome step back in the right direction.[28]

In order to create a more biophilic society, we must surely start by ensuring that kids understand the facts about what is happening to our planet and appreciate why it matters.

The Covid-19 pandemic has demonstrated beyond question the threats that arise from our complete domination over nature. As the natural world declines, so does our relationship to it. Yet nature is not some external construct 'out there' ... we are very much part of it. We ignore this interconnectedness at our peril.

Perhaps the last word on this should go to Richard Louv, author of the seminal book *Last Child in the Woods*: 'Passion is lifted from the earth itself by the muddy hands of the young; it travels along grass-stained sleeves to the heart. If we are going to save environmentalism and the environment, we must also save an endangered indicator species: the child in nature.'[29]

A great leveller?

Many people are predicting that the Covid-19 pandemic is destined to change the way we work forever, yet I think it is still too early to call. For those of us with experience, desks and gardens at home, being away from the office during lockdown imposed no hardship; many of my colleagues appreciated the saving of time and money on commuting and enjoyed their improved work-life balance. For others, confined to a small flat and trying to work with a laptop balanced on an ironing board while young children screamed for their attention, it was little short of a nightmare.

One thing that is clear, however, is that for the young Covid-19 has brought nothing but bad news. Not only have they lost an irreplaceable part of their education and endured the chaos of cancelled exams and estimated grades, they have also sacrificed formative moments in their careers and face limited job prospects going forwards. The Chancellor Rishi Sunak's Kickstart job placement scheme is a useful attempt to repair the damage, but all businesses should now focus on bringing young people into the workforce.

Mentoring and training the young is the best argument I know for getting back to conventional working patterns. There is no doubt that new starters learn more readily through direct interaction in an office than they ever will through Microsoft Teams or Zoom meetings, and I suspect that ideas are also more likely to be generated by everyone through face-to-face engagement.

We must also face the fact that the whole economy as we know it will suffer grievously if city centre offices remain permanently empty. But perhaps a balance is achievable: a more flexible approach that combines home and office working, encourages the regeneration of affordable housing in city centres to cut travelling time, lowers air pollution and perhaps even helps to address the UK's long-standing productivity issues by cutting the huge amount of time British workers waste commuting.

Whatever else it may have been, coronavirus was certainly no leveller. Public Health England statistics showed that the poorest were twice as likely to die of Covid-19, with black people and ethnic minorities disproportionately affected.[30] While research by the Resolution Foundation think tank found that lower-income households were twice as likely as richer ones to have increased their debts during the crisis.[31]

This has gravely exacerbated a problem that was already commanding my attention before the crisis struck. Although Britain is a rich country with an expanding economy, child poverty has increased relentlessly over the decade since the financial crisis of 2008, with 4.2 million children classified as living in poverty in 2019.[32] (A statistic already mentioned in the Introduction, but one that is so important I wanted to repeat it again.) That is a quarter of all the kids in the UK – families that Iceland reaches through its customer base every week. And yet, nearly 3 million of these kids have working parents – often juggling more than one job. The rise of the gig economy of zero hours contracts means that many of these parents are not only cash poor, but phenomenally time poor as well.

Pre-Covid-19, we could clearly see these problems around the country. By the end of 2019, Shelter estimated that 135,000 children were homeless on Christmas Day.[33] Over 7 million people have gone hungry during Covid-19, and the NHS now sees over 100 people admitted to hospital with malnutrition every week.[34]

But we could also see these socio-economic problems reflected directly in our own sales performance. Throughout 2018 and 2019, our transaction frequency and basket spend were less buoyant in the more deprived northern regions of the UK than in the south, and we could see just how the rollout of Universal Credit was impacting our customers' spending power. And in some instances, we realised that we were starting to lose customers altogether to poverty – not just to food banks, but in too many instances simply to starvation.

The rise of child poverty had been driven by a range of factors including the shortage of affordable social housing, and the failure to increase child benefit in line with inflation, so that its value has fallen by almost a quarter in real terms since 2010.[35] Then there was the 'two child rule' limiting benefits for larger families, that took effect in 2017, and the disastrously botched introduction of Universal Credit.[36]

However well-intentioned this project might have been, it surely did not take a genius to answer the question 'What could possibly go wrong?' if we suddenly expected people who had been used to receiving their income every week to switch to monthly budgeting, and we stopped paying their rent direct to landlords at the same time. The vast majority of our colleagues are paid weekly. I know that they are sensible and responsible individuals; I also know that many of them would struggle to budget if we suddenly switched to paying their salaries gross of rent, once a month.

Add to that the long delay in receiving an initial payment when a claimant is moved onto Universal Credit, and you have a potent recipe for human misery. I visited a food bank in Ellesmere Port and listened to a newly unemployed father in tears as he explained how he has worked hard all his life, but had been left with no state support for over a month.

It is undeniable that Covid-19 has made life harder for the most vulnerable groups. The Institute for Fiscal Studies have said that the pandemic risks entrenching deep class, ethnic, gender, educational, generational and geographic divides unless inequality is systemically tackled.[37]

Disturbingly, in August 2020, the ONS reported that since March 730,000 people had lost their jobs; the worst drop in over a decade.[38] This figure didn't even include self-employed workers and will only worsen as government job retention schemes end. Indeed, the

Office for Budget Responsibility forecasted in November 2020 that 2.6 million people, or 7.5 per cent of the UK workforce, could be out of work by the second quarter of 2021.[39] One in seven businesses polled at the time said that they fear they won't survive 2021.[40]

The collateral damage of the Covid-19 pandemic and the resultant lockdowns will be wide-ranging and long-lasting. From a health perspective, for every Covid-19 death another life was being lost to cancer, the ex-health secretary Jeremy Hunt said in October 2020.[41] Add to that the backlog of heart disease appointments, or even dentistry visits, and the physical health impacts are serious.

Psychologically, by late 2020, the UK was a nation riddled with fear and anxiety about a virus that, while highly contagious, had sharply falling estimations as to its lethality that was highly concentrated on the eldest age groups.[42] Yet, according to the Police Federation, associated mental health impacts such as depression and even suicide were rising across all ages.[43] Then consider the job losses, indebtedness, bankruptcies and evictions – not to mention the missed schooling – and for once I agreed with President Trump when he tweeted that the cure might be worse than the disease.[44] Time will tell.

There are, however, some people who instinctively understand just how acute the problems of inequality, poverty – and in particular child poverty – are. Throughout 2020 the Manchester United and England footballer Marcus Rashford led a series of campaigns to help raise money for hungry kids and called upon the government to provide them with more support. He managed to secure extensions of free school meals for children through the holidays and pushed for an increase in the value of Healthy Start Vouchers (a food voucher scheme for families with young children or for women who are pregnant and receiving benefits).

In our stores up and down Britain we see clearly the issues that Marcus is campaigning on. Towns like Wythenshawe, where the footballer benefited from free school meals himself while growing up. Iceland has the highest participation of any food retailer for Healthy Start Vouchers, because our store locations are the most correlated with areas of high deprivation. We were delighted to support Marcus's campaigns, urged the government to do the same and became the first retailer to provide financial backing by giving free frozen vegetables to any customer with Healthy Start Vouchers.[45]

The issue of family poverty is a complex one. The vagaries of Universal Credit mean it is hard for many hard-working families to budget effectively, so they have sudden, unplanned drops in income. Even before the pandemic, the 14 million people living in poverty[46] within our communities struggled to access mainstream credit to smooth their finances and were forced to rely on friends and family, high interest 'rent to own' or doorstep lenders, payday loans or, even worse, loan sharks.

It seems to me that some of the solutions lie in innovation and collaboration. Throughout the pandemic, Iceland has been quietly working with the not-for-profit ethical lender, Fair for You, to trial a new FinTech product, in the form of a food club. Our mission is to understand how to help families keep their independence, buy healthy food and use good credit without getting trapped in a spiral of debt they cannot escape from. The technology was developed thanks to funding provided by the innovation foundation Nesta and the Treasury, and the club allows customers to take out affordable micro-loans, on flexible terms – supported by the lender rather than put under pressure.

The initial results show that while most food club members previously struggled to buy essential items and half used a food bank, more than 80 per cent no longer visit a food bank or have to rely on family and friends, are able to buy healthy food and have enough to eat. Seventy-three per cent expect an improvement in their children's diet and 80 per cent expect to be less anxious or depressed as a result.

Iceland's grocery market share increased to a record level during the Covid-19 crisis, when analysts reported that we were often the fastest growing food retailer.[47] I am particularly pleased that this growth allowed us to offer continuing employment to more than 3,500 of the extra colleagues we had taken on to help us trade through lockdown.

The pandemic showed that those businesses who had focused on a broader stakeholder approach, gave priority to protecting their employees and the communities that they serve, were more resilient through the crisis. Those that stuck with the old concept of shareholder primacy – pursuing excessive bonuses or special dividends above sound financial prudence – were found wanting.

. . . .

By late 2020, any lesser person would be fully justified in using the phrase, 'I told you so!' But rather than gloating, as ever Bill Gates was simply seeking to improve things. Locked down in his $100 million Seattle mansion, he was busy connecting the dots between health, nature and climate. In a livestreamed TED conversation in March he said 'As we get past this ... that idea of innovation and science and the world working together ... is totally common between these two problems [climate change and Covid-19] ... I don't think this has to be a huge setback for climate.'[48]

Let's make sure that this time, we listen to Bill. Covid-19 has given us a wake-up call and an opportunity, to rethink and act differently. To harness the power of innovation and society by building future resilience for our health, our economy and our planet.

Nature-based solutions

One idea to come out of the pandemic that I really like the sound of is the establishment of a National Nature Service (NNS)[49] – emulating America's Civilian Conservation Corps of the 1930s, which found work for 3 million people following the Great Depression, by installing nationwide flood defences, planting billions of trees and establishing 700 new national parks.

As the UK looks to rebuild its economy post-Covid, mass re-employment could come from a series of large-scale initiatives – such as restoring natural habitats like peatlands and grasslands, creating urban parks, sustainable building projects and refocusing on renewable energy infrastructure. A NNS should prioritise disadvantaged communities and upskill workers in new, greener industries. Putting people back to work, improving wellbeing and expanding access to nature – while also building our defences for a changing climate – sounds like exactly the sort of ambitious project the government should get behind. As the financier and environmentalist Ben Goldsmith writes, 'Such a plan would leave a legacy of a healthier, more employable workforce, an infrastructure for ongoing community and volunteer work in nature, and ecosystems across our country restored to health and abundance.'[50]

And the concept of 'rewilding' – of taking a step back and letting nature follow its course – has gone from the niche passion of a few environmentalists to becoming mainstream thinking. The theory of traditional conservation, which can often be very time-consuming and expensive, has been turned on its head by pioneering rewilding projects at farms such as Knepp, in West Sussex, which has witnessed an unparalleled restoration of nature by using free-roaming grazing animals to create new habitats for wildlife.[51]

As over-intensified farmland across the world becomes redundant, the case for landscape-scale rewilding is compelling. Not only does nature bounce back dramatically, but the restoring of degraded lands and seas is a highly effective (and cheap) way to store carbon. According to research published in the journal *Nature*, by restoring only a third of the planet's most degraded areas, and if environments still in good condition were robustly protected, enough carbon would be stored to balance half of all greenhouse gases caused by humans since the Industrial Revolution.'[52]

It seems that political momentum is gathering behind these ideas, too. Just before the October 2020 virtual UN biodiversity summit, more than 60 countries pledged to put wildlife and climate at the heart of their post-Covid recovery plans.[53] In his keynote speech at the conference, President Xi Jinping of China told his fellow leaders that 'We need to respect nature, follow its laws and protect it.'[54] Having seen the consequences of what happens when we do not protect nature, suddenly leaders the world over are calling for nature-based solutions with growing urgency.

Never waste a good crisis

Milton Friedman once observed that 'Only a crisis – actual or perceived – produces real change', and we can see many examples in history of pandemics leading to tectonic shifts in human society. The Black Death in the 14th century ended the Hundred Years' War between England and France, and ultimately brought about the downfall of the feudal system. The flu pandemic of 1918–19, far more deadly in its impact than the World War I, contributed to a process of radical societal change that culminated in the establishment of the NHS and the foundation of the modern welfare state – though it took the further pressure of World War II to reach that destination.

Wars have a proven track record of acccelerating technological change, for good or ill (the tank, the jet engine, rocketry, the atom bomb, the wristwatch) and also of promoting national solidarity. We saw something of the Blitz spirit during lockdown in the UK – a shared feeling that 'we can only get through this together' – and I hope this will lead to a continuing sense of collective responsibility: valuing the smaller things in life and making sure that we take care of each other.

I think that most people's priorities were well captured in an Instagram meme I was sent during the depths of lockdown: 'Have we realised it yet? That nobody is missing the material things. We all miss the company of others, great conversations, a hug ... That's what life is all about.'

I would like to think that this moment of darkness will also prove to have been a moment of truth, when we reached our limit as peak consumer and began to think about acting more like citizens first. We have the opportunity to redefine history as 'BC' and 'AC' – Before and After Covid-19. I feel sure that future generations will look back and say that this was – or could have been – the key turning point. We certainly want to avoid returning exactly to our old ways in the inevitable post-Covid-19 boom.

It's all very well having the power and influence to affect change which comes with running a big business, but the question that I am most often asked is 'What can we do as *individuals* to help?' My standard response is simple: 'Shop at Iceland!'

Joking aside, this question is one that has been asked with increasing frequency since March 2020, as people are becoming more concerned about our impact on the planet, and perhaps valuing our relationship to it with greater importance.

This book is not an attempt to focus on what individuals should be doing in order to play their part. There are many good books on the subject, such as Mike Berners-Lee's *There Is No Planet B*.

However, while holed up in our house night after night, one thing we did debate and create as a family during lockdown was our own Family Sustainability Plan – a set of principles we want to try to live by in an attempt to have a greener lifestyle. I thought it would be worth sharing with you. I am acutely aware that my personal circumstances are more comfortable than most, and so my list will not be applicable to everyone. But hopefully it will prompt your own thoughts as to what actions you can take to make a difference ...

THE WALKER FAMILY SUSTAINABILITY PLAN

TAKE UK HOLIDAYS
Britain is full of beauty and adventure. When you do fly, offset your emissions – it's low cost and better than nothing.

DON'T THROW FOOD IN THE BIN
Wrong on many levels, not least because if food waste was a country, it'd be the #3 global greenhouse gas emitter.

EAT BEEF NO MORE THAN ONCE A WEEK
It takes vast amounts of land, water and greenhouse gases to produce beef. For the sake of the environment, as well as our health, moderating consumption is key.

DE-PLASTIC OUR LIVES
Go wooden!

ONLY BUY A PIECE OF CLOTHING IF WE'LL COMMIT TO MORE THAN 30 WEARS
Fashion is a dirty business – as consumers we have the power to make it more sustainable.

SWITCH TO A 100 PER CENT RENEWABLE ENERGY SUPPLIER
The energy we consume in our homes is, on average, 26 per cent of our individual carbon footprint. Bulb is one such company, run by my friend Hayden Wood ... it takes two minutes to switch, saves you money and makes you feel great.

IF YOU HAVE THE CHOICE, DRIVE AN ELECTRIC VEHICLE (EV)
I had a hybrid car for a few years ... but they're more about saving tax than petrol. The technology has improved, and the price has dropped to the extent that full EVs are now the smarter choice.

RE-WILD THE GARDEN (OR A SPACE IN YOUR COMMUNITY)
We don't have a big garden, yet it's amazing what insects you can attract simply by not cutting a patch of grass.

DIVEST OUR PENSIONS FROM ALL FOSSIL FUEL COMPANIES
Read about the Make My Money Matter campaign in Chapter 2.

NEVER PREACH
I am certainly not perfect and full of contradictions.

Throughout history, collective individual actions can amount to a tidal wave of change. As citizens and consumers, we have the power to change what sometimes can seem like an environmental apocalypse. But as he summarised in Sir David Attenborough's closing remark for the BBC One documentary *Extinction: The Facts*, the broadcaster said, 'What happens next is up to every one of us.'

Of course, such demand-side emission reductions can't just be left to the lifestyle decisions of earnest eco-warriors like you and me. We need to make low carbon and nature positive choices easy and convenient for everyone – and they need to be fair, so the poor aren't subsidising the high energy lifestyles of the rich, and developing countries aren't paying the price on behalf of the developed world.

Through a series of sticks and carrots, the government must set about restructuring the business landscape to ensure that the private sector starts making the right choices and avoids the wrong ones.

Over the next chapter, I look at both how we can put our economy back together in a greener and more resilient way, and beyond the immediate concern of a post-Covid-19 recovery to what actions the UK government can take in order to create a more socially equitable society.

CHAPTER 6
SPEAKING OUT

What the government
needs to do

'WE CANNOT BE RADICAL ENOUGH.'
SIR DAVID ATTENBOROUGH[1]

There is a great line at the start of Isabel Hardman's book *Why We Get the Wrong Politicians*. A newly elected politician, when met by her best friend, is asked a very blunt question: 'Oh my God – what the fuck have you done?!' It neatly summarises the exceptionally low esteem in which government ministers, politicians and our whole political system are held.

An Ipsos MORI poll conducted just before the December 2019 election showed that politicians were trusted the least out of every professional class – less than bankers, estate agents or advertising executives, with only 14 per cent of respondents believing they tell the truth.[2] The 'Westminster bubble' is broadly judged to contain a mistrusted class of egomaniacs and liars, who are in it for themselves and out of touch with the real lives of normal people.

In an age of increasing polarisation and division, many of us point simplistic fingers at politicians as the bad guys and blame them for society's problems. Yet as Hardman explains, most politicians are good people who go into politics to try and make the world a better place. In the UK, it is the political system itself that is broken, forcing MPs to be both part-time frustrated Westminster legislator and part-time glorified constituency social worker. At the same time, the public are now expecting instant accessibility via social media platforms such as Twitter.

In fact, politicians in any democratic nation are merely a reflection of ourselves. As the adage goes: we get the politicians we deserve. The problem we really need to solve is that of how we *relate* to each other. We are now more judgemental and binary in our views than ever before – particularly on social media. We need to take more time to listen, create more space for challenging discourse and be accepting of ambiguity.

My approach to politicians is to try and be more empathetic and less subjective. The partisan animosity that defines the American political system has led to an ugly impasse, where critical issues such as climate change are viewed exclusively through the prism of Republican or Democrat. If we are to make genuine progress on the key issues of our time, we have to become more respectful of politicians and open-minded to alternative ideas, escaping our own echo chambers.

Given the fact that I run a business, it should come as no surprise that my personal economic philosophy is that of a free marketeer. The best way for the private sector to operate is within a market system that is largely self-regulated, unencumbered by onerous regulations, tariffs or trade restrictions. The laws of supply and demand inevitably lead to the highest levels of competition, the strongest amount of innovation and therefore the best deal for consumers.

People often forget the immutable economic law that it is free enterprise which generates the money from which all our public institutions are funded. When politicians talk about 'investing', they are in fact talking about spending public income that is raised through taxation – which in itself comes exclusively from business activity. Taxing public sector workers and institutions, who are funded from the nation's purse, is merely a recirculation of cash.

The private sector is therefore vital as the engine from which central government, local governments and public corporations are run. Moreover, by providing employment and opportunity, capitalism really is the only system we have of ensuring provision and progression. An open market system that rewards ambition and hard work, which provides the fuel for government to look after its citizens and run its national institutions, is therefore the best way of ensuring that societal issues such as inequality are improved.

At least that is what's supposed to happen. As I'll discuss later in this chapter, recently capitalism seems to be heading in the wrong direction.

Yet when it comes to the existential environmental issues that we face today we simply cannot rely on market forces alone to reach the right solutions — at least not quickly enough. As someone operating within the business sector and being around the business community, it has become clear to me that a more interventionist approach from government on issues such as climate change and biodiversity loss is the only way to go.[3] A bit like politicians, the vast majority of business people are not inherently bad. But we operate within a system which frankly takes too long for the most sustainable businesses to rise to the top, and for the bad ones to be extinguished.

Over the course of this chapter, I will attempt to unpack these issues by looking at how we can attune the power of business to help push a more radical government agenda that I believe we now so desperately need. In order to do this, we will first have to find more compassion and objectivity – and be open to shedding our old ways of thinking and seeking out new ideas.

Politics needs business

It should be the purpose of any government to develop and enact laws, taxes and spending which facilitate the running of the country – in other words, to get stuff done. Without support from the private sector, this becomes very difficult. It's a smart move for any administration to be business friendly, and make allies in the corporate world, because ultimately it will help to push through their own agenda.

The same goes for business – they need to be proactive too. Gone are the days where business leaders can hide behind being 'apolitical'. Business needs more of a public face. My Dad often gives me a hard time about appearing on *Question Time*, saying that he can't see the benefit to the business (only to my ego!). Fair enough. But I can't just sit there every week shouting at my TV from behind four walls – I want to make a stand and do what is right for my family, the world we live in, the business and our customers. I want to talk about things like climate change, poverty, inequality, diversity, jobs, Brexit or the Chancellor's latest budget. Iceland provides the perfect barometer for what is really happening in communities up and down the UK.

Look at what happens when a young, brave footballer speaks out about what is important to him: the poorest kids in the UK don't go hungry during the school holidays any more. We need more leadership from outside the political sphere to guide and lead to real change.

I strongly believe that our society *needs* business to engage more with the public sector – otherwise government, politicians and politics will never change. And the role of business in politics need not be corrosive to society – so long as the money is kept out of it. Fortunately, in the UK, our highly regulated and transparent donation system provides an essential check to excessive corporate lobbying.

When businesses are siloed from the public sector, and communication channels dry up, a lack of collaboration leads to a lack of progress in solving big issues.

Good and bad policies

A particular area of concern is the alarming rise in food banks. The government seems to be outsourcing a societal problem to businesses and charities, who are being encouraged to supply food banks with food – and in effect propping up failed policy. Yet far from being a successful collaboration as many would portray it, I believe that it is a modern-day tragedy.

I said as much to prime minister Boris Johnson during a supermarket CEO virtual roundtable meeting in late 2020. In turn, each and every one of my competitors proclaimed that I was completely wrong, and that food banks are a wonderful way of empowering communities, solving 'food' poverty and dealing with food waste. Yet the donation of surplus food does not solve the underlying issue of people not being able to afford to eat, as philanthropy is not a solution to social problems. People can't have dignity if they are relying on handouts. Rather, as I see it, the major supermarkets are now fuelling the boom in food banks because it gives them an outlet for over-production while also getting great PR in the process. In Britain, one of the biggest economies in the world, no one should be going hungry – and the real solutions require systemic collaboration between the private, public and third sectors. That's why Emma Revie, the boss of The Trussell Trust (a charity that supports a nationwide network of food banks) says we need to work towards putting them out of business.[4]

On the other hand, the government's plans to introduce green-coloured number plates for electric cars as part of their £1.5 billion Road to Zero Strategy, is a smart initiative.[5] Having consulted with car manufacturers and trade bodies, business knows that the idea will appeal to the psyche of drivers wanting to show off their green credentials (as well as benefit from incentives such as cheaper parking and the use of bus lanes).

Business can also help inform government to create better long-term policy decisions, such as addressing the systemic decline of the UK's high streets, which has only been accentuated by the Covid-19 shutdown. This should be a concern to us all: not only is the retail sector the UK's largest private sector employer with 2.9 million employees[6], but high streets are the backbone of communities up and down the country.

Business rates are a significant element of Iceland's annual tax bill, currently costing us over £40 million each year. But these rates are an outdated tax mechanism designed for a different era, when 'bricks and mortar' shops were the only type of retailing that existed. This rapidly changing environment has seen online's share of UK retail sales almost double since 2014 to account for nearly 20 per cent of the total market by March 2019. During the pandemic, by May 2020 online retail sales had jumped to almost 33 per cent.[7]

I shop online myself and I have absolutely no desire to stand in the way of customers getting what they want. Indeed, as I noted in Chapter 1, we have an extremely fast-growing online business ourselves.

But I do have a big problem with the online behemoths simply not paying their fair share of tax. Amazon, for example, has paid just £62 million in UK corporation tax over the last two decades.[8] Such online-only businesses use our national transport infrastructure for free. If their warehouses catch fire, they won't put the blaze out on their own. Their employees need the support of the NHS and other public services just like everyone else's.

While the online companies, including some of the biggest in the world, get a free ride, traditional retail has seen increases in rates year after year. Indeed, as central government funding has evaporated over the last decade, rates have become the principal revenue-raising lever for local authorities. This growing burden is simply killing our traditional retailers.

In an attempt to level the playing field, in his Autumn 2018 budget the then Chancellor Philip Hammond announced a digital services tax, from which he hoped to raise £400 million a year.[9] That sounds a lot, but it's peanuts ... as I said before, we are a relatively small retailer, and our own business rates bill alone is equal to 10 per cent of the hoped-for revenue.

As part of his support package to help retailers through the Covid-induced economic shutdown, the Chancellor Rishi Sunak announced a temporary suspension of all business rates for one year.[10] While it is unrealistic to hope that this moratorium lasts any longer than necessary, at least it has created a blank sheet of paper from which business can help government think up a new taxation system that protects our town centres, rather than kills them.

In December 2020, Iceland took some heat because we were one of the few retailers not to pay back the business rates relief.[11] Reluctantly, many of the bigger, listed supermarkets abruptly paid back the support they had received as pressure started to mount from the press with increasing righteousness. Fiscal support, they argued, was not fair given that supermarkets had been lucky enough to be allowed to stay open throughout 2020.

As a private company, we never have to bow to financial journalists' opinion – yet I can't pretend that the episode wasn't uncomfortable for our business, when we have always prided ourselves in 'Doing It Right'. While ministers described those companies who had paid back the relief as 'real models of good, healthy capitalism'[12], Iceland was left out in the cold.

But if we were told it was only a loan, then we would have acted differently. The reality was that I didn't think we should pay the rates back – and nor could we have afforded to anyway. If did, we would have had to unhire the 3,500 new permanent jobs we created in 2020, ask all our colleagues for their special bonus and pay rises back, pay back the millions of pounds of Covid-related costs and return the company to its previous foreign owners. Unlike many of our peers, we took no dividends through the pandemic, and put not a single person on furlough. Like all of them, we had donated to good causes throughout.

Sometimes, doing the right thing can be uncomfortable and you have to hold your nerve, despite public pressure. If we really want more social justice from business, we should be focusing on making the likes of Amazon pay their way – rather than supporting a broken business rates system that is widely recognised to be killing off the high street.

I am a realist and so cannot see scope for a dramatic reduction in the taxes levied on traditional retailers, given that non-domestic rates are currently generating nearly £25 billion a year for local authorities[13], and play a key role in funding all their work from roads to refuse collection, schools to adult social care.

But we do need a much more level playing field for those retailing through physical stores and those selling online. It is clear to me that we need an online sales tax. It has been argued that such a tax would only penalise consumers, but you can apply precisely the same argument against business rates and every other tax that retailers currently pay. Ultimately, they are all costs that we have to recover from the consumer through selling prices, once we have done our best to maximise our own efficiency.

Business can also work with government to look at ways of relaxing and reforming our sclerotic town centre planning system – something that Boris Johnson promises he is keen to do.[14]

Making it easier to convert unused retail premises into apartments, for example, would help rejuvenate our high streets into places where young people actually want to live and work. This would be much better for productivity, the environment and socialising when compared to the car-based lifestyle that is required when living on an out-of-town housing estate. Likewise, user restrictions need to be lifted in order to transform redundant city warehousing into flexible co-working space.

Through the patchwork of shops and local offices around the UK, business not only helps people economically, but also provides an anchor to communities' sense of place. And if the government wants to do anything in order to make people feel like their lives have been improved, it should focus on policies that facilitate the enhancement of their local areas and the reclaiming of civic pride to reverse the structural decline of many of our town centres.

Business can also help stop the government making bad policy. The shambolic introduction of Universal Credit, for example, would have benefited hugely from some pragmatic business sense. When the roll-out brought delays in benefit payments, and the switch to a gross, monthly pay-out overwhelmed those who have only ever been used to weekly budgeting (not to mention having to pay their rent directly to their landlord for the first time), we felt the real economic impact it was having on people at our tills. Store colleagues told us about families unable to feed their children and horror stories about the reality of the 'poverty premium', where people unable to get traditional credit pay astronomical amounts of interest to doorstep lenders and 'rent-to-own' schemes.

Another example is that of the 10pm curfew abruptly imposed by the government in September 2020 in an attempt to limit the spread of Covid-19. Any restaurateur could have told them that this would be a death sentence for many restaurants that rely on tables being turned two or three times in an evening in order to make a profit.

And Iceland has borne the brunt of civil service idiocy in our prolonged battle with the National Minimum Wage Taskforce, which deemed our optional employee Christmas Savings Club a technical breach of the national minimum wage rules. Yet this is a scheme that was encouraged by government in order to help colleagues save for Christmas time, and is hugely popular.

Governments should consult with business, benefit from the private sector's practical opinions and real-world experiences, before introducing policies in order to avoid such unintended consequences.

Perpetual growth on a finite planet

At the beginning of this chapter, I said that capitalism is really the best option we have of ensuring broad societal support and improvement. Indeed, since the emergence of the concept of consumers and producers in the 17th century, capitalism has literally lifted billions of people out of poverty and misery.

As the late Hans Rosling explained in his thought-provoking book *Factfulness*, infant mortality caused by basic medical infrastructure limitations, is thankfully now at record lows; while socio-economic improvements mean that female education has never been so high. In many ways, we have never had it so good.[15]

Over the last 20 years the proportion of people living in extreme poverty worldwide has halved and families are living healthier lives. It is an indisputable fact that over the last 400 years economic growth has been the silent driver of human progress. We all need jobs and income to survive and get on in life.

And yet in recent years, inequality across developed economies has grown dramatically. Take the country that is home to the 'American dream', where *anyone* is supposed to be able to achieve success as long as they work hard enough. According to official Census Bureau data, in 2019 income inequality reached its highest level for at least 50 years, with many Americans no longer able to afford basic healthcare.[16] This was despite a strong, growing economy.

The UK isn't doing much better. According to the Equality Trust, in 2018 the richest fifth of households had an income of more than 12 times the amount earned by the poorest fifth.[17] Wealth is even more unequally distributed, with the ONS calculating that in 2016 the richest 10 per cent of households held 44 per cent of wealth; whereas the poorest 50 per cent held just 9 per cent.[18]

Across advanced economies, two-thirds of the population are on track to be poorer than their parents.[19] People are starting to question whether the structure of capitalism relieves inequality or reinforces it.

So what on earth happened? And should we be surprised at the growing youth disengagement from business people or the wider capitalist system?

It is little wonder that there are growing calls from fashionable economists such as Thomas Piketty to introduce global progressive taxes on extreme wealth and reinvest the windfall in working people. Once seen as the exemplars of our capitalist system, billionaires the world over are now under attack as never before.

While I don't think such a blunt taxation on the accumulated results of success is the right way to go, there is clearly a need for more radical ideas and ambitious policies. It should not be anathema to make a lot of money, and billionaires should not be demonised – so long as they genuinely contribute to helping the problems of the world in the process.

I do find an alternative idea, that of a Universal Basic Income (UBI), particularly interesting. UBI gives everyone a guaranteed monthly wage that provides a cushion for their most basic needs. Crucially, it would also provide equal opportunity for everyone in society to develop new concepts, businesses and products. As technology continues to disrupt the job market and careers become less stable, a UBI would replace existing tax breaks and benefits, which often flow to the wrong places.[20] Such noble ideas come at a price, however. And so, people who have been lucky enough to benefit from the incumbent capitalist system – people like me – should pay for it.

Unless we get serious about bending the exponential curve of growing inequality, I fear for the long-term future of our capitalist system. We must properly consider ideas such as a UBI, alongside many others. The coming Fourth Industrial Revolution, which will see ever-increasing technological changes, will benefit society in many ways but is also a serious threat to the future of manual, administrative and even managerial jobs. As we look to reinvent business models and even our whole economic system in order to keep up, we need to be mindful of ensuring that social justice is improved along the way, not degraded.

As we set out on this exciting but uncertain future, I believe that the over-arching problem for governments is how they currently measure their nation's economic success. In the post-war era, all around the world governments have become myopically obsessed with one single yardstick: GDP.

Following the Great Depression in the 1920s, the US economist Simon Kuznets was called upon to develop an accounting system that would trace the monetary value of all the goods and services produced within the economy. His resulting metric, Gross National Product, was the precursor to GDP. As Kate Raworth explains in her book *Doughnut Economics*, the appeal of such a simplistic indicator to measure year-on-year economic progress took hold and is now both a political necessity and a de facto policy goal. Today, the overriding objective of countries around the world is what has been termed 'growthism' – to pursue the highest rate of GDP growth possible, for its own sake.

Yet Kuznets himself was eager to point out the limitations to his new calculation. GDP only captures the cold economic output of production, rather than the intrinsic value of goods and services produced within households and by society. While it may capture the economic output of a person's office job, it would not measure how fulfilled that person is within their job. It would capture the material value extracted from a coalminer's work, but could not factor the impacts of that work on his health. GDP values the sale of a throwaway coffee cup, but not the reuse of a cup. According to GDP, the destruction of an ancient forest for timber or plundering of ocean fish stocks is beneficial. The danger of governments using GDP as the preeminent policy goal becomes clear.

Two other major problems present themselves.

First, GDP growth doesn't capture how income and consumption is distributed across society – which has enabled the shockingly high levels of wealth inequality that we see today. Even the OECD, whose charter goal is to 'promote policies designed to achieve the highest sustainable rate of economic growth'[21], suggests that policies aimed solely at growth might be responsible for the rise in income inequality seen across most OECD countries during the last two or three decades.[22] This makes logical sense, because money follows money in search of ever-higher returns, and 'trickledown' benefits do not keep pace. Beyond a certain point, GDP growth is also inversely linked to human wellbeing. Today's high-income nations saw happiness levels peak long ago. Britons, for example, are less happy than in the 1950s, despite the fact that today we are three times richer.[23]

Second, what is the end goal of continual GDP growth? How much growth is enough, and for how long? No government or economist in the world could answer these questions – we are simply stuck on a treadmill of chasing endless growth, for growth's sake, without considering the ecological consequences. And because this is compound growth – growth on growth – policy makers numbly expect the GDP curve to rise exponentially, for ever.

Our planet is already breaking down under the weight of humanity's relentless search for growth. Yet if we take a fairly standard economic policy of 3 per cent annual growth, in 200 years GDP would be *1,000 times* bigger than today. Assuming China's current GDP growth rate of around 5 per cent is maintained, in 40 years' time the planet would have to cope with over four times as many Chinas as we have today. As Paul Hawken, the author of *The Ecology of Commerce* put it, 'At present we are stealing the future, selling it in the present, and calling it gross domestic product.'[24]

Yet economic growth has actually benefited the environment, at times. From 1998 to 2015 there was a 25 per cent *reduction* in forest area burned around the globe[25] – a fact many eco-alarmists do not want to hear or believe. This decrease in forest fire loss came mainly from economic growth in developing countries, with urban jobs driving people away from rural slash-and-burn farming. Another obvious example would be localised littering and its associated pollution of waterways, which is much lower in developed economies because of their ability to invest in decent waste management infrastructure.

The problems start when economies reach their natural maturity – the limits to the possible growth they can achieve. Indeed, many western economies find themselves in such low or no growth scenarios – yet have not amended their growthism ideology. So rather than benefit from natural headline growth that comes from an emerging economy, we 'must pursue relentless productivity savings in order to prop up GDP. This 'productivity trap' manifests itself in the form of dismantling workers' rights, reducing community resources and lowering environmental protections. As Jason Hickel puts it in his book *Less is More*, 'We are in the absurd position of needing perpetual growth just in order to avoid social collapse.'[26]

It makes good sense that developing nations with low GDP per capita should seek 'clean' or 'green' growth as their primary economic policy (using solar, not coal, for power – which is both cheaper and non-polluting). This is the clearest way of enhancing life for all their citizens. But it makes little sense that developed nations should pursue the same metric. Rather, we should be seeking to provide everyone with a solid social foundation, without wrecking the planet. As Kate Raworth puts it, 'Today we have economies that need to grow, whether or not they make us thrive; what we need are economies that make us thrive, whether or not they grow.'[27]

We must face up to the reckless idiocy of pursuing perpetual growth on a finite planet. So, what is my alternative suggestion? Well, I'm afraid that I don't actually have one. There are people far cleverer than me who are currently trying to work that out. A vast array of alternative indices have been developed, and in some cases they have been adopted as a secondary background measure to GDP – such as the United Nations Human Development Index or the Genuine Progress Indicator. These seek to enlarge the accounting lens in order to consider social aspects (such as health and poverty) and environmental sustainability (such as resource depletion and pollution).[28]

The highly regarded prime minister of New Zealand, Jacinda Ardern, announced in 2019 a 'wellbeing budget', making New Zealand the first western country to design its entire budget around issues such as mental health, family violence and child poverty.[29] And later that year, the Icelandic prime minister Katrín Jakobsdóttir teamed up with Scotland's first minister Nicola Sturgeon by putting wellbeing ahead of GDP in their respective budgets, and urging other governments to prioritise similar green and family-friendly metrics. Shift is happening – at least from the world's female leaders.

In 2007, the European Commission set up the Beyond GDP initiative, a group comprising many of the world's pre-eminent think tanks, NGOs and quangos, to consider better-suited metrics for social, economic and environmental progress. As they state on their website:

> *The Beyond GDP initiative is about developing indicators that are as clear and appealing as GDP, but more inclusive of environmental and social aspects of progress. Economic indicators such as GDP were never designed to be comprehensive measures of prosperity and wellbeing. We need adequate indicators to address global challenges of the 21st century such as climate change, poverty, resource depletion, health and quality of life.'[30]*

Drawing down

While per capita GDP growth is religiously tracked and published every quarter, an indicator that isn't but should be is that of carbon emissions on a per capita basis.[31] In fact, given that in May 2019 the UK parliament declared a climate emergency[32], and soon after the then government committed itself to reaching net zero emissions by 2050[33], it is crazy to think that we are not carefully monitoring, reporting and comparing the root cause of the problem.

Yet one has to ask – as Extinction Rebellion do – whether that 2050 commitment actually matches the scale of the challenge. If we really are facing an emergency, surely there is a crying need to achieve net zero much earlier – why not 2040, at the very latest? Hey, let's be bold: 2030!

But nobody has a serious plan for 2030. Considering the emissions curve has risen exponentially since the dawn of the Industrial Revolution, aspirations of hitting net zero within a decade would require an immediate halt to life as we know it. No more meat, dairy, flights, cars or heating. No more holidays in the sun or new clothes. No more iPhones or cloud storage. When people demand 'TELL US THE TRUTH!'... well, there it is. And I think that truth once quantified is so absolutely unpalatable and unrealistic that no democratic country would ever allow it to happen.

Over the past decade, global carbon emissions have been going up by about 1 per cent per year, according to Corinne Le Quéré, the UK government's adviser on how to get to net zero emissions by 2050. In an interview with the *New Scientist* magazine, the climate scientist estimated that 2020 will show a reduction in emissions of between 4 and 7 per cent as a direct result of the economic shutdown caused by the Covid-19 pandemic.[34]

This is, of course, dramatic progress – but it's also not nearly enough. To reach net zero by 2050, we actually need to halve our global carbon emissions by 2030. Even in a year when over one-third of the world's population was locked down, and planes, trains and automobiles were temporarily abandoned, we are still left with more than 90 per cent of the hard yards to travel if we are to meet our global decarbonisation obligations under the Paris Agreement (which specified holding global warming within a target range of between 1.5 and 2.0°C for this century, compared to pre-industrial levels).

It is what happens next that is important. Le Quéré went on to explain: 'In 2009, during the financial crash, emissions dropped 1.4 per cent. They then grew more than 5 per cent in 2010, which brought us exactly back to where we were.'

So, we need to be realistic about the pace of change and imagine a future that we can look forward to rather than be afraid of. People must feel like they have agency and choices. Climate activists will never win the debate, let alone the cause they are fighting for, otherwise.

All of that being said, the UK's own independent government adviser, the Climate Change Committee (CCC), published a report in July 2019 that left no doubt that nowhere near enough is being done to reduce Britain's 435 million tonnes of annual greenhouse gases.[35] Greenpeace UK's Chief Scientist Doug Parr described the report as 'a truly brutal reality check on the government's current progress in tackling the climate emergency. It paints the government as a sleeper who's woken up, seen the house is on fire, raised the alarm and gone straight back to sleep.' [36][37]

Yet the government's actual target is for an 80 per cent gross reduction in carbon emissions by 2050, with the remaining 20 per cent netted off by technologies known as 'carbon capture and storage' (CCS). The big hitch, however, is that CCS technology barely exists. In 2019, according to the Global CCS Institute the world's total CCS capacity was a meagre 40 million tonnes (including 'projects under construction').[38] For context, the 2019 CCC report estimated that the UK would need to capture 175 million tonnes of CO_2 a year from the atmosphere – as well as 300 million tonnes of annual reduction from 2017 levels.[39]

To meet the more ambitious Paris Agreement target of 1.5°C, global emissions would need to drop by 7.6 per cent every year between now and 2030, according to the UN.[40] But you don't need to be a climate expert to understand the cold reality that we are simply not going to get there. That's not pessimistic, it's realistic. And it's certainly not giving up hope – in business we always try to face up to reality so that we can deal with the problem head-on.

It is high time for a reality check on our legally binding net zero goals. If we are going to get there, I believe that we urgently need to introduce a clear, consistent carbon tax.

Such a tax would both expedite the drawdown of emissions, while also raising capital to invest in low-carbon infrastructure and technology. This is not such a radical idea – the UK already has carbon taxes, of a sort: namely fuel duty and utility taxes. Yet flights are effectively subsidised. And it is this policy inconsistency that is slowing overall market behaviour change.[41]

Regarding how to expedite behaviour and market change in order to restore nature, a clear and simple concept was proposed to me by my friend James Byrne from The Wildlife Trusts: a de minimis levy on any goods sold, which goes towards a Nature Restoration Fund. A sort of 'biodiversity levy'.

Conservationists know exactly where the problems are and what to do about them – the problem is having enough of a war chest to enact their plans at scale. According to the pressure group Natural Climate Solutions, ecological restoration projects only receive around 2.5 per cent of the money allocated for climate mitigation, despite the interconnectedness of the two issues.[42]

Natural England, whose responsibilities include monitoring key wildlife sites, advising on planning applications and paying farmers to protect wildlife, has seen its funding by DEFRA cut by £180 million since 2009.[43] The Chairwoman of the Environment Agency, Emma Howard-Boyd, said in December 2020 that the government-funded body no longer had enough money to do its job – blaming cuts of more than 50 per cent to its enforcement budget.[44] This is probably because government money tends to follow corporate money, and many corporates still aren't really interested. According to Natural Climate Solutions, the beauty of ecological restoration is that it is different everywhere – which makes it difficult to attract corporate capital, which favours large-scale, highly controlled monocultures offering economies of scale.

A government-imposed fractional levy – of perhaps 0.001 per cent of any goods sold – would get around this issue. I tried to interest one of Boris Johnson's special advisers in this concept not long before the December 2019 general election, but the objection immediately became clear: the expected consumer backlash against 'yet another tax'. True, the run-up to an election was maybe not the most propitious time to propose this. Yet once explained, one would hope that society would see the sense in foregoing an unnoticeable amount of money in exchange for our survival on this planet.

With the UK on track for a record £400 billion deficit by the end of 2020, it might seem that the nation's credit card is maxed out on dealing with the corona pandemic. Yet according to Greenpeace, the government should be spending at least 2 per cent of GDP per year on a 'climate and nature emergency budget'.[45] Therefore, we must look towards raising the money that we so desperately need to spend on environmental initiatives.

A carbon tax or a biodiversity levy could have a big impact on the world's fight to limit climate change and enhance nature, and this is despite the fact that the UK itself accounts for only just over 1 per cent of global production emissions.[46] It is particularly important for the UK government to act because so many of the world's largest companies are incorporated here and have their primary listings on the London Stock Exchange. Hence, we have a unique responsibility to enact positive taxation and regulations that will deliver genuinely world-class environmental stewardship. Not a bad pitch to the world for a post-Brexit Britain.

However, even more challenging than introducing new taxes is to rationalise existing ones. Yet this is precisely what needs to be done if we want tangible progress on greening consumer and business behaviour. The playing field, currently lop-sided towards fossil fuels, needs to be levelled. I discuss later in this chapter the subsidies that the aviation and oil and gas industries currently enjoy. But many other examples abound: people will suffer 20 per cent VAT to install a solar panel on their roof, compared to 5 per cent VAT for coal to heat their home, for instance. Another is the tax relief that promotes the building of new homes rather than refurbishing existing, because VAT is levied on the latter but not the former. Consumers currently face a myriad of overlapping carbon taxes, which are at odds with the government's long-term green policies and require urgent harmonisation.[47]

Building back better

The prolonged, national lockdown afforded an opportunity to reflect upon what really needs to change in our society. In May 2020, I signed a joint letter to the prime minister – along with many other business leaders, charities and experts – calling for the UK government to prioritise a green economic recovery following the pandemic. We argued that the unplanned 'great global pause' provided the best chance we were ever likely to get to change direction and behave more responsibly.[48]

Most of the business world is now aligned in its focus on driving a greener economy, tackling the climate crisis, and reversing the decline in global biodiversity. With fossil fuel prices at rock bottom, and old industries already painfully readjusting, there will never be a better opportunity to achieve radical change in our economic base.

A green economy will be a stronger economy. Smart, low carbon technologies such as hydrogen power – where the UK has an opportunity to lead the world in terms of research and development – will increase efficiency and productivity, while also offering new employment opportunities across the country. If that sounds like a pipedream, the UK already has form: 20 years ago, we had only two offshore wind turbines; now we have more offshore wind capacity than any other country in the world.[49]

Or take the government's target of upgrading the UK's 19 million homes to an acceptable Energy Performance Certificate standard by 2035. This is estimated to require the creation of an additional 220,000 jobs in the first year alone.[50] New buildings that support a net zero emissions future would also increase export opportunities because of the UK's expertise in green building design and architecture.

The many investments and policy levers required to deliver a green recovery would also help level up communities across the UK by stimulating local economies. Think of the potential for making offshore wind the backbone of the UK's energy system, and the resultant jobs rescued from the declining North Sea oil and gas industry. Considering that renewables are now the cheapest form of electricity generation, with the potential to offer lower household bills, and the recent rapid improvements to battery storage technologies, such a push into wind and solar would also save money for both businesses and consumers, make supply chains more resilient, cut pollution and improve health.

Why would any sane country continue propping up old, dirty industries that have no long-term future when we could be investing in business activity that reduces carbon, helps the planet and provides secure 'green-collar' jobs in entirely new sectors instead? That is why it is vital that the government's post-pandemic economic stimulus must have green strings attached – and ensure that business delivers a more resilient, low carbon and resource-efficient society.

The bailout packages and fiscal policies that governments around the world will be implementing over the next 18 months – amounting to trillions in spending – must be concurrent with positive environmental goals. They cannot prop up carbon intensive industries that we should be transitioning away from.

If a proportion of the huge wave of forthcoming government spending is properly linked to climate action, we can change our current trajectory. If it is not ... that trajectory will only accelerate. Therefore the 10 years that the Intergovernmental Panel on Climate Change (IPCC) warned us we have left to solve the climate crisis has shortened to probably 18 months. Our window for environmental change has collided with the Covid-19 pandemic. It has both sped up the opportunity but also severely curtailed our timescale to take action.

Early signs are encouraging. A report by DNV GL published in autumn 2020 forecast that Covid-19 will represent a watershed moment for the global energy transition, with the pandemic having long-lasting effects on energy use, investment decisions and CO_2 emissions.[51] In turn, oil prices may have already peaked. Increased home working, fewer business air miles and a boom in electric vehicles all combined to prompt the oil and gas majors to cut thousands of jobs and write down billions in dollar assets.[52][53]

The startling drop in global oil prices should not, however, be used as a reason to pull investment in renewable technologies and industries. Rather, governments should accelerate the retraining of workers and the switch of skills from declining fossil fuel industries into growing renewables ones. According to the International Renewable Energy Agency, investing in renewables would increase jobs in the sector to 42 million globally by 2050 – four times today's level. They also forecast that it would boost global GDP by $98 trillion, returning between $3 and $8 on every dollar invested.[54]

Such returns are attractive to private capital, but it also makes sense to spend taxpayers' money on investing in such nationwide green technologies, promoting new industries and employment opportunities, as well as supporting workers through a just transition.

But where will this public money initially come from? Additional funds could be raised from the introduction of a carbon tax. And the pandemic has proved that governments can spend as much as they like in an emergency, as administrations around the world are rediscovering the concept of running large deficits, which modern economics had previously thought unthinkable. As governments turn their attention from Covid-19 to biodiversity decline and climate change, this is a lesson worth remembering.

A pretty obvious pot of money which we could redeploy is the huge subsidy that oil and gas exploration and extraction currently enjoy. The International Monetary Fund estimated that 2017 saw a staggering \$5.2 trillion go towards global fossil fuel subsidies, making the sector by far the most heavily subsidised in the world.[55] In 2019 the European Commission reported that the UK alone gave £10.5 billion a year of taxpayers' money to fossil fuels, leading all of the European Union countries.[56] This was £3 billion more than was spent on the renewable energy sector[57] and vastly higher than the pitiful £40 million offered up by the UK government for their showpiece Green Recovery Challenge Fund announced in response to Covid-19.[58]

The science is clear and yet we continue with a system that is designed to maximise fossil fuel exploration and burning. In order to avoid an economic shock of a 'jump-to-distress' in terms of job losses and stranded financial assets, we must start de-subsidising the grossly over-supported fossil fuel sector without delay.

In the post-Covid-19 world we need to be focusing on 'soft' infrastructure projects such as the nationwide rollout of superfast fibre broadband, given the huge growth in home working. Stepping up the electrification of our vehicle fleet is essential – ensuring that all new cars and vans are electric by 2030 would not only provide around 30 per cent of the emissions reductions needed to keep the UK on track towards its net zero target[59], but would also provide a boost to the UK economy.

Pre-Covid plans for 'hard' infrastructure investments in concrete and steel should be reconsidered, from the

Heathrow third runway to the £27 billion road building programme scheduled until 2025.[60]

The UK's HS2 vanity project cries out to be ditched. HS2 didn't even show a return for the taxpayer before the pandemic[61], and post-Covid-19 all the assumptions about future travel on which it is based have now been blown out of the water.

The original budget was estimated at somewhere around £30 billion but has since spiralled out of control with estimates now at over £100 billion.[62] That would make it the costliest infrastructure project in Europe, possibly the world.

Then there is the environmental cost. According to the Woodland Trust, 108 irreplaceable ancient woods are threatened with loss or damage from the proposed route.[63] On top of that, countless old meadows, wetlands and Sites of Special Scientific Interest (supposedly protected by UK law) are also under threat. As The Wildlife Trusts put it: 'In this time of climatic and ecological crisis, the risks to nature HS2 poses are unacceptable. The route risks pushing nature closer to the brink, with local species extinctions, destruction of carbon-storing habitats and biodiversity irreversibly damaged.'[64]

For me – a northern-based businessman who commutes regularly via train to London – HS2 represents a very southern-based 'Establishment' view of the north: to help us level up we need quicker journey times to London. But if that does anything, it will simply suck more jobs and prosperity out of the north. Much more sensible would be to invest in northern east–west rail connections instead and drop this white elephant. And productivity would be better improved by simply installing decent wifi on our existing trains.

We must also thoroughly review the taxation and subsidies of air travel. Of course, we must not deny the family that saves all year to reward themselves for their annual week or fortnight in the sun. There is nothing better calculated to raise the hackles of the public than being lectured about the need for self-denial by plutocrats and politicians who have just flown in their private jets to gather at some exotic resort for yet another climate change conference.

But with Zoom and Teams meetings becoming the new corporate norm, the pandemic has made it patently clear that we just don't need to travel as much for work as we thought we did. Pre-Covid, there were many wealthy (mostly male) business people who were seemingly addicted to the escapism of business air travel. We should start with attacking that culture of unnecessary flying, focusing on the frequent business traveller, rather than the occasional, well-earned holidaymaker.

An escalating frequent flyer tax seems to me like a no-brainer ... it has been estimated that 1 per cent of people cause half of global aviation emissions; so it makes sense to focus on those 'super emitters'.[65] And if airlines and airports are going to need government support (which they clearly will), then they need to commit to reducing emissions and developing new technologies, such as hybrid fuel planes and sustainable aviation fuels.

What the government must not do is view the pandemic as a reason to weaken existing environmental laws and protections. We are already hearing the siren voices of Big Plastic calling for a climbdown on planned legislation for plastic and packaging taxes.[66] We must not fall for it. Covid-19 is not an excuse for breaking promises, as we have demonstrated at Iceland by continuing to pursue our plastics removal programme regardless.

Likewise, policymakers have no time to lose as well. At the time of writing in early 2021, the government must press ahead urgently with the Environment Bill and detailing the new Agriculture Act – once-in-a-generation opportunities to change the trajectory we currently find ourselves on. Prepared over two years previously by a different government, they set out a range of actions to enhance the environment for the next generation, from ending plastic pollution to reforming our agricultural and fishing industries so they are more sustainable.

But much work needs to be done.

Specifically, the concept of 'public money for public goods', as a way of redirecting farming subsidies to nature-positive land management practices post-Brexit, should be kept as ambitious as when it was announced by then Environment Secretary Michael Gove in 2018.

The proposed post-Brexit Environmental Land Management Scheme (ELMS) for England, and Sustainable Land Management Scheme (SLMS) for Wales, are fantastically exciting prospects that give us the best hope we will have of restoring our farmland nature in the UK. For more than 40 years, the European Union's Common Agricultural Policy (CAP) has dictated how we farm. By paying farmers solely on the size of their landholding and scale of their output, it has led to devasting declines in wildlife across the UK.

The idea of both ELMS and SLMS is to redesign agricultural policy to allow us to meet our environmental ambitions, while also supporting farmers, foresters and other land managers. The trick will be to engender healthier soils, wetlands, hedgerows and woodlands, while also maintaining productivity and livelihoods. The new subsidy system will have to be carefully channelled to the right places in order to ensure the crucial support of the farming and rural communities.

The government should also mandate the establishment of local nature recovery networks, as The Wildlife Trusts have been calling for, so as to embed environmental restoration into strategic guidance at a local level. These need to be applied across all four nations of the UK and include local government as well.

The new Office for Environmental Protection needs to be given real teeth by being made independent and empowered to act as a watchdog. It needs to be accountable to Parliament, rather than to the government of the day, and to have the power to issue fines where these are needed to drive change. Long-term, legally binding targets need to be introduced so that we can restore nature, improve air and water quality and cut down resource use.

There should be radical targets to reduce the production of single-use plastic – by at least 50 per cent. And as discussed in Chapter 3, we were also part of a campaign to lobby the mandating of companies to fully disclose their plastic footprints, as an addendum to the Environment Bill.

Finally, we must use the legislation to learn the fundamental lesson of Covid-19 and ensure that the UK becomes serious about the protection of natural habitats, from Marine Protected Areas to local nature reserves.

New order

A greener economy and society does now appear to be what people actually want: an Ipsos MORI poll in April 2020 showed that two-thirds of people globally consider long-term climate change as serious an issue as Covid-19, and most want to see the climate prioritised in recovery plans (albeit most see it as someone else's problem to solve).[67]

Yet it's difficult for any government to win elections by telling the voters things that they do not want to hear: eat less meat, turn down the heating, ask whether their journeys are really necessary and take fewer flights.

Sanctimonious preaching from global elites or political leaders about the need to limit our emissions comes with real risk. Populist backlashes are brewing all around the world over the issue of climate change. While government officials everywhere are busy drafting ambitious 'green new deals' to reorientate economies, there is very little thought from within policy units as to how such measures will impact low-income voters.

Ditching old cars, cheap flights or gas boilers may sound palatable to those who can afford it, but it is the vast majority who are struggling to get by who would feel such changes most keenly. People who already feel left behind are in no mood to be lectured at by globalist elites. As the rage against higher fuel taxes by France's *gilets jaunes* protesters showed, condescending politicians should beware.

One clear way for the UK to push ahead with a positive green agenda, alongside keeping the playing field level for all its citizens, is to ensure that any new trade deals we sign maintain or enhance our current environmental standards.

It would also help businesses with the difficult task of trying to deal with emission reductions far up their international supply chains. As discussed in Chapter 1, Iceland has made solid progress in reducing carbon through our direct operations over the last nine years. Yet I am far from happy with that progress. In many ways the actions we took represented the low hanging fruit of cost savings that were sure to win approval from the finance department.

Scope 3 emissions – which account for by far the largest share of the total – comprise all the indirect carbon that our business is responsible for, both upstream and downstream. It is an identical story for the UK as a whole. While the UK has done pretty well at cutting its Scope 1 and 2 (i.e. direct) emissions, as I have previously explained, this has largely been done simply by offshoring manufacturing to the likes of China.

Iceland can do a much better job of applying pressure up our supply chain. Inspired by conversations with Christiana Figueres, in 2021 Iceland will become the first food retailer to sign The Carbon Pledge, which sets a net zero target of 2040 – inclusive of Scope 3. From working with the Carbon Trust, we are now mapping our supply chain emissions and collating information from our supplier base to target and track reductions via a public annual report.

But to speed up the momentum of Scope 3 carbon reduction also requires governmental action and diplomatic pressure, to ensure the maintenance and improvement of high standards throughout the food supply chain, for the protection of consumers, animal welfare and the environment alike.

Upcoming trade negotiations with Brazil should be linked to tackling fires in the Amazon, halting deforestation and stopping indigenous rights abuses, for example. The current US trade deal being negotiated by the UK government must not allow a race to the bottom in animal welfare standards, by allowing products such as chlorinated chicken or hormone-injected beef to flood the market.

Of course, the UK can't solve the climate and nature emergency alone. And 2021 presents the opportunity for us to set an example on the world stage. Looking beyond domestic policies, UK ministers and civil servants can showcase the credentials of a post-EU Britain by showing global leadership – with the UK both hosting COP26 and holding the G7 Presidency in 2021.

Climate conferences have a long history of breakthrough highs and impassable lows; yet it feels that this time we really have all the justifications we could ever need to step up to our responsibility of being the last generation to be able to avert climate and ecological breakdown.

Make no mistake: the world's upcoming green transition will create nothing short of a new geo-political order, and the UK needs to be at the heart of it.

Since the onset of Covid-19, demand for oil dropped by more than a fifth and prices collapsed.[68] Stalwarts of the old energy landscape such as ExxonMobil were ejected from the Dow Jones Industrial Average in 2020, having been a member since 1928.[69] The clean energy industry is gaining momentum, with stocks up 45 per cent in the year to September 2020.[70]

Politicians around the world are seizing the moment, seeing both the chance to flatten the climate curve and future-proof their nation's economies. The European Union, striving to be the first climate-neutral continent, has pledged at least €100 billion to support a shift to the green economy from 2021 to 2027.[71]

Today, it is the US that dominates the global energy market – of which 85 per cent still comes from burning fossil fuels.[72] Yet as the new energy system emerges, petrostates will be forced to reform and become more democratic, as they seek taxation from their own citizens.

And it is China which has the biggest opportunity to consolidate its lead as the world's biggest force in green technologies and supply chains. China is rapidly building a world-beating renewable energy platform. Today, Chinese firms produce 45 per cent of the world's wind turbines, 69 per cent of its lithium-ion batteries and almost three-quarters of its solar modules.[73] In September 2020, China's leader, President Xi Jinping made the ground-breaking announcement that the country would aim to be carbon neutral by 2060.[74]

Sometimes, it does seem that the best responses to environmental challenges or even pandemics have come from authoritarian states. The West does not envy the Chinese state's restrictions on free speech, the surveillance of its citizens or its treatment of minorities, but it does envy its ability to get things done. One party states can take decisive action to go green. In early 2018, for example, China simply reassigned 60,000 soldiers to plant trees around Beijing in a bid to fight pollution.[75]

Limiting the warming of the planet to 1.5°C will require the sort of radical action that may well prove easier for a dictatorship than a democracy. In both the World Wars of the 20th century, Britain's main political parties found it necessary to shelve their differences and work together in the national interest. The war on climate change is certainly no less of a challenge than Kaiser Wilhelm or Hitler, and I hope that politicians will not take too long in coming to appreciate this.

According to *The Economist*, some 69 per cent of Britons are now dissatisfied with the way democracy is currently working.[76] In response, all around the world – including the UK – there are Citizens' Assemblies forming in an attempt to better reflect the views of normal people in order to deal with existential issues like climate and social justice. 'Politics as usual' is no longer an option for many.

This is no doubt a well-intentioned endeavour to find out how the great British public would prefer the goal of net zero carbon emissions to be achieved. I sincerely wish them well in their deliberations, but my own painful experience of attempting to reach business decisions through unwieldy consultation is that you always end up with an over-compromised answer that ultimately satisfies none of the participants and does not deliver the desired results.

My company has functioned well for years under the benign dictatorship of its founder, so I am perhaps naturally more sympathetic than most to that model of governance. I have seen how well it can work. That is why, when it comes to the multiple environmental and social emergencies that we face today, our leaders should decide on an urgent course of action themselves by adopting the proven Iceland model of JFDI: Just Fucking Do It.

. . . .

As our society and economy awakens from the Covid-19 pandemic, and sets about tackling the social, climate and nature crisis through the 2020s, we will need a comprehensive set of policies and programmes.

So many business leaders are scared of turning consumers off, or saying the wrong thing and being trolled on social media, that they don't become involved in the public debate. I think our country suffers as a result. All of us – especially business leaders – need to take a stand, rather than just point fingers. We need to lean into the issues that impact our country by listening to one another and making our opinions heard.

I'm not necessarily saying that these are all the right ideas; my hope is that they will promote debate around those which are.

But when we look at the broad sweep of challenges that we face today – from rebuilding our economy and society post-Covid, to the UK making its own way in the world having left the European Union, the twin environmental emergencies of a dramatically warming climate and plummeting biodiversity, to the alarming rise in social inequality – new ideas are what we so desperately need from our politicians. Business must speak out, rather than hide in the shadows, and help to support political decision-making and policy implementation for all our sakes.

MY KEY RECOMMENDATIONS FOR GOVERNMENT

RETHINK OLD NORMS
Be agnostic about GDP.

RADICAL TIMES NEED RADICAL IDEAS
Overhaul our welfare state and introduce a Universal Basic Income.

USE THE POWER OF THE STATE TO QUICKLY REDUCE CARBON AND RESTORE NATURE
Harmonise existing taxation to make it pro-green, impose a carbon tax and a de minimis biodiversity levy.

IMPROVE PEOPLE'S COMMUNITIES AND 'OUR SENSE OF PLACE'
Free up the planning system, overhaul business rates and introduce an online sales tax.

FOCUS ON 'AFTER COVID-19' SOFT INFRASTRUCTURE PROJECTS AND DITCH THE 'BEFORE COVID-19' ONES
Scrap HS2 and the Heathrow third runway. Fire up our nation's broadband.

FACE REALITY
We need an escalating frequent flyer tax and a consumption tax.

STOP DOING STUPID THINGS
We need to urgently taper down fossil fuel subsidies and redirect them into green industries.

DON'T LOSE OUR AMBITION
We should push for a gold-plated Environment Bill, with the concept of 'public money for public goods' at its heart. We must properly protect 30 per cent of our land and sea by 2030. Create a National Nature Service.

BAILOUT PACKAGES SHOULD HAVE GREEN STRINGS ATTACHED
We must not waste the opportunity to genuinely 'build back better'.

LINK FUTURE TRADE DEALS WITH STRONG ENVIRONMENTALISM AND HIGH ANIMAL WELFARE
Let's enhance, not diminish, our agricultural standards.

CONCLUSION
THE KINDNESS CONNECTION

Why I'm optimistic

'BELIEF IS IRRESISTIBLE.'

PHIL KNIGHT[1]

As a family we have been visiting Norway for years. For some time in her early 20s my wife lived in Tranby, a chocolate-box village outside Oslo surrounded by rolling hills and pine forests, where she would cross country ski to the local school to teach English. While there, Rebecca learned the language and developed some life-long friendships.

As well as its dramatic natural beauty, Norway is a country with a deep social conscience and strong national identity. Most houses proudly fly the traditional red, white and indigo Norwegian flag. Their *Nasjonaldagen* (National Day) on 17 May is a major public holiday and a spectacle to behold. Across the country residents dress up in their traditional rural outfits, known as *Bunad*, and parade through every town and village. It's a light-hearted, celebratory day that centres around children and brings families together.

This sense of patriotism, however, is not driven through looking inwards – quite the opposite. Norway boasts an immigrant population of almost 17 per cent[2], with the country receiving tens of thousands of asylum seekers during the European migrant crisis of 2015.[3] It is also a country with high egalitarian values, evidenced by Norway's low Gini coefficient (which ranks countries by wealth and income distribution).[4] On top of that, the Norwegians somehow manage to balance being the most productive country in the world[5] with being the healthiest[6] – and one of the happiest, according to the 2019 *World*

Happiness Report. Their famous 'high tax, high welfare' approach seems to be working out pretty well.

But what impresses me most of all about Norway is their concept of *dugnad*: a long-established cultural tradition where community members work together towards a common goal, for the greater good of all. In the 14th and 15th centuries it was used by farming communities to prepare for impending winters, with everyone playing their part to ensure mutual survival. In the 20th century *dugnad* manifested itself through the country's labour movements, informing today's strong sense of equality. Social democratic ideals that value justice and community above individualism and consumerism (plainly evident when driving through the country by the lack of top-end sports cars ... or old bangers ready for the scrapheap).

And the tradition was used more recently to galvanise the nation on 12 March 2020, when prime minister Erna Solberg called upon Norwegians for a national *dugnad* in order to fight Covid-19. In a televised address announcing a national lockdown, she explained:

It has now become absolutely crucial that all of the country's citizens and residents participate in a national dugnad *to slow down the spread. We are doing this in solidarity with the elderly, chronically ill, and others that are especially vulnerable in developing this serious disease. We have to protect ourselves in order to protect others. We will stand together through this period in time – not with hugs and handshakes – but by keeping our distance from one another. It will require a lot from each and every one of us. We need to care about one another*

and help each other the best we can. We have gotten
ourselves through tough times before – I am absolutely
certain that we will achieve this once again.

What I think *dugnad* really signifies is people's
commitment to helping one another. As the Norwegian
people showed through their Covid-19 lockdown, it can
be just as relevant for the whole of society as for any
single community.

And *dugnadsand* (the spirit of dugnad) should
translate across borders, beyond a traditional Norwegian
custom, to serve as an inspiration for all societies.

. . . .

Yet we all want to get the most out of life, because life is
short. A more sustainable lifestyle would require us to
forego greed. Is the answer that we must change human
nature, in order to secure our survival as a species?

To make sense of this, we really need to unpack
the conundrum of capitalism, and our relationship with
it. Despite being the best system we've got, capitalism
and its pursuit of economic growth is coming off
the rails. Kate Raworth neatly sums up our challenge in
Doughnut Economics when she states: 'No country has
ever ended human deprivation without a growing
economy. And no country has ever ended ecological
degradation with one.'[7]

The town of Whitehaven, next to England's north-west
Lake District National Park, distils this conundrum
perfectly. In late 2020, environmentalists were outraged
when Cumbria County Council approved the UK's first
deep coal mine in 30 years. Such coking coal extraction

will undoubtedly contribute towards climate change, yet Whitehaven is located within an economically depressed region. As the local mayor put it, 'These type of investment opportunities into the local community come around not even once in a lifetime.'[8]

Growing numbers of people around the world are starting to be left behind, while at the same time our unabated drive for consumerism is also wrecking the planet, destroying our natural world and hurtling us towards climate change that will be catastrophic (for us humans, at least).

We all know this. In fact, deep down, we've known it for a very long time. None of these problems are new.

As Nathaniel Rich explains in *Losing Earth*, a depressing chronology of the wilful lack of political progress on climate policy throughout 1980s America: 'Nearly everything we understand about global warming was understood in 1979.'[9] And yet since that time, with our full realisation of the consequences, we've committed the crimes. From 1990, we've emitted more carbon than since the dawn of the Industrial Revolution.[10] And since 1970, over half the world's wild animals have disappeared due to human activity.[11]

To pose a blunt question: what is wrong with us?

As if we needed reminding that the Covid-19-induced pause in our rampant upwards emissions spiral was only temporary, at the end of June 2020 a small Siberian town sent the world a stark message. Verkhoyansk in Russia recorded the highest temperature ever seen within the Arctic Circle – a tropical 38°C. Scientists had previously predicted that such temperatures would not be reached in that region until perhaps 2100. However, throughout the summer of 2020 (at the same time that the western media was flooded with calls for a 'green recovery') Siberia was amid the grip of a heatwave, causing wildfires that sent smoke stretching for thousands of miles.

And yet we relentlessly continue to increase global emissions. What is *wrong* with us?

Avoidance behaviour by those who do know and indeed care is, in fact, entirely natural. Behavioural economists term it 'hyperbolic discounting' – a grand way of saying that when offered two rewards, the human brain opts for the quickest one and discounts the value of the longer-term one ... rather like opting for £10 today instead of £20 next week. We tend to make decisions for the short term that our future selves would disagree with. We would rather opt for convenience and comfort now rather than stop to think about the consequences. And we are only powerfully motivated to avoid threats if they are immediate – when walking down a dark alley at night for example, we naturally become more vigilant and quicken our pace.

Others are still prepared to ignore the overwhelming scientific consensus on climate change. Some citizens, business people and politicians simply do not care. Such people actively seek out or only accept information that squarely fits with their beliefs – and reject outright facts that do not. Social media platforms, whose core objective is to maximise time spent engaging with their content, accentuates this confirmation bias by inclining users towards those who share their incumbent views. This is achieved via an infinitely optimised and synthetic experience, which deliberately reinforces prejudices simply to hold attention.

Others might feel the overwhelming sense of helplessness that can grip us when faced with such an existential threat. I've come to realise that the eco-alarmists – those prophets of doom who fuel their righteousness by lecturing others on impending catastrophes caused by our imperviousness – will never win. People simply shrug their shoulders and tune out.

But the overwhelming reason, something that some environmentalists forget or simply do not understand, is that many people have more immediate concerns to worry about. Many people today are simply struggling to make ends meet – and saving the planet isn't exactly top of their hierarchy of needs. In order to make genuine progress, the green agenda must become relevant and meaningful to regular people.

The big tendency is for those who think they know best to patronise others in society they consider too dim to make the right lifestyle choices for themselves. I've never believed that the environmental debate will be won by telling people not to do things – fly less, eat less meat and so on. As someone who constantly reviews marketing slogans and straplines, I know that you'll never inspire action if you come at it from the point of view of cost and consequence. The debate needs reframing to focus on the opportunity and benefits.

President Joe Biden does this perfectly, by linking positive environmental action with green-collar opportunity. 'When I think about climate change, the word I think of is "jobs"', Biden said in a 2020 address.[12] Such statements are no longer hypothetical – the green economy now employs 10 times as many people as the fossil fuel industry in the US, representing nearly 10 million jobs.[13] Just after the November 2020 US election, over in the UK Boris Johnson announced that his Green Industrial Revolution would create 250,000 jobs, in overlooked places like the North East, Yorkshire and the Humber, the West Midlands, Scotland and Wales – and spur three times that number from the private sector.[14] Our leaders need to start having normal conversations with us about the benefits to society of ambitious green policies. A green future must be a jobs-first future.

It's also an inconvenient truth, to use Al Gore's rather sanctimonious phrase, that many of those telling others to live more simply are doing the exact opposite themselves. The battering Prince Harry got in the British press in 2019 for telling people to reduce their emissions, while also flying around on a private jet, shows the contempt people feel for hypocrites. In my own business life, I have literally lost count of the number of global sustainability conferences on the other side of the world I have been invited to fly over to. And woe betide any business that tries to dictate to its consumers what they must do.

What we actually need is a healthy debate on crucial issues like climate that includes *all* of society's stakeholders. If real people are empowered to have a voice, we might actually make some progress. Without their input, we are not having a proper debate – and without proper debate there is just polarisation.

At the moment, we are seemingly stuck within a buck-passing circle ... society blames business for our environmental ills, while business people bemoan the confines of the market they operate within – and the limits to what the consumer will accept before shopping somewhere else. Governments are often blamed for their short-termism due to electoral cycles lasting a few short years; yet politicians will point towards the limitations of what voters find politically palatable. As the West talks of the vast pollution and emissions that are now produced by countries such as India and China, developing nations say that they merely want to play catch-up by having the same carbon budgets as their wealthier counterparts. Instead of implying that they must not be allowed to live like us, maybe we should question whether *we* should be allowed to live like us.

To borrow Hans Rosling's phrase: when the finger-pointing starts, the thinking stops.

. . . .

The UN's 17 Sustainable Development Goals already provide nations with a detailed blueprint to advance social justice, ensure economic progression for all, as well as live within our planetary limits. But how can we balance such lofty globalist aspirations with the hard reality on the ground, in places like Whitehaven?

For certain, many of the answers lie with national and local governments. A 'political *dugnadsand*' would surely accept the sheer illogicality of pursuing perpetual growth on a finite planet, and instead seek to create more inclusive economies. We need radical new ideas that challenge economic orthodoxy – such as prioritising happiness and egalitarianism over growth and consumerism.

Yet it is private enterprise – as the job, wealth and tax creators – that will actually enable such action. Business, alongside the third sector, is the delivery partner for the public sector. And it is business alone that pays for it all.

Governments merely set the parameters – and they need to do a better job of ensuring the playing field is levelled to facilitate climate, nature and social justice.

As well as doing and delivering, business can also use their brands to inspire and engage consumers around an issue. I'm particularly impressed with the craft beer company BrewDog, who in their disruptive, punkish style, have used 'F**k You CO_2' as their campaign slogan for becoming a carbon-neutral brewer.

Furthermore, as governments aren't acting quickly enough, business can and should be making public policy interventions. It is no longer enough for business people to hide away in the shadows on the big issues of our time. Nowadays, we have an obligation to speak out – particularly on behalf of those whose voices aren't being heard. The vast array of businesses stepping up to agitate governments for meaningful climate and nature policies in the run-up to November 2021's COP26 conference is testament to that growing realisation. We, as business leaders, can play a positive role in delivering a more sustainable society, but only within a system that allows wealth creators to flourish, create jobs and pay taxes. Any alternative ideology that kills ambition and aspiration will dilute rather than deliver the answers.

I have talked repeatedly about a multi-stakeholder approach to business; how we need to recognise our duty to both the wealth of society and the environment. I have shown how Iceland has inspired people from all walks of life on issues such as plastic reduction, rainforest protection and nature engagement. I know that understanding and reducing our business's impacts is critical, as is sharing what we learn with others along the way.

Ultimately, I think what we really need is more 'corporate *dugnad*': business people treating their business like it's a community. Business is, after all, just a bunch of people working together, for the benefit of other people. We're all interconnected. Society, business and government have responsibilities to each other.

Such a radical approach necessitates acting with both kindness and empathy towards the vast array of people that private enterprise affects – from suppliers and employees, to consumers and communities. Business needs to be mindful of the consequences of our actions on both society and the planet, and link our sense of human compassion with the environment.

This view of business leadership, which is becoming increasingly clear to me, doesn't always sit comfortably with older and more established players who relentlessly focus on shareholder profit. Instead, I look to the more holistic approach of some smaller, disruptive businesses, who see the benefit of creating purpose-driven value for customers, colleagues – and perhaps, most importantly, for future generations.

I believe more than ever that kindness is not just the prerogative of a good business – in fact, kindness is the currency of a healthy society. The 2020 pandemic had a devastating impact on our world, with a great deal of collateral damage to economies and communities. It brought out the worst in people, but also the best.

Within the business sector, it drove extraordinary collaboration, innovation and a rethinking of what's normal. In such moments, whatever is broken in business and society is revealed. But it is also an opportunity to glimpse how we might do things better. There is an opening for change and reflection that just wasn't there before.

It's made us face up to the reality of inequality and power dynamics, of what's important in society and the kind of future we want to live in. Suddenly, kindness matters more than anything.

You don't see kindness on an MBA syllabus. So, what do I mean by kindness and what does it have to do with business leadership? By 'kindness', I am not just talking about a word that ticks a CSR box. Genuine kindness is not something you consciously adopt, but rather the output from a set of values. My values come from the way I was brought up, the embedded culture that has been curated within our business over 50 years, and my life experiences along the way.

I've discovered that I make better decisions if I put myself in other peoples' shoes. Because change comes about not from what I do or say, but how I make others feel. If they are inspired to action, real change happens.

Kindness is the result of empathy.

The explosion of the Black Lives Matter movement laid bare many issues, not least the deep divisions across societies that have resulted in a lack of empathy to one another. As H.R. McMaster said on BBC Radio 4's *Rethinking Empathy*: 'Lack of empathy is rooted in ignorance and an unwillingness to listen.' The podcast went on to say, 'Indeed, so much of life today pushes against the nurturing of our empathetic instincts; yet if we cultivate empathy for one another, we can strengthen our world.'[15]

It's not just about the beauty of the nature that's around us – it's about caring about the poorest in our society, those who are overlooked, the developing world, inequality, diversity, health and education. Business does not operate within a vacuum, and the tribulations of the world today are very much on our watch. It's time to deal with the causes, and not just the symptoms.

Social justice, a safe climate for humanity and a flourishing natural world are all inextricably linked. You cannot consider one without the others. When fighting for a social foundation for all, we must repair the multiple ecological ceilings that we are currently breaching.

The only way to make people really care about environmentalism – to make it more accessible – is to inspire belief. Yet belief will only happen if people are shown why something should matter to them. And issues only matter to people if they are made relevant.

Our customers were motivated to avoid GM foods because they didn't want their families to gamble with the unknown consequences of 'Frankenstein foods'. The public became advocates against tropical rainforest deforestation because they didn't want to inadvertently drive the orangutan to extinction. People become inspired if they can relate to issues – and simply don't care if they cannot.

So how can the people of Whitehaven ever be so inspired by climate change that they would forego the only realistic opportunity of job security they are likely to get? The answer is simple: they won't be – and nor should they.

On the road that lies ahead, we need to rediscover how to have meaningful conversations, laced with nuance and ambiguity. When fervent environmentalists present their views as binary choices, it merely adds to many others feeling annoyed, alienated or overlooked.

We need to build coalition, not division.

Paradoxes are found everywhere. Norway's credentials are to be applauded – yet thanks to its vast oil reserves, it is also the seventh-largest exporter of greenhouse gas emissions.[16] From a corporate perspective, as I have explained, there is actually no such thing as a sustainable business; we can only seek to minimise our impacts. The very phrase 'corporate activism' is contrastive.

Personally, I am full of contradictions: a supporter of equality and a wealthy businessman; an environmentalist, who loves going on adventures to the other side of the planet; someone who cares deeply about the health of our ecosystems, who also runs a food business that often scores low on many environmental surveys.

We cannot solve all these problems at once, but we can recognise them and deal with each one in turn, depending on what is pragmatically possible. That's what we have tried to achieve at Iceland, in our role as a corporate activist. I've found that it involves trade-offs and tough choices at every turn; but we keep moving towards our goals.

If the world waits for perfect solutions with no contradictions, we will stand still. We all need to do our very best, and to not be frightened of criticism or threatened by getting things wrong. We need to take pride in the difference that we can all make – and most importantly, take action. That is *how* we will improve our world.

As citizens, we have choices over who we vote for, where our savings are invested, being a conscious consumer and reducing our own environmental footprints. These all make a difference. Combined, they make all the difference.

As the polar-explorer-turned environmentalist Robert Swan put it, 'The greatest danger to our planet is the belief that someone else will save it.'[17]

. . . .

I'll let you into a secret: every single day I fret about whether I'm making best use of my life. After all, there isn't a sequel for any of us. I've been ridiculously lucky to be born into a world that has so many doors open to me, and I sometimes feel guilty that I am not charging through as many of them as possible.

Considering that in 2018 the IPCC warned us that we only have 12 years left to stop runaway climate change[18] (a deadline now less than a decade away) – am I really having maximum impact doing what I'm doing? Was I *really* put on this planet to sell frozen peas?

Of course, the official answer is that by helping to run Iceland and by making it successful, I can use it as a vehicle for corporate activism – and have more social and environmental influence than anywhere else. But I have to keep reminding myself of that fact. Sometimes the daily grind of running a budget supermarket, in one of the most competitive markets in the world, at a time of great disruption and intense competition ... well, it can be a bit overwhelming.

I also feel an enormous sense of responsibility, not just for continued business success, but also to meet the targets we've set ourselves around plastic elimination, palm oil, food waste, carbon and everything else in between. These are all, of course, things that I'm determined to do – however 'impossible' or whatever vitriol is thrown at me.

And I feel an even greater sense of responsibility to our customers and colleagues. Of course, I'm sure there are some who would be happy to see the back of me ... but I know there are also many who are pinning their hopes on me. Willing me on to succeed. Believing in me.

I've always been fascinated by successful organisations, businesspeople, activists and politicians. Like many others, I've often looked for the common thread in their behaviour or actions. Less *what* they've done, but *how* they've done it. I want to know their secret formulas and decode their magic.

Inspiration can come from the most unlikely places, too. From the army of everyday people with learned experience, who intuitively know what the barriers to change are, and know how to fix things if you simply take the trouble to ask them.

Someone once described me as 'a new car with high mileage'. The truth is that I often blag the number of miles I've travelled; and I'm no longer that new either. But what I have come to learn on my journey through life is that success comes from having courage. Courage to believe and to give others that same belief. Because once belief sets in, any mission is possible. Even missions as impossible as reducing inequality, reaching net zero carbon emissions or restoring nature that's been lost by human activity.

And the greatest tool that any government, business or organisation can deploy is to harness the power of collective belief. Attempting significant change alone is foolish, but convincing others to join you is powerful.

I like to think that my father has showcased an

excellent example of the power of belief. In the 50 years since he started Iceland, he has been through countless challenges and tough times. Recessions, inflation, deflation, competition and regulation. As we often say, Iceland today is an oddity: a company with just over 2 per cent market share, focusing on frozen food yet only earning 30 per cent of its sales from that category. Convenient stores to shop in, yet not convenience stores per se. In summary: a business model that has evolved over time yet not something you would make up in a business plan today. And yet I don't think he has ever wavered in his belief. Our secret weapon is that our army of colleagues share in that belief too.

That's the sort of 'stubborn optimism', as Christiana Figueres and Tom Rivett-Carnac term it in their book *The Future We Choose*, which is required when facing up to today's existential challenges. Optimism can wrongly be inferred as a weakness of the naive. In business, I have found the opposite – it is a trait inherent in the most hard-nosed and pragmatic of entrepreneurial minds.

Having the courage of your conviction is contagious and will make people believe in you and want to follow you. It's all very well having an idea but having the single-minded determination to see it through to fruition is something quite rare. I've seen that quality repeatedly in Dad – coming up with esoteric ideas, ignoring the eye-rolling, the sceptics and making things happen.

Sometimes I wish I was running a company like Patagonia. Their customers are, by definition, outdoor enthusiasts who buy the company's premium-priced products in order to help Patagonia in their unequivocal mission: 'to help save our home planet'.

If Iceland had such a natural fit between customer, product and environment I could really dial up our corporate activism. And yet the reality is we don't. The majority of our customers are chiefly concerned with putting food on the table for their families rather than saving the planet. We're shopkeepers, not an NGO. I have to recognise that fact and sometimes that's frustrating.

But as I have explained throughout this book, this reality also presents an important opportunity to make these links between our customers and environmental issues where normally they might not happen. To 'democratise environmentalism' – making ethical choices available to everyone, not just the privileged.

Any business – large or small – must of course work within the confines of the markets they operate in and the internal politics that exist. But that should never be an excuse for inaction or looking the other way. With the enormous challenges humanity now faces, it is surely incumbent on all organisations to question what they can pragmatically do to change and how they can be better stewards of our planet.

Yet to succeed it is simply not enough to pay lip-service to such initiatives; we must believe in them too.

. . . .

Despite the wildfires, the droughts, the human health consequences and rising levels of inequality, undeterred by the apocalyptic warnings of ecological tipping points impacting the most vulnerable or the effects of nature's unrelenting diminishment – I certainly do not despair. In fact, I see opportunity and encouragement on a daily basis from a multitude of places.

By late 2020, not only had China set its ambition of carbon neutrality by 2060 and was vocally encouraging world leaders to respect and restore nature, but Joe Biden had won the White House, which is set to turbocharge a massive wave of green investment and a long hoped-for Green New Deal. This will trigger a domino effect: positive policy loops across the world, not least in the UK where prime minister Boris Johnson is planning a wind, hydrogen and nuclear-powered revolution in order to accelerate significant carbon reduction by 2030.

Across the private sector, businesses large and small are embracing the opportunities and responsibilities that the green revolution will bring. From the net zero and nature restoration goals of big business, to the hugely exciting technologies being embraced by start-ups, shift is happening.

Importantly, the money is following – in October 2020, NextEra (a clean-power utility) had surpassed ExxonMobil to become America's biggest energy firm.[19] The EV manufacturer Tesla now has a bigger market capitalisation than General Motors, Ford and Fiat Chrysler combined.[20] Investors can see the writing on the wall: EVs will reach cost parity with petro and diesel by 2023, but with much lower operating costs.[21]

With the plunging cost of renewables, the decarbonisation calculus is completely changing. Around the world, countries are transitioning to a low carbon infrastructure. According to the energy tracker MyGridGB, coal accounted for less than 2 per cent of the UK's energy mix in 2020.[22] The International Energy Agency (IEA) have announced that globally, wind and solar power will overtake oil and gas by 2024.[23]

With rapidly increasing technological innovation, businesses and jobs in entirely new sectors are emerging. These range from the large-scale 'blue water farming' of kelp, which both sequesters carbon and produces a variety of raw material uses, to the highly productive insect farms creating protein for animal feedstocks, and are now attracting huge investor interest.

Following a visit to Solar Foods, the writer George Monbiot described how the Finnish company is literally turning water into food by brewing microbes fuelled by hydrogen to create flours intended for feedstocks. But with a few tweaks, the bacteria can be modified to replace palm and fish oils, or the proteins needed for lab-grown meat, milk and eggs. The future possibility of actually being able to feed the estimated 9 billion people on our planet sustainably suddenly seems possible.[24]

Communities are also taking matters into their own hands. By November 2020, 1,830 jurisdictions in 31 countries had declared a climate emergency – amounting to over 820 million citizens around the world.[25] Greta Thunberg had become a global icon, inspiring a new generation of climate activists.

Christiana Figueres has termed these twin narratives 'competing exponential curves'; whereby we are now seemingly facing both an ever-increasing cycle of ecological destruction ... and a fresh wave of recognition and activism from politicians, corporations and communities.[26] Both curves are rapidly sharpening, month by month, day by day and hour by hour. We urgently need to make sure that the right curve wins.

I firmly believe it will.

ENDNOTES

Prologue

[1] *Do Purpose*, Hieatt (2014)

Introduction

[1] https://www.facebook.com/NgoziOkonjoIweala/posts/1124830400900556:0
FaceBook post by Ngozi Okonjo-Iweala from 2 April 2016
[2] Which I named Peak Rhianydd after my Mum: http://publications.americanalpineclub.org/articles/13201214451/Central-and-Western-At-Bashi-Pik-Rhianydd-and-Other-Ascents
[3] My Dad and I set the targets of trying to reach the mountain's North Col at 23,000ft and raise £1 million for Alzheimer's – we successfully achieved both: https://about.iceland.co.uk/wp-content/uploads/2017/12/Iceland_Everest_Expedition-launch_25211.pdf
[4] https://www.edelman.co.uk/research/edelman-trust-barometer-2020
[5] Ibid
[6] Our sustainability website is: https://sustainability.iceland.co.uk
[7] https://plasticoceans.org/the-facts/
[8] https://www.shropshirestar.com/news/business/2020/06/09/shropshire-founded-iceland-back-in-british-hands/
[9] US research has shown that privately held companies, free to take a longer-term approach, invest at almost 2.5 times the rate of publicly held counterparts in the same industries: https://www.ft.com/content/bce20202-d703-11e4-97c3-00144feab7de
[10] https://www.telegraph.co.uk/business/2019/06/12/average-tenure-ftse-100-boss-grows-first-time-three-years/
[11] https://cpag.org.uk/child-poverty/child-poverty-facts-and-figures
[12] www.trusselltrust.org
[13] https://www.independentliving.co.uk/advice/malnutrition-on-the-rise/
[14] https://www.thelondoneconomic.com/news/food-banks-now-outnumber-mcdonalds-in-britain/09/12/
[15] https://news.un.org/en/story/2020/01/1055681
[16] https://oxfamilibrary.openrepository.com/bitstream/handle/10546/620599/bp-public-good-or-private-wealth-210119-en.pdf?utm_source=indepth
[17] https://www.theguardian.com/environment/2018/jun/11/chris-packham-springwatch-warns-of-ecological-apocalypse-britain
[18] https://www.plantlife.org.uk/uk/about-us/news/real-action-needed-to-save-our-vanishing-meadows
[19] https://www.iucn-uk-peatlandprogramme.org/about-peatlands/peatland-damage
[20] https://www.sciencedirect.com/science/article/pii/S0006320718313636
[21] https://news.brown.edu/articles/2014/09/extinctions
[22] https://www.climatecentral.org/gallery/graphics/top-10-warmest-years-on-record
[23] https://www.ncei.noaa.gov/news/projected-ranks#:~:text=The%20warmest%20years%20globally%20have,Courtesy%20of%20NOAA%20NCEI
[24] https://www.climatecentral.org/gallery/graphics/top-10-warmest-years-on-record

25 http://www.fao.org/publications/sofi/en/
26 https://www.theguardian.com/environment/2019/
feb/04/a-third-of-himalayan-ice-cap-doomed-finds-shocking-report
27 http://www.globalforestwatch.org/topics/biodiversity/#intro
28 https://gfw.global/34CobMb
29 https://www.theguardian.com/science/2020/oct/27/sleeping-giant-arctic-methane-deposits-starting-to-release-scientists-find
30 *The Nature of Nature*, Enric Sala (2020)
31 https://news.mongabay.com/2018/03/amazon-forest-to-savannah-tipping-point-could-be-far-closer-than-thought-commentary/
32 https://www.nature.com/articles/s41586-020-3010-5
33 https://globalfishingwatch.org
34 https://www.ellenmacarthurfoundation.org/publications/the-new-plastics-economy-rethinking-the-future-of-plastics-catalysing-action
35 https://www.theworldcounts.com/challenges/planet-earth/oceans/coral-reef-destruction/story
36 https://www.iea.org/articles/global-co2-emissions-in-2019
37 https://www.mckinsey.com/~/media/mckinsey/business%20functions/strategy%20and%20corporate%20finance/our%20insights/how%20executives%20can%20help%20sustain%20value%20creation%20for%20the%20long%20term/corporate-long-term-behaviors-how-ceos-and-boards-drive-sustained-value%20creation.pdf
38 https://climateactiontracker.org/publications/global-update-paris-agreement-turning-point/

Chapter 1

1 One of Dad's favourite and oft-repeated phrases, which sums up his determination, commitment and will to win at whatever he puts his mind to.

2 For a riveting account of how my Dad started and grew the business, and the many twists and turns he faced along the way, look no further than his 2013 autobiography *Best Served Cold*.

3 Forty-five years later, in a populist pre-election move, the Icelandic government took out legal action against Iceland Foods for breach of copyright: https://www.theweek.co.uk/79097/iceland-the-country-sues-iceland-the-supermarket-over-name I suppose we can blame Mum for that!

4 He paid her back.

5 Freezing food at source makes slower forms of transportation possible to the end retailer. The greenhouse gas emitted from air-freighting fresh Norwegian salmon is significantly higher than freezing it and transporting via container ship: https://www.researchgate.net/publication/256048653_The_Carbon_Footprint_of_Norwegian_Seafood_Products_on_the_Global_Seafood_Market.

6 A good example is the month-old 'fresh' turkey consumers buy at Christmas: https://www.dailymail.co.uk/news/article-7794155/Supermarkets-conning-shoppers-paying-fresh-turkeys-slaughtered-November.html

7 An excellent summary of the issues by people from all sides of the debate (along with the benefit of 20 years' worth of hindsight) was the BBC's *The Reunion* podcast. There's an

audio clip of an old interview with my Dad at 13 minutes in, with a notably stronger Yorkshire accent than he has today. Time has clearly made him smoother around the edges: https://www.bbc.co.uk/programmes/m000mbpp

[8] Ibid

[9] Ibid

[10] Ibid

[11] Ibid

[12] https://books.google.co.uk/books?id=88WLT_oPLdcC&pg=PA14&lpg=PA14&dq=GM+campaign+Iceland+launch+1998&source=bl&ots=oFCcTyCHjl&sig=ACfU3U1yxmKL-1bXKuOTvnd_tYxY5amexg&hl=en&sa=X&ved=2ahUKEwj12_m375XqAhUElFwKHaeDCWQ4ChDoATABegQIBxAB#v=onepage&q=GM%20campaign%20Iceland%20launch%201998&f=false

[13] Monsanto, now owned by Bayer, insisted that Roundup was safe, and announced that it would appeal: https://www.telegraph.co.uk/news/2019/05/14/california-jury-orders-monsanto-pay-2-billion-damages-couple/

[14] For a simplified but watchable summary of some of the issues, the Netflix documentary *Kiss the Ground* is well worth a watch.

[15] A great book to read on the thorny topics for environmentalists of genetic engineering, geoengineering and nuclear power is *Whole Earth Discipline* by Stewart Brand (2009)

[16] The Montreal Protocol, originally signed in 1987 and revised numerous times over the succeeding decades, set out to protect ozone depletion by phasing out substances such as CFCs. It is heralded as one of the most successful examples of a truly global environmental treaty, delivered with exceptional international cooperation. But it is also a sobering example of unintended consequence: CFCs were replaced in air conditioning and refrigerants by HFCs. While HFCs are not harmful to the ozone layer, their capacity to warm the atmosphere is 1,000–9,000 times greater than carbon dioxide. Indeed, according to Project Drawdown HFC removal has been calculated as the number one action the world can take to alleviate global warming (https://www.drawdown.org/solutions/refrigerant-management). Despite challenging global politics, the Kigali Amendment to the Montreal Protocol was reached in 2016, which phases out HFCs through the 2020s. Iceland is now working with suppliers to research and trial HFC substitutes for our freezers, including natural refrigerants such as propane and ammonia.

[17] See: *Ahead of the Curve: Cases of Innovation in Environmental Management*, Green, K. Groenewegen, P. and Hofman, P.S. (Eds) (2001) and: *Business Ethics: Managing Corporate Citizenship and Sustainability in the Age of Globalization*, Crane, A. and Matten, D. (2007)

[18] https://www.shropshirestar.com/entertainment/attractions/2020/06/03/chester-zoo-at-risk-of-extinction-as-gates-remain-closed/

[19] https://www.dailymail.co.uk/news/article-8403033/Iceland-supermarket-adopts-Chester-Zoos-penguins-help-attraction-raise-funds.html

[20] https://about.iceland.co.uk/great-place-to-work/

[21] Proving that a sense of being valued and respected by employees is paramount.

[22] https://www.bbc.co.uk/news/uk-44720109

[23] And if you raise an eyebrow at the £5,000 a head carbon extravagancy of the trip, you'd of course be right. But remember that for many this was a rare long-haul flight, and for all it was the trip of a lifetime. If you're going to fly, as people sparingly should, make sure you make the most of it.

24 https://www.theguardian.com/society/2020/jun/26/millions-went-hungry-during-first-months-of-uk-lockdown-figures-show-coronavirus

25 https://en.wikipedia.org/wiki/Disappearance_of_Patrick_Warren_and_David_Spencer

26 https://www.campaignlive.co.uk/article/iceland-launches-milk-carton-initiative-missing-people/856538

27 https://www.bbc.co.uk/news/world-europe-13364178

28 https://blogs.scientificamerican.com/plugged-in/un-says-that-if-food-waste-was a country-ite28099d-be-the-3-global-greenhouse-gas-emitter/

29 https://www.nationalgeographic.com/foodfeatures/feeding-9-billion/

30 https://www.foodmanufacture.co.uk/Article/2020/09/03/Food-production-reform-urged-to-cut-greenhouse-gas-emissions

31 https://www.wrap.org.uk/sites/files/wrap/Food%20Surplus%20and%20Waste%20 in%20the%20UK%20Key%20Facts%2011%2010%2018.pdf

32 https://www.iceland.co.uk/birds-eye-and-iceland-june-release/birds-eye-and-iceland-june-release.html

33 'The impact of food preservation on food waste', *British Food Journal* 119 (12) 2510-2518, Martindale W. & Schiebel W. (2017) http://bfff.co.uk/wp-content/uploads/2015/03/Frozen-Food-and-Food-Security-in-the-UK-Executive-Summary.pdf

34 https://wrap.org.uk/sites/files/wrap/Food_%20surplus_and_waste_in_the_UK_key_facts_Jan_2020.pdf

35 https://sustainability.iceland.co.uk/our-planet/food-waste/

36 Ibid

37 Ibid

38 Ibid

39 Ibid

40 https://about.iceland.co.uk/wp-content/uploads/2020/05/Iceland-announces-23-food-waste-reduction-and-launches-nationwide-colleague-food-redistribution-trial.pdf

41 https://www.feedingamerica.org/about-us/partners/become-a-product-partner/tax-benefits-for-your-company

42 https://www.legco.gov.hk/research-publications/english/1617in18-food-donation-policies-in-selected-places-20170830-e.pdf

43 https://www.telegraph.co.uk/news/2020/02/10/almost-half-councils-fail-collect-food-waste-households/

44 https://deframedia.blog.gov.uk/2020/02/10/household-food-waste-to-be-collected-separately-by-2023-and 50000 city-trees-to-be-planted-in-urban-tree-challenge-fund/

45 http://sustainability.iceland.co.uk/wp-content/uploads/2020/07/Carbon-Our-Story-So-Far-2020.pdf

46 Ibid

47 Ibid

48 While calls for a much higher 'Real Living Wage' superficially sound like the right thing to do, the reality is that such a large cost increase would put impossible pressure on the operating margins of many large employers – including Iceland – and this means that it is simply not a viable option. If such a scheme were made compulsory, it would inevitably lead to companies raising prices, reducing contracted hours for staff, and ultimately result in job losses.

49 https://about.iceland.co.uk/our-performance/

50 https://ifcf.org.uk/our-story/

51 https://www.ons.gov.uk/peoplepopulationandcommunity/healthandsocialcare/
causesofdeath/articles/leadingcausesofdeathuk/2001to2018
52 https://www.dementiastatistics.org/statistics-about-dementia/human-and-financial-
impact/
53 In 2015–16, UK dementia research charities funded approximately £23m of research in
2015–16, compared to 13 times the amount (£310m) of charity research funding for
cancer: https://www.dementiastatistics.org/statistics/funding-comparisons/
54 Liverpool's Alder Hey having previously been a predictably popular charity partner.
55 A link to the DRI can be found here: https://www.ucl.ac.uk/uk-dementia-research-
institute/
56 *Doing It Right*, Peter Pugh (1991)

Chapter 2

1 *Business As Unusual: The Journey of Anita Roddick and The Body Shop*, Anita Roddick
(2000). A great book recounting Anita's ideology of corporate responsibility and
accountability.
2 https://www.bbc.co.uk/news/uk-england-london-50079716
3 *Business As Unusual*, Anita Roddick (2000)
4 https://6fefcbb86e61af1b2fc4-c70d8ead6ced550b4d987d7c03fcdd1d.ssl.cf3.rackcdn.
com/cms/reports/documents/000/002/327/original/Carbon-Majors-Report-2017.
pdf?1501833772
5 https://www.economist.com/special-report/2006/11/23/a-heavyweight-champ-at-five-foot-two
6 https://www.johnobrien.world
7 https://www.edelman.com/research/2018-edelman-trust-barometer
8 *Trailblazer*, Marc Benioff (2019)
9 The only time I met Philip Green was at a wake. I walked up to him, alongside my Dad.
Philip smirked and said 'Hello Malcolm' … before poking him in the groin. Even from that
fleeting encounter, I would say that Steve Coogan's 2019 portrayal of him in the film
Greed was entirely accurate.
10 https://www.bbc.co.uk/programmes/m000cz18
11 https://blogs.microsoft.com/blog/2020/01/16/microsoft-will-be-carbon-negative-
by-2030/
12 https://www.fsb.org.uk/uk-small-business-statistics.html
13 https://govandbusinessjournal.ng/the-impact-of-smes-on-global-economy-the-new-
perspective/
14 https://www.intracen.org/news/SMEs-drive-world-trade-and-economic-growth/
15 An example: rather than spending £20,000 on joining the Roundtable on Responsible
Soy Association (which seeks to alleviate deforestation caused by soy farmers), as I
discuss in Chapter 4, Iceland will spend that money instead on sourcing a chicken
product that hasn't been fed on soy whatsoever – a market first.
16 A good example: https://www.theguardian.com/sustainable-business/2015/sep/03/
diageo-results-drinks-multinational-sustainability-targets-corporate-commitments
17 *The Future We Choose*, Christiana Figueres and Tom Rivett-Carnac (2020)
18 https://www.goodreads.com/quotes/19742-success-is-stumbling-from-failure-to-
failure-with-no-loss

[19] https://medium.com/@amazonemployeesclimatejustice/public-letter-to-jeff-bezos-and-the-amazon-board-of-directors-82a8405f5e38

[20] https://www.independent.co.uk/voices/jeff-bezos-firefighter-cosplay-money-amazon-climate-environment-billionaire-a9343061.html

[21] Examples abound, such as the carcinogenic drinking water resulting from the chemical manufacturer DuPont's illegal contamination of a West Virginian town at the turn of the millennium, as profiled in the 2019 film *Dark Waters*.

[22] 'Why we need to put a number on nature', Gillian Tett, *FT Magazine* (26 September 2020)

[23] *Financing Nature*, Paulson Institute, The Nature Conservancy and Cornell University (2020)

[24] https://www.bp.com/en/global/corporate/news-and-insights/reimagining-energy/web-summit-2020.html

[25] https://www.upi.com/Top_News/World-News/2019/12/01/UN-secretary-general-appoints-new-special-envoy-for-climate-action-ahead-of-COP25/2761575224153/

[26] https://www.accountingtoday.com/news/big-four-firms-release-esg-reporting-metrics-with-world-economic-forum

[27] *Green Swans*, John Elkington (2020)

[28] Ibid

[29] https://www.azquotes.com/author/20919-Herb_Kelleher

[30] https://www.ft.com/content/e7040df4-fa19-11e8-8b7c-6fa24bd5409c

[31] https://imagine.one

[32] Ibid

[33] https://www.gov.uk/government/groups/council-for-sustainable-business

[34] A once-in-a-generation and hugely ambitious framework. For further detail, see: https://www.gov.uk/government/publications/25-year-environment-plan

[35] https://councilforsustainablebusiness.com

[36] https://www2.deloitte.com/tr/en/pages/about-deloitte/articles/millennialsurvey-2018.html

[37] https://www.edelman.com/research/2019-edelman-trust-barometer

[38] At the end of 2018, Iceland's YouGov Brand Buzz score (a measure of trust, consideration, and perceptions of quality and value) was the highest for a decade. Consumer consideration of Iceland grew to the highest of any retailer, placing Iceland ahead of Waitrose. The palm oil campaign lifted the brand's 'talkability' score, making Iceland the second-most-talked-about supermarket brand after Aldi. Before the campaign, Iceland was ranked seventh.

[39] https://www.ft.com/content/e7040df4-fa19-11e8-8b7c-6fa24bd5409c

[40] https://www.ft.com/content/e61046bc-7a2e-11e8-8e67-1e1a0846c475

[41] https://www.economist.com/leaders/2019/02/09/the-truth-about-big-oil-and-climate-change

[42] https://www.telegraph.co.uk/finance/personalfinance/investing/9021946/How-long-does-the-average-share-holding-last-Just-22-seconds.html

[43] *Prosperity: Better Business Makes the Greater Good*, Colin Mayer (2018)

[44] https://www.blackrock.com/corporate/investor-relations/larry-fink-ceo-letter

[45] http://www.irn-research.com/market-research-reports/uk-pension-market-market-trends-report-2020/

[46] https://nordeainvestmagasinet.dk/sites/default/files/inline-files/Regnestykke-baggrund.pdf

[47] https://makemymoneymatter.co.uk/

[48] https://uk.reuters.com/article/uk-bp-writeoffs/bp-to-take-up-to-13-9-billion-writedown-lowers-oil-outlook-idUKKBN23MON3

[49] https://www.forbes.com/sites/lbsbusinessstrategyreview/2020/01/29/why-sustainability-was-the-star-at-davos-2020/#25754ac776a3

[50] https://www.rt.com/business/467366-energy-worst-performing-sector/

[51] https://www.bbc.co.uk/ideas/videos/theres-a-danger-of-losing-our-tenure-on-this-plane/p06yyqvc?playlist=extraordinary-pioneers

[52] https://www.airspacemag.com/daily-planet/how-much-worlds-population-has-flown-airplane-180957719/

[53] https://www.ipcc.ch/report/ar5/wg3/

[54] https://trackingsdg7.esmap.org/data/files/download-documents/2019-Tracking%20SDG7-Full%20Report.pdf

[55] For a definitive guide to the most promising current and future solutions that will decarbonise our world, see: www.drawdown.org

[56] Summary of 'What if carbon removal becomes the new Big Oil?' and 'What if technology tracked all carbon emissions?' From 'The World If' series by *The Economist* (July 2020)

[57] https://www.ukgbc.org/climate-change/

[58] In the UK, we have a planning system that makes any 'change of use' exceptionally timely and costly – such as converting offices into residential. We also charge VAT on renovating homes, whereas new-build houses are VAT exempt, encouraging the building of new over the repurposing of old. As a result, there are around 200,000 dilapidated houses according to the charity Empty Homes.

[59] https://www.academia.edu/18481731/Embodied_energy_analysis_of_fixtures_fittings_and_furniture_in_office_buildings

[60] https://www.rypeoffice.com

[61] https://www.ons.gov.uk/peoplepopulationandcommunity/personalandhouseholdfinances/expenditure/bulletins/familyspendingintheuk/april2018tomarch2019

[62] https://www.independent.co.uk/news/uk/home-news/survey-of-family-spending-charts-half-century-of-consumer-culture-775185.html

[63] https://nbn.org.uk/stateofnature2019/

[64] https://www.thetimes.co.uk/edition/news/free-range-egg-farms-choking-life-out-of-the-wye-rt3c763qc

[65] Personal email correspondence (January 2020)

[66] White-shelled eggs are laid by less aggressive birds that don't need to have their beaks trimmed.

[67] https://www.bbc.co.uk/sounds/play/p08k0jj0

[68] https://ourworldindata.org/food-ghg-emissions

[69] As a window into what these might be, in 2016 startling images emerged from the Chinese province of Sichuan showing workers hand-pollinating pear blossoms with long feathered sticks. Following decades of intensive insecticide spraying, local bee populations have disappeared – along with their essential services. See: https://www.huffingtonpost.co.uk/entry/humans-bees-china_n_570404b3e4b083f5c6092ba9

[70] http://www.fao.org/soils-2015/events/detail/en/c/338738/

[71] For further info, see: https://www.no-meat.co.uk
[72] *Ecological Intelligence*, Daniel Goleman (2009)
[73] *The responsible company*, Yvon Chouinard and Vincent Stanley (2012)

Chapter 3

[1] *Frankenstein*, Mary Shelley (1818)
[2] https://www.bpf.co.uk/article/bpf-response-to-icelands-announcement-1261.aspx
[3] Tweet by Theresa May (17 January 2018)
[4] Personal correspondence from Michael Gove MP to Malcolm Walker (16 January 2018)
[5] Cross-party letter to then Tesco CEO Dave Lewis urging the company to follow Iceland's lead, co-written by Catherine West MP and Sue Hayman MP and signed by more than 200 additional MPs (18 January 2018)
[6] https://www.thegrocer.co.uk/power-list/packaging-power-list-the-10-most-powerful-people-in-fmcg-packaging/566888.article
[7] https://www.weforum.org/agenda/2016/10/every-minute-one-garbage-truck-of-plastic-is-dumped-into-our-oceans/
[8] https://www.theguardian.com/environment/2018/jan/17/nearly-1m-tonnes-every-year-supermarkets-shamed-for-plastic-packaging
[9] https://www.ft.com/content/981f3f16-9625-4c47-b67d-0a4dd23cbd79
[10] https://www.nationalgeographic.co.uk/environment-and-conservation/2018/05/plastic-bag-found-bottom-worlds-deepest-ocean-trench
[11] https://www.newplasticseconomy.org/assets/doc/EllenMacArthurFoundation_TheNewPlasticsEconomy_Pages.pdf
[12] At a very special dinner organised by a friend, the astronaut Buzz Aldrin told me how upon finding himself stuck on the Moon (due to a broken switch on the Apollo 11 lunar module), he used a plastic biro to unjam it – enabling take-off and their safe return home. He still has his lucky plastic pen.
[13] https://plasticoceans.org/the-facts/
[14] https://www.theguardian.com/books/2016/apr/01/generation-anthropocene-altered-planet-for-ever
[15] https://www.ciel.org/wp-content/uploads/2019/05/Plastic-and-Climate-FINAL-2019.pdf
[16] https://journals.plos.org/plosone/article?id=10.1371/journal.pone.0200574
[17] https://www.ciel.org/wp-content/uploads/2019/02/Plastic-and-Health-The-Hidden-Costs-of-a-Plastic-Planet-February-2019.pdf
[18] https://www.sciencedirect.com/science/article/abs/pii/S0025326X16307639
[19] http://www.ecotox.ugent.be/microplastics-bivalves-cultured-human-consumption
[20] https://wwfeu.awsassets.panda.org/downloads/plastic_ingestion_web_spreads_1.pdf
[21] https://www.ncbi.nlm.nih.gov/pmc/articles/PMC4428475/
[22] https://www.dailymail.co.uk/news/article-5351661/Chemicals-plastic-90-teenage-bodies.html
[23] https://www.nationalgeographic.com/science/2020/01/pfas-contamination-safe-drinking-water-study/
[24] https://www.theguardian.com/lifeandstyle/2018/feb/19/are-we-poisoning-our-children-with-plastic
[25] *The Complete Guide to Environmental Packaging*, Aldridge and Miller (2012)
[26] https://www.paradise11.co.uk
[27] https://www.chathamhouse.org/sites/default/files/publications/2018-06-13-making-

concrete-change-cement-lehne-preston-final.pdf

[28] https://www.keepbritaintidy.org/sites/default/files/resource/KBT17_Policy_Position_Chewing_Gum_Litter.pdf

[29] https://www.seeturtles.org/ocean-plastic

[30] https://www.thetimes.co.uk/article/scourge-of-more-than-1-billion-plastic-bags-for-life-cjg0cm8ds

[31] http://sustainability.iceland.co.uk/wp-content/uploads/2020/03/Iceland-Plastics-Annual-Report-2019.pdf

[32] A must-read for anyone wanting to understand and reduce their personal plastic footprint.

[33] https://www.economist.com/graphic-detail/2018/03/06/only-9-of-the-worlds-plastic-is-recycled

[34] https://en.wikipedia.org/wiki/Recycling_rates_by_country

[35] Jambeck J.R. (2015); Hoornweg, D. Bhada-Tata, P. (2012)

[36] https://en.wikipedia.org/wiki/China%27s_waste_import_ban

[37] https://www.economist.com/international/2020/06/22/covid-19-has-led-to-a-pandemic-of-plastic-pollution

[38] https://www.ufz.de/export/data/2/149396_EGU_2017_Schmidt.pdf#search=%22plastic%20rivers%22

[39] Norway is seen as the global leader when it comes to DRS, with statistics showing it has a 96 per cent recycling rate of plastic bottles since its introduction in 1999.

[40] Now an annual event, and a heck of a party: https://www.plasticfreeawards.com

[41] https://www.statista.com/statistics/281241/online-share-of-retail-trade-in-european-countries/

[42] https://unearthed.greenpeace.org/2020/08/30/plastic-waste-africa-oil-kenya-us-trade-deal-trump/

[43] https://www.economist.com/international/2020/06/22/covid-19-has-led-to-a-pandemic-of-plastic-pollution

[44] https://unearthed.greenpeace.org/2019/05/10/industry-calls-on-philip-hammond-to-weaken-his-planned-plastics-tax/

[45] http://sustainability.iceland.co.uk/wp-content/uploads/2020/09/Iceland-Plastic-Packaging-Footprint-2019.pdf

[46] https://corporate.lidl.co.uk/sustainability/plastics

[47] The Environment Bill, stymied by the Covid-19 pandemic, is finally back in the House of Commons at the time of writing in January 2021 – more than a year since it was introduced for debate.

[48] Sustainable Business Leadership Survey, edie (2019)

[49] https://wedocs.unep.org/bitstream/handle/20.500.11822/25398/WED%20Messaging%20Two-Page%2027April.pdf?sequence=12&isAllowed=y

Chapter 4

[1] Statement on being Awarded the Schlich Forestry Medal (29 January 1935)

[2] And I found it perplexing that such as scandal was apparently an 'open secret', well known to industry and government (https://www.ft.com/content/c2e42868-bf8f-11ea-9b66-39ae33ea12cb). Rather than wasting years pursuing their entirely spurious case against Iceland's Christmas Savings Club, the National Minimum Wage taskforce should

have taken enforcement action in Leicester years ago.

[3] https://www.thetimes.co.uk/article/blood-batteries-fuel-the-fortune-of-elon-musk-qkhlvp5dr

[4] http://ecological-problems.blogspot.com/2008/06/borneo-deforestation-and-endangered.html

[5] *How We're F***ing Up Our Planet*, Tony Juniper (2019)

[6] https://twitter.com/nature_org/status/601785680058916864

[7] You don't have to travel to the other side of the world to experience the beauty of rainforests. I would strongly recommend visiting the Eden Project's rainforest biome in Cornwall or reading Tony Juniper's book *Rainforest*. Both cheaper, less polluting options – without the risk of being chased by a jaguar.

[8] *Lord Leverhulme's Ghosts: Colonial Exploitation in the Congo*, Jules Marchal (2008)

[9] https://greennews.ie/biofuels-the-cure-worse-than-the-disease/#:~:text=The%20study%20analyses%20how%20on,and%20three%20times%20worse%20respectively.

[10] *Oil World Annual* (2019)

[11] https://www.transportenvironment.org/press/100-times-more-palm-oil-eu-diesel-all-oreo-cookies-world

[12] https://www.transportenvironment.org/what-we-do/biofuels/why-palm-oil-biodiesel-bad

[13] http://www.palmoilworld.org/about_malaysian-industry.html

[14] https://eur-lex.europa.eu/resource.html?uri=cellar:b160eb62-4580-11e9-a8ed-01aa75ed71a1.0008.02/DOC_1&format=PDF

[15] https://www.statista.com/statistics/613471/palm-oil-production-volume-worldwide/

[16] http://blog.globalforestwatch.org/data-and-research/global-tree-cover-loss-remains-high-and-emerging-patterns-reveal-shifting-contributors/

[17] The *Faces of Palm Oil* smear video was mostly met with derision and failed to gain any new supporters. My mates thought the video hilarious, however, and it's worth a watch: https://twitter.com/PalmOilFarmer/status/986725495420186624

[18] https://www.aljazeera.com/indepth/inpictures/2015/10/southeast-asia-hazardous-haze-151007061537973.html

[19] https://www.rainforest-rescue.org/topics/palm-oil#start

[20] https://www.dol.gov/ilab/reports/pdf/tvpra_report2014.pdf

[21] '2017 Trafficking in Persons Report', US State Department (2017), https://www.state.gov/documents/organization/271342.pdf page 208 (Indonesia) and https://www.state.gov/documents/organization/271343.pdf page 264 (Malaysia).

[22] https://www.thejakartapost.com/news/2018/11/03/farmers-dispute-palm-oil-prosperity-claims-environment.html#:~:text=Farmers%20have%20challenged%20claims%20that,to%20meet%20their%20basic%20needs

[23] https://chainreactionresearch.com/report/future-smallholder-deforestation-possible-palm-oil-risk/#:~:text=As%20independent%20smallholders%20are%20confronted%20with%20a%20large,five%20years%20before%20the%20new%20trees%20become%20productive

[24] https://www.wri.org/blog/2018/03/smallholder-farmers-are-key-making-palm-oil-industry-sustainable

[25] Unknown to me, *The Times* even ran an investigation and editorial into the 'highly personal online character assassination': https://www.thetimes.co.uk/article/palm-oil-lobby-smears-iceland-boss-richard-walker-tqldz85dh

[26] https://unearthed.greenpeace.org/2019/03/18/palm-oil-indonesia-malaysia-biofuels-eu/

[27] https://www.hellenicshippingnews.com/indonesias-palm-oil-export-drifts-down-11-pct-in-h1-as-epidemic-suppresses-demands/

[28] http://www.jonathonporritt.com/iceland-palm-oil-and-empty-pr-stunts/

[29] https://www.radiotimes.com/tv-programme/e/ghzryd/red-ape-saving-the-orangutan---e4-red-ape-saving-the-orangutan/

[30] https://www.cell.com/current-biology/fulltext/S0960-9822(18)30086-1

[31] 'Take time out to save the world', *The Times* (15 August 2019)

[32] https://www.thirdsector.co.uk/campaigns-good-awards-charity-ngo-category-winners-revealed/communications/article/1590264

[33] https://rspo.org/news-and-events/news/rspo-members-agree-on-new-palm-oil-standard-to-halt-deforestation-and-improve-human-rights-protection

[34] https://www.wilmar-international.com/docs/default-source/default-document-library/highlights/sustainability/latest-updates/news-release-10-dec-18-wilmar-leads-palm-oil-industry-to-be-deforestation-free.pdf

[35] https://www.nst.com.my/business/2019/03/466143/malaysia-cap-65m-ha-oil-palm-plantations-2023

[36] https://www.ft.com/content/b032046a-1360-11e9-a168-d45595ad076d

[37] For a summary of the BBC exposé see: https://www.bbc.co.uk/news/uk-46969920

[38] https://www.telegraph.co.uk/news/2019/05/12/no-good-companies-woke-customers-brexiteer-tories/

[39] Selling a Greener Future, *Creative Review* (August 2020)

[40] https://sustainability.iceland.co.uk/news/1-million-mangrove-trees-planted-as-part-of-icelands-50th-birthday-celebrations/

[41] Getting Amazon Destruction Off Your Dinner Plate: Forest Campaign 2020–21, Greenpeace UK (2020)

[42] In November 2020, the UK government announced its intention to introduce a new 'due diligence' law to stop businesses from using commodities linked to illegal deforestation, which is an excellent step in the right direction. See: https://assets.publishing.service.gov.uk/government/uploads/system/uploads/attachment_data/file/933985/due-diligence-forest-risk-commodities-government-response.pdf

[43] https://www.bbc.co.uk/news/business-55016453

[44] Under the trading scheme, countries and corporations can continue to pollute if they purchase carbon credits to offset their emissions. Furthermore, what count as 'credits' can seem disingenuous – the carbon not released from a standing forest that was under threat from deforestation, for example.

Chapter 5

[1] Interview with *The Times* entitled 'Bill Gates: from Microsoft to saving lives with Gavi and the Global Fund', Alice Thomson (published 16 March 2019)

[2] https://ipbes.net/covid19stimulus

[3] https://www.iucnredlist.org

[4] https://www.theguardian.com/environment/2019/feb/10/plummeting-insect-numbers-threaten-collapse-of-nature

[5] *A Life on Our Planet*, Sir David Attenborough (2020)

[6] https://www.kew.org/sites/default/files/2020-09/Kew%20State%20of%20the%20Worlds%20Plants%20and%20Fungi.pdf

7 https://ipbes.net/news/Media-Release-Global-Assessment

8 *The Nature of Nature*, Enric Sala (2020)

9 https://www.bbc.co.uk/news/science-environment-48169783

10 https://www.mckinsey.com/business-functions/sustainability/our-insights/valuing-nature-conservation#

11 http://www3.weforum.org/docs/WEF_New_Nature_Economy_Report_2020.pdf

12 https://www.bcg.com/publications/2020/the-staggering-value-of-forests-and-how-to-save-them

13 https://ipbes.net/covid19stimulus

14 https://www.gov.uk/government/news/supermarkets-to-join-forces-to-feed-the-nation

15 https://www.express.co.uk/news/uk/1265190/Iceland-coronavirus-shopping-latest-high-street-online

16 https://www.unilad.co.uk/news/fish-return-to-venices-canals-as-water-becomes-cleaner-during-coronavirus-lockdown/

17 https://www.dailymail.co.uk/sciencetech/article-8109819/Coronavirus-lockdown-Italy-leads-notable-drop-air-pollution.html

18 https://www.forbes.com/sites/jeffmcmahon/2020/03/22/video-watch-from-space-as-air-pollution-vanishes-over-china-during-coronavirus-lockdown-then-returns/#474c09c835f0

19 Well worth a watch: https://www.theguardian.com/uk-news/video/2020/mar/31/goats-take-over-empty-welsh-streets-llandudno-coronavirus-lockdown-video

20 http://www.fieldsintrust.org/News/latest-green-space-index-highlights-importance-of-parks-and-green-spaces

21 https://friendsoftheearth.uk/trees/beth-collier-nature-accessible-everyone

22 https://www.bbc.co.uk/news/world-53181112

23 https://www.dailymail.co.uk/news/article-7354627/Four-five-British-children-recognise-bee-half-know-stinging-nettle-is.html

24 *The Lost Words*, Robert Macfarlane and Jackie Morris (2017)

25 https://www.theguardian.com/environment/2016/feb/10/concerns-raised-over-amount-of-children-not-engaging-with-nature

26 https://www.theguardian.com/commentisfree/2012/nov/19/children-lose-contact-with-nature

27 https://www.theguardian.com/environment/2013/mar/17/climate-change-cut-national-curriculum

28 https://www.telegraph.co.uk/news/2020/05/29/natural-history-gcse-set-taught-schools-2022-bbc-broadcaster/

29 *Last Child in the Woods*, Richard Louv (2005)

30 https://assets.publishing.service.gov.uk/government/uploads/system/uploads/attachment_data/file/908434/Disparities_in_the_risk_and_outcomes_of_COVID_August_2020_update.pdf

31 https://www.resolutionfoundation.org/app/uploads/2020/06/Return-to-spender.pdf

32 https://cpag.org.uk/child-poverty/child-poverty-facts-and-figures

33 https://england.shelter.org.uk/media/press_releases/articles/a_child_becomes_homeless_in_britain_every_eight_minutes

34 https://www.independent.co.uk/news/uk/home-news/food-poverty-hunger-child-malnutrition-hospital-layla-moran-coronavirus-a9615161.html

35 https://cpag.org.uk

36 https://www.theguardian.com/society/2019/jun/26/two-child-benefit-limit-pushes-

families-further-into-poverty-study

[37] https://www.ifs.org.uk/publications/14879

[38] https://news.sky.com/story/coronavirus-730000-have-lost-their-job-since-lockdown-began-12046850

[39] https://www.ft.com/content/8250fec7-0581-477e-a525-bc2ab2dd5a11

[40] https://www.theguardian.com/business/2020/nov/19/one-in-seven-uk-businesses-in-fear-of-collapse-survey-shows

[41] https://www.thesun.co.uk/news/12816845/every-coronavirus-death-another-lost-cancer-jeremy-hunt/

[42] https://theconversation.com/coronavirus-why-arent-death-rates-rising-with-case-numbers-145865

[43] https://www.independent.co.uk/news/uk/home-news/coronavirus-suicide-rates-uk-mental-health-support-a9451086.html

[44] https://twitter.com/realDonaldTrump/status/1241935285916782593

[45] https://sustainability.iceland.co.uk/news/iceland-offers-free-frozen-veg-with-healthy-start-vouchers/

[46] https://fair4allfinance.org.uk/wp-content/uploads/2020/05/Mapping-the-groups-most-financially-impacted-by-the-economic-fallout-of-the-Coronavirus-pandemic-1-4.pdf

[47] https://www.kantar.com/inspiration/fmcg/uk-grocery-sales-reach-new-high-as-shoppers-remain-cautious/

[48] https://www.ted.com/talks/bill_gates_how_we_must_respond_to_the_coronavirus_pandemic#t-3031532

[49] Sign the petition and lobby your local MP here: https://www.nationalnatureservice.org

[50] https://reaction.life/britain-needs-a-national-nature-service-to-power-a-green-recovery/

[51] The rewilding project at Knepp is documented by the estate's owner Isabella Tree in her brilliant book *Wilding*.

[52] https://www.nature.com/articles/s41586-020-2784-9.epdf

[53] https://www.leaderspledgefornature.org

[54] https://news.cgtn.com/news/2020-09-30/Full-text-Xi-Jinping-s-speech-at-UN-summit-on-biodiversity-Udo37GZogE/index.html

Chapter 6

[1] Speaking at the Business, Energy and Industrial Strategy Committee (9 July 2019)

[2] https://www.ipsos.com/ipsos-mori/en-uk/trust-politicians-falls-sending-them-spiralling-back-bottom-ipsos-mori-veracity-index

[3] For example, take plastic pollution, where a modest charge for plastic bags led to near 90 per cent reduction in the numbers being handed out by supermarkets almost overnight. From the Clean Air Act of 1956 to the Climate Change Act of 2008, government intervention to expedite positive environmental action can work very well.

[4] https://www.theguardian.com/society/2018/apr/24/food-banks-norm-trussell-trust-emma-revie

[5] https://www.gov.uk/government/news/green-number-plates-get-the-green-light-for-a-zero-emission-future

[6] https://www.retailappointment.co.uk/career-advice/talking-shop/uk-retail-facts-and-

figures
[7] https://www.ons.gov.uk/businessindustryandtrade/retailindustry/timeseries/j4mc/drsi
[8] https://www.mirror.co.uk/news/uk-news/amazon-storm-over-tax-bill-13936012
[9] https://www.telegraph.co.uk/technology/2018/10/29/hammond-unveils-digital-services-tax-make-tech-giants-pay-fair/
[10] https://www.retailgazette.co.uk/blog/2020/03/chancellor-extends-one-year-business-rates-holiday-for-all-retailers/
[11] 'Rates rebel under pressure', Ben Marlow, *Daily Telegraph* (5 December 2020)
[12] 'Four refuse to return rates', *Daily Mail* (5 December 2020)
[13] https://www.bbc.co.uk/news/uk-england-48854450
[14] https://www.bbc.co.uk/news/uk-53669432
[15] *Factfulness*, Hans Rosling (2018)
[16] https://www.washingtonpost.com/business/2019/09/26/income-inequality-america-highest-its-been-since-census-started-tracking-it-data-show/
[17] https://www.equalitytrust.org.uk/scale-economic-inequality-uk
[18] https://www.ons.gov.uk/peoplepopulationandcommunity/personalandhouseholdfinances/incomeandwealth/bulletins/wealthingreatbritainwave5/2014to2016
[19] https://www.mckinsey.com/featured-insights/employment-and-growth/poorer-than-their-parents-a-new-perspective-on-income-inequality
[20] The manageress of our store in Byker once told me how a criminally convicted alcohol and drug addict, who was banned from the shop, received more in monthly benefits than she did in salary ... as well as having two full-time carers. I am not making value judgements about this particular person, merely observing that she was trapped within a welfare system that only facilitated her addiction and criminality.
[21] http://www.oecd.org/greengrowth/1869800.pdf
[22] http://www.oecd.org/economy/growth-and-inequality-close-relationship.htm
[23] https://www.independent.co.uk/voices/editorials/leading-article-an-index-of-happiness-is-at-least-a-worthwhile-endeavour-2143897.html
[24] *The Ecology of Commerce*, Paul Hawken (2010)
[25] https://science.sciencemag.org/content/356/6345/1356
[26] *Less is More: How Degrowth Will Save the World*, Jason Hickel (2020)
[27] *Doughnut Economics*, Kate Raworth (2017)
[28] http://www.consultmcgregor.com/documents/resources/GDP_and_GPI.pdf
[29] https://www.theguardian.com/world/2019/may/30/new-zealand-wellbeing-budget-jacinda-ardern-unveils-billions-to-care-for-most-vulnerable
[30] https://ec.europa.eu/environment/beyond_gdp/background_en.html
[31] In his book *Factfulness*, Hans Rosling explains how he lobbied the Swedish government to do this very thing, yet they are still the only country to do so.
[32] https://www.bbc.co.uk/news/uk-politics-48126677
[33] https://www.gov.uk/government/news/uk-becomes-first-major-economy-to-pass-net-zero-emissions-law
[34] https://www.newscientist.com/article/mg24632891-100-we-can-fix-the-climate-as-we-reboot-the-economy-heres-how/

[35] https://www.theccc.org.uk/publication/progress-in-preparing-for-climate-change-2019-progress-report-to-parliament/
[36] https://www.greenpeace.org.uk/news/committee-climate-change-report-greenpeace-

reaction/
[37] On the very day the report was released, I personally challenged the then prime minister, Theresa May, about it at a business roundtable. Despite receiving a text from one of her key advisers before the meeting, warning me not to 'go too heavy on climate change', I asked why the UK was not doing much more. Before I had even managed to finish my opening remarks, the PM interrupted me – with a ferocity of spirit I had not previously seen in her premiership – and insisted that the UK has already done more than any other developed nation to reduce its emissions. This is an often-used piece of total greenwash: in fact, all we have done is offshored our emissions to the likes of China. While production in the UK has indeed gone down, our consumption continues to go up and up. All we have done is to shift the problem out of sight by exporting so much of our manufacturing industry.
[38] https://www.globalccsinstitute.com/resources/global-status-report/download/
[39] Ibid
[40] https://www.unenvironment.org/news-and-stories/press-release/cut-global-emissions-76-percent-every-year-next-decade-meet-15degc
[41] According to the UK's Department for Business, Energy and Industrial Strategy, a carbon tax priced at £80 a tonne is required to realign prices which will keep global warming within our Paris Agreement obligations. Yet drivers currently pay £109 a tonne, whereas electricity is priced at £41 a tonne, according to the think tank Energy Systems Catapult.
[42] https://www.naturalclimate.solutions/full-rationale
[43] https://www.theguardian.com/environment/2020/may/18/natural-england-funding-boost-gets-cautious-welcome-aoep
[44] https://www.thetimes.co.uk/article/we-dont-have-the-money-to-beat-polluters-environment-agency-admits-dqhrtxxbr
[45] https://static1.squarespace.com/static/58b40fe1be65940cc4889d33/t/5d10b62345897f000114c54b/1561376292241/TTIN_A5_lobby_leaflet_AW_3.pdf
[46] https://ourworldindata.org/co2/country/united-kingdom?country=~GBR
[47] Summarised in BusinessGreen's overnight email entitled *Taxing anomalies* (23 November 2020)
[48] https://mk0ossociety9jn92eye.kinstacdn.com/wp-content/uploads/2020/06/ResilientRecovery-LetterToThePrimeMinister-08.05.2020.pdf
[49] https://www.renewableuk.com/news/405601/RenewableUK-releases-new-global-offshore-wind-market-rankings.htm
[50] http://parityprojects.com/net-zero-housing-workforce/
[51] https://eto.dnvgl.com/2020/index.html#ETO2019-top
[52] https://www.businessgreen.com/news/4016248/bp-confirms-job-cuts-reasserts-clean-energy-pledge
[53] https://www.businessgreen.com/news/4019071/carbon-tracker-oil-gas-giants-usd87bn-hit-assets-months
[54] https://energypeople.com/news/story/green-energy-could-drive-covid-19-recovery-with--100tn-boost
[55] https://www.imf.org/en/Publications/WP/Issues/2019/05/02/Global-Fossil-Fuel-Subsidies-Remain-Large-An-Update-Based-on-Country-Level-Estimates-46509
[56] https://eur-lex.europa.eu/legal-content/EN/TXT/PDF/?uri=COM:2019:1:FIN&from=EN

[57] https://www.theguardian.com/environment/2019/jan/23/uk-has-biggest-fossil-fuel-subsidies-in-the-eu-finds-commission
[58] https://www.heritagefund.org.uk/funding/green-recovery-challenge-fund
[59] https://www.green-alliance.org.uk/acting_on_net_zero_now.php
[60] https://assets.publishing.service.gov.uk/government/uploads/system/uploads/attachment_data/file/872252/road-investment-strategy-2-2020-2025.pdf
[61] https://www.telegraph.co.uk/politics/2020/01/04/taxpayers-will-suffer-40billion-loss-hs2-goes-ahead-official/
[62] https://www.building.co.uk/news/governments-own-review-says-hs2-will-exceed-100bn/5103791.article
[63] https://www.woodlandtrust.org.uk/protecting-trees-and-woods/campaign-with-us/hs2-rail-link/
[64] https://www.wildlifetrusts.org/sites/default/files/2020-01/What%27s%20the%20damage%20-%20Full%20Report%20digital2_0.pdf
[65] https://www.theguardian.com/business/2020/nov/17/people-cause-global-aviation-emissions-study-covid-19
[66] https://www.forbes.com/sites/patrickgleason/2020/03/17/pandemic-prompts-call-to-suspend-or-repeal-bag-bans--taxes/
[67] https://www.ipsos.com/en-za/two-thirds-citizens-around-world-agree-climate-change-serious-covid-19
[68] https://www.economist.com/leaders/2020/09/17/is-it-the-end-of-the-oil-age
[69] https://www.investopedia.com/shakeup-dow-industrials-exxon-out-5075621
[70] Ibid
[71] https://ec.europa.eu/info/strategy/priorities-2019-2024/european-green-deal_en
[72] Ibid
[73] Ibid
[74] https://www.economist.com/china/2020/09/24/china-aims-to-cut-its-net-carbon-dioxide-emissions-to-zero-by-2060
[75] https://www.independent.co.uk/news/world/asia/china-tree-plant-soldiers-reassign-climate-change-global-warming-deforestation-a8208836.html
[76] https://www.economist.com/international/2020/09/19/citizens-assemblies-are-increasingly-popular

Conclusion

[1] *Shoe Dog – A Memoir by the Creator of NIKE*, Phil Knight (2016)
[2] https://www.ssb.no/en/befolkning/statistikker/innvbef/aar/2016-03-03
[3] https://snl.no/asylsituasjonen_i_Norge_2015_og_2016
[4] https://www.cia.gov/library/publications/the-world-factbook/rankorder/2172rank.html
[5] https://www.bls.gov/fls/intl_gdp_capita_gdp_hour.pdf
[6] United Nations (November 2012). *Human Development Report 2013. UNDEP*
[7] *Doughnut Economics*, Kate Raworth (2017)
[8] https://www.bbc.co.uk/news/uk-england-cumbria-54393345
[9] *Losing Earth*, Nathaniel Rich (2019)
[10] https://thecorrespondent.com/751/weve-emitted-more-co2-in-the-past-30-years-than-in-all-of-history-these-three-reasons-are-to-blame/99422365889-1d29a874

[11] Ibid

[12] https://www.washingtonpost.com/opinions/2020/07/15/big-bold-normal-biden-speech-climate-change/

[13] https://bigthink.com/technology-innovation/rise-of-the-green-economy?rebelltitem=1#rebelltitem1

[14] https://www.gov.uk/government/news/pm-outlines-his-ten-point-plan-for-a-green-industrial-revolution-for-250000-jobs

[15] https://www.bbc.co.uk/programmes/p08jq3n7

[16] https://theconversation.com/norways-supreme-court-set-to-rule-on-whether-the-country-can-keep-searching-for-new-arctic-oil-148485

[17] https://www.huffpost.com/entry/robert-swan-antarctica_b_1315047

[18] https://www.theguardian.com/environment/2018/oct/08/global-warming-must-not-exceed-15c-warns-landmark-un-report

[19] 'Breaking Through', *The Economist* (31 October 2020)

[20] https://www.fool.com/investing/2020/02/04/teslas-now-bigger-than-ford-gm-and-fiat-chrysler-c.aspx

[21] 'Grasping the climate nettle will open door to an industrial revolution', *Daily Telegraph* (19 November 2020)

[22] http://www.mygridgb.co.uk/last-12-months/

[23] https://www.resilience.org/stories/2020-11-12/iea-wind-and-solar-capacity-will-overtake-both-gas-and-coal-globally-by-2024/

[24] https://www.theguardian.com/commentisfree/2020/jan/08/lab-grown-food-destroy-farming-save-planet

[25] https://climateemergencydeclaration.org/climate-emergency-declarations-cover-15-million-citizens/

[26] 'BP's Road to Rebuilding Trust with CEO Bernard Looney', *Outrage + Optimism* podcast (2020)

LIST OF TERMS AND ABBREVIATIONS

B Corp	Benefit Corporations measures companies on the impact and value they add to workers, community, environment and customers
BPA	Bisphenol A
Brand Buzz	https://www.brandindex.com
CAP	Common Agricultural Policy
CCC	Climate Change Committee
CCS	Carbon capture and storage
CFC	Chlorofluorocarbons
CIEL	Center for International Environmental Law
CLT	Cross Laminated Timber
COP26	UN Climate Change Conference Glasgow, November 2021
CSB	Council for Sustainable Business
CSR	Corporate and Social Responsibility
DEFRA	Department for Environment, Food and Rural Affairs
DRS	Deposit return scheme

edie	A media brand to make business more sustainable
ELMS	Environmental Land Management Scheme (England)
ESG	Environmental and Social Governance
EV	Electric vehicle
FTSE 100	Financial Times Stock Exchange 100 Index
G7	Group of top industrial nations
GDP	Gross Domestic Product
GM	Genetically modified
HFC	Hydrofluorocarbons
IPBES	Intergovernmental Science-Policy Platform on Biodiversity and Ecosystem Services
IFCF	Iceland Foods Charitable Foundation
IPCC	Intergovernmental Panel on Climate Change
IUCN	International Union for Conservation of Nature
MURF	Mixed use recycling facility
NGO	Non-governmental organisation
NNS	National Nature Service
OECD	Organisation for Economic Co-Operation and Development
ONS	Office for National Statistics
PCB	Polychlorinated biphenyl
PET	Polyethylene terephthalate, a form of polyester
PFA	Per and Polyfluoroalkyl substances
POIG	Palm Oil Innovation Group
PRN	Packaging Recovery Note
PVC	Polyvinyl chloride, the world's third most widely produced synthetic plastic polymer
REDD	Reducing Emissions from Deforestation and Degradation
RSPO	Roundtable on Sustainable Palm Oil
S&P	500 A US stock market index
SLMS	Sustainable Land Management Scheme (Wales)
SME	Small and Medium Enterprise
TED Talks	Influential videos/podcasts from expert speakers on education, business, science, tech and creativity
UBI	Universal Basic Income
WRAP	The Waste and Resources Action Programme. The UK's circular economy and resource efficiency experts
WWF	World Wide Fund for Nature (World Wildlife Fund in the US and Canada)

RECOMMENDED READING

Business and Management

Beautiful Corporations, Paul Dickinson (2000)

Best Served Cold: The Rise, Fall And Rise Again Of Malcolm Walker, Malcolm Walker (2013)

Business As Unusual: The Journey of Anita Roddick and The Body Shop, Anita Roddick (2000)

Confessions of a Radical Industrialist: How Interface Proved That You Can Build A Successful Business Without Destroying The Planet, Ray Anderson with Robin White (2009)

Eco Barons: The New Heroes of Environmental Activism, Edward Humes (2009)

Ecological Intelligence: The Coming Age of Radical Transparency, Daniel Goleman (2009)

Green Swans: The Coming Boom in Regenerative Capitalism, John Elkington (2020)

Let My People Go Surfing: The Education Of A Reluctant Businessman, Yvon Chouinard (2005)

Prosperity: Better Business Makes the Greater Good, Colin Mayer (2018)

The Ecology of Commerce: A Declaration of Sustainability, Paul Hawken (1993)

The Power of Purpose, John O'Brien and Andrew Cave (2017)

The Responsible Company: What We've Learned From Patagonia's First 40 Years, Yvon Chouinard and Vincent Stanley (2012)

Trailblazer, Marc Benioff (2019)

Climate Change

Drawdown: The Most Comprehensive Plan Ever Proposed to Reverse Global Warming, Paul Hawken (Ed.) (2017)

How Bad Are Bananas? The Carbon Footprint of Everything, Mike Berners-Lee (2010)

How We're F***ing Up Our Planet: and What We Can Do About It, Tony Juniper (2018)

The Future We Choose: Surviving the Climate Crisis, Christiana Figueres and Tom Rivett-Carnac (2020)

The Uninhabitable Earth: Life After Warming, David Wallace-Wells (2019)

There Is No Planet B: A Handbook for the Make or Break Years, Mike Berners-Lee (2019)

This Changes Everything, Naomi Klein (2014)

Whole Earth Discipline, Stewart Brand (2009)

Economics

Doughnut Economics: Seven Ways to Think Like a 21st-Century Economist, Kate Raworth (2017)

Grow the Pie: How Great Companies Deliver Both Purpose and Profit, Alex Edmans (2020)

Less is More: How Degrowth Will Save the World, Jason Hickel (2020)

Prosperity Without Growth: Foundations For the Economy of Tomorrow (Second Edition), Tim Jackson (2017)

Small is Beautiful: A Study of Economics As if People Mattered, E.F. Schumacher (1973)

Inspiration

A Life on Our Planet: My Witness Statement and a Vision for the Future, David Attenborough (2020)
English Pastoral: An Inheritance, James Rebanks (2020)
Factfulness: 10 reasons We're Wrong About The World – and Why Things Are Better Than You Think, Hans Rosling (2018)
How Will You Measure Your Life?, Clayton M. Christensen (2017)
No One is Too Small to Make a Difference, Greta Thunberg (2019)
The Man Who Planted Trees, Jean Giono (1954)

Nature

Dirt to Soil: One Family's Journey into Regenerative Agriculture, Gabe Brown (2018)
Feral: Rewilding the Land, Sea and Human Life, George Monbiot (2013)
Last Child in the Woods: Saving Our Children From Nature-deficit Disorder, Richard Louv (2005)
Losing Eden: Why Our Minds Need the Wild, Lucy Jones (2020)
Rainforest: Dispatches From Earth's Most Vital Frontlines, Tony Juniper (2018)
The Lost Words, Robert Macfarlane and Jackie Morris (2017)
The Nature of Nature: Why We Need the Wild, Enric Sala (2020)
The Silent Spring, Rachel Carson (1962)
Wilding: The Return of Nature to a British Farm, Isabella Tree (2018)

Plastic Pollution

How to Give Up Plastic: Simple Steps to Living Consciously on our Blue Planet, Will McCallum (2019)
Our Stolen Future, Theo Colborn, John Peterson Myers and Dianne Dumanoski (1996)
Plastic Soup: An Atlas of Ocean Pollution, Michiel Roscam Abbing (2019)
Turning the Tide on Plastic: How Humanity (and You) Can Make Our Globe Clean Again, Lucy Siegle (2018)

Politics

Environmental Politics: A Very Short Introduction, Andrew Dobson (2016)
Global Planet Authority: How We're About to Save the Biosphere, Angus Forbes (2019)
How Did We Get into This Mess?, George Monbiot (2017)
Losing Earth: The Decade We Could Have Stopped Climate Change, Nathaniel Rich (2019)
Why We Get the Wrong Politicians, Isabel Hardman (2018)

Social Change

Humankind: A Hopeful History, Rutger Bregman (2020)
New Power: How It's Changing the 21st Century – and Why You Need to Know, Jeremy Heimans and Henry Timms (2018)
The Inner Level: How More Equal Societies Reduce Stress, Restore Sanity and Improve Everyone's Well-being, Richard Wilkinson and Kate Pickett (2018)

ABOUT THE AUTHOR

Richard Walker was born in Chester in 1980. After graduating from Durham University in 2001 with a degree in geography, he travelled extensively across Russia, China, India, South East Asia and South America before qualifying as a chartered surveyor in London. In 2006 he moved to Poland to found Bywater Properties, of which today he still remains Chairman. The company has a commercial property investment and development pipeline of over £250 million.

In 2012 he joined Iceland Foods, the supermarket established in 1970 by his parents. He worked full-time as a shelf-stacker and cashier in Iceland stores in London for a year, before becoming a store manager and then moving to head office roles. After spells running Iceland's International Division and The Food Warehouse,

Iceland's chain of larger stores, he took responsibility for the group's sustainability initiatives in 2017 and became managing director of Iceland Foods in 2018.

Richard is an honorary fellow of University College London, a World Economic Forum Young Global Leader, a member of the DEFRA Council for Sustainable Business, a Sustainable Business Ambassador for HRH The Prince of Wales, an Ambassador for The Wildlife Trusts, chairman of Surfers Against Sewage and a trustee of several leading environmental charities. He has written opinion pieces on business, politics and sustainability for many of the UK's national newspapers, and is a regular panellist on shows such as BBC1's *Question Time*. He is married with two daughters.

Outside family and business, his greatest passions are trail running, skiing, surfing and climbing all over the world. His notable climbing achievements include a 2011 expedition to Everest, scaling the Old Man of Hoy in Scotland in 2020, and a 2017 trip to Kyrgyzstan where he notched up several first ascents of previously unclimbed mountains – one of which he named Peak Rhianydd, in honour of his mother. Surfing-wise, he is yet to get barrelled.

Instagram: @richardiceland
Twitter: @icelandrichard

AUTHOR'S ACKNOWLEDGEMENTS

I had no idea what writing a book actually entails. Following an unsuccessful attempt to delegate the whole thing, I was struck by the reality that I would actually have to *write* my own book.

It was a long and halting process that took the best part of two years, alongside juggling the many work hats I wear, family life, personal commitments and a global pandemic. Yet I found it utterly absorbing and enjoyable.

I'd like to thank the many things that got me through that time: such as 5 o'clock starts before work, weekends, thesaurus.com, coffee, noise-cancelling headphones, and my 'Writing' playlist on Spotify. Also: wine (on occasion ... albeit not at 5am).

But I'd particularly like to thank: my wife, Rebecca, and our kids Sophie and Rosalie, for their patience, enthusiasm and understanding. I love you.

When I started out in retail, I thought that it merely consisted of plonking something on a shelf and watching it sell. Likewise, the act of producing a book has been a voyage of intrigue and discovery for me. The people who played key roles in making it possible and deserve special thank-yous are: my agent Gordon Wise (who managed to find someone actually interested in publishing it); said commissioning editor Stephanie Milner (who saw the potential for this 'eco-paperback original'); Keith Hann (who provided much helpful input throughout); Hilary Berg (my campaigning partner in crime); and my wonderfully proficient editor Fiona Holman. My old

English teacher, Sandy Mackinnon, encouraged me to find my descriptive writing voice. Big thank-yous also to Tom Gooding, Nick Gardner and John Sauven for reading the manuscript, offering comments and suggestions and for not telling me it was daft. Thank you also to all the team at DK, including Bess Daly for design, Nicola Powling for cover design, Katie Hewett for proof reading and Angie Hipkin for indexing, and our PR agency Weber Shandwick for bringing the whole project to life.

The subject matter, and indeed the world generally, was very fluid at the time of writing. This book can only provide a momentary snapshot. I tried to keep track of events via endless notes, emails to myself and voice memos. I hope that I have attributed everything properly – apologies if I unintentionally missed anything out.

To everyone who provided a supportive quote: it is massively appreciated!

Business is all about people: Iceland has 30,000 amazing, hard-working colleagues without whom we wouldn't exist – they enable all our corporate activism, and indeed this book. I'd especially like to thank Michaela Stretton, for holding my life together; and Tarsem Dhaliwal, for allowing me to pretend to be the boss sometimes. I'd also like to thank Patrick O'Gorman and Theo Michell for steering Bywater Properties: the future is bright (and sustainable).

Thank you to my Dad for your endless provision of motivation and brilliance; and, of course, to my Mum – you continue to inspire me.

January 2021

Index